D0746658

The Sand Canyon
Archaeological Project
A Progress Report

OCCASIONAL PAPERS OF THE CROW CANYON ARCHAEOLOGICAL CENTER

William D. Lipe, General Editor

MEMBERS OF THE BOARD

Raymond T. Duncan (Chairman)
Stuart Struever (President)
Stephen H. Lekson (President-elect)

Richard G. Ballantine   C. Paul Johnson
George W. Bermant   John O. Lohre
Albert L. Blum   Mark O. L. Lynton
Robert W. Cox   Marianne O'Shaughnessy
Marjorie Y. Crosby   Burton R. Rissman
Sally C. Duncan   Michael D. Searle
Peggy V. Fossett   William R. Thurston
Alden C. Hayes   Gerald L. Vincent
Clayton R. Jackson   Edward B. Wasson
            Gordon P. Wilson

CROW CANYON ARCHAEOLOGICAL CENTER

Crow Canyon Archaeological Center is a private, independent, not-for-profit organization committed to excellence in sustained interdisciplinary archaeological research integrated with experiential education programs. The Center seeks to broaden public involvement, awareness, and support for the conservation of our cultural heritage and resources, and to increase public knowledge of prehistoric and contemporary Native American cultures.

Crow Canyon Archaeological Center
23390 County Road K
Cortez, Colorado 81321

Telephone: 303-565-8975
FAX: 303-565-4859
Bitnet: alr@csn.org

The Sand Canyon Archaeological Project
A Progress Report

Edited by William D. Lipe

OCCASIONAL PAPER NO. 2
CROW CANYON ARCHAEOLOGICAL CENTER
Cortez, Colorado
1992

This book is printed on recycled acid-free paper.

© 1992 Crow Canyon Archaeological Center
ISBN 0-9624640-1-5
Library of Congress Catalog Card Number: 91-76231

Contents

Illustrations

Tables

Acknowledgments

Publication of this volume was made possible through the generosity of the Scott Family Foundation, and it is dedicated to the memory of David N. Scott, who loved and studied archaeology all of his life. The Crow Canyon Archaeological Center also wishes to thank Wesley M. Dixon, Jr. and Kenneth and Harle Montgomery for their sustained support of the long and complex laboratory research process that has enabled the Center's archaeologists to achieve many of the interpretations contained in this volume. Without the long-term, continuing encouragement and financial support of the Center's Board, Chairman's Council, and Members, the Sand Canyon Archaeological Project would not have been possible. Essential financial assistance for specific aspects of the research was provided by grants from the National Science Foundation, the National Geographic Society, the Wenner-Gren Foundation for Anthropological Research, the Ballantine Family Foundation, and the Colorado Endowment for the Humanities, as noted in the various chapters of this monograph.

The development of the research publications program has been greatly aided by advice and support received from the Crow Canyon Center's Research Advisory Committee. The members are: Nance Creager, Marjorie Crosby, George Feldman, Charlotte Gibson, David Gibson, Alden Hayes, John Hopkins, William McLaughlin, Stuart Patterson, Jim Porter, John Pryor, Nancy Todd, and Robert Wickham.

Surveys, excavations, and testing were done on Bureau of Land Management lands under Archaeological Resources Protection Act permits and a cooperative agreement between the Crow Canyon Center and the Bureau's San Juan Resource Area Office in Durango, Colorado. Special thanks go to Kristie Arrington, Resource Area Archeologist, and Sally Wisely, Resource Area Manager, for their cooperation and assistance. Collections from sites on Bureau of Land Management administered lands will be curated at the Bureau's Anasazi Heritage Center, in Dolores, Colorado. Thanks go to Shela McFarlin, Director of the Heritage Center, and to Susan Thomas and other members of the Heritage Center staff for their assistance and advice on numerous matters relating to conservation and curation of collections. Surface examination of sites in the Goodman Point unit of Hovenweep National Monument, and the mapping of the main Goodman Point site were done with permission of Robert Heyder, Superintendent of Mesa Verde National Park. Dr. Jack Smith, Park Archeologist, kindly provided access to records and collections resulting from previous surveys in the Goodman Point unit. The Colorado State Archaeologist, Dr. Susan Collins of the Colorado Historical Society, provided helpful guidance regarding questions of state law and permits.

Landowners in the Goodman Point and Sand Canyon areas were generous in sharing their knowledge of the prehistory and history of the area and in providing permission for surface survey of archaeological sites on their land. Test excavations at several of the sites discussed in this volume could not have been done without the permission and cooperation of the owners of these sites. Troy and Shorlene Oliver gave permission for test excavations at Troy's Tower, Shorlene's site, Kenzie Dawn Hamlet, and the midden section of Roy's Ruin. Roy and Lillian Retherford, who passed away after the testing program began, gave us the opportunity to test Lillian's site and the main portion of Roy's Ruin. Their daughters, Glenna Harris and Guyrene McAfee, permitted us to excavate at G and G Hamlet. Catherine Stanley and her son Stanton Stanley gave access through their land so we could test Catherine's site and Stanton's site.

Virtually every spoonful of dirt excavated from the sites reported here was removed by adult and student participants in the Center's educational programs, working closely with Crow Canyon staff members. These participants, who cumulatively number in the several thousands, also contributed to the basic processing and analysis of specimens from the excavations. The curiosity, care, dedication, and enthusiasm which these members of the lay public have brought to the Sand Canyon Project have been a source of continuing energy and renewal for the Center's professional staff.

Amaterra, a non-profit volunteer organization based in Tucson and directed by Dr. Roger Irwin, provided numerous types of assistance during the summer excavation seasons at Sand Canyon Pueblo. These included refurbishing and maintaining two trailers and a ramada as a field station; constructing trails for visitors to the site and giving tours as needed; assisting in the collection of environmental data; giving educational programs; and providing a variety of informal intellectual, emotional, and physical support services for staff and participants.

A number of key staff members and associated researchers on the Sand Canyon Project are represented as authors of the various chapters of this monograph. In addition, however, many other field, lab, and administrative staff members, student interns, volunteers, and outside researchers made essential contributions to the project. They are too numerous to name here, but their contributions are recognized and valued.

Editing and production of the book was capably directed by Lynn Udick, Research Publications Manager, with essential help from Louise Schmidlap, Editorial Assistant. Fiorella Ljunggren, a program participant, volunteered her professional editorial skills to give the manuscript a quick but intensive copyedit. Her careful work made the text much clearer and more consistent. The majority of the figures were drafted by Tom May and Neal Morris; Carla Van West furnished Figures 9.3 and 9.4. The cover was designed by Nancy Leach of Graphic Interpretations, in Durango, Colorado, and the book was printed by Thomson-Shore, Incorporated, of Dexter, Michigan.

William D. Lipe

List of Contributors

KAREN R. ADAMS (Ph.D., University of Arizona, 1988) directs the Environmental Archaeology program at the Crow Canyon Archaeological Center and is also an independent consultant in archaeobotany in Tucson, Arizona.

MICHAEL A. ADLER (Ph.D., University of Michigan, 1990) is Assistant Professor of Anthropology at Southern Methodist University, Dallas, Texas, and Director of the Archaeological Field School at the Fort Burgwin Research Center, Taos, New Mexico. He is also a Research Associate of the Crow Canyon Archaeological Center.

BRUCE A. BRADLEY (Ph.D., Cambridge University, 1976) is Senior Research Archaeologist at the Crow Canyon Archaeological Center.

MARJORIE R. CONNOLLY (M.A., Northern Arizona University, 1988) is an Archaeological Educator at the Crow Canyon Archaeological Center.

CAROL L. GLEICHMAN (M.A., Arizona State University, 1979) is a Historic Preservation Specialist in the Western Office of Project Review, Advisory Council for Historic Preservation, Denver, Colorado.

PETER J. GLEICHMAN (B.A., University of Colorado, Boulder, 1976) is Principal Investigator and Director of Native Cultural Services, Boulder, Colorado.

EDGAR K. HUBER (M.A., University of Colorado, Denver, 1984) is a Ph.D. candidate in anthropology at Washington State University and a Research Affiliate of the Crow Canyon Archaeological Center.

JAMES H. KLEIDON (B.A., Fort Lewis College, 1977) is an independent archaeological consultant in Dolores, Colorado, and a former Assistant Archaeologist at the Crow Canyon Archaeological Center.

KRISTIN A. KUCKELMAN (M.A., University of Texas, Austin, 1977) is an Assistant Research Archaeologist at the Crow Canyon Archaeological Center.

WILLIAM D. LIPE (Ph.D., Yale University, 1966) is Director of Research at the Crow Canyon Archaeological Center and Professor of Anthropology at Washington State University, Pullman, Washington.

CARLA R. VAN WEST (Ph.D., Washington State University, 1990) is a Principal Investigator for Statistical Research, Inc. in Tucson, Arizona, and a Research Associate of the Crow Canyon Archaeological Center.

MARK D. VARIEN (M.A., University of Texas, Austin, 1984) is a Research Archaeologist at the Crow Canyon Archaeological Center and a student in the Ph.D. program in anthropology at Arizona State University.

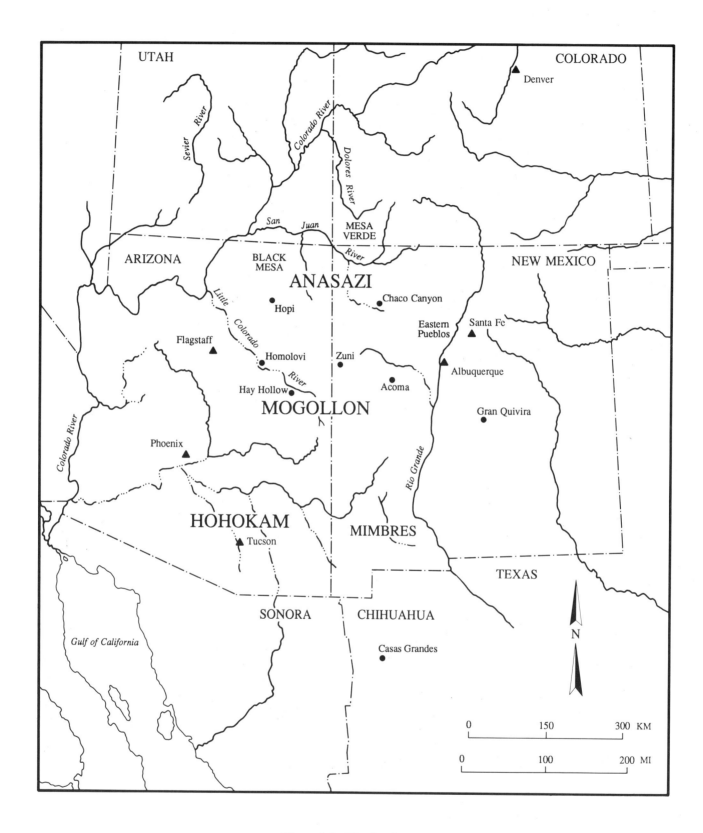

Figure 1.1. The Southwest.

1

Introduction

William D. Lipe

The Crow Canyon Archaeological Center of Cortez, Colorado, is pursuing a continuing research program focused on the Anasazi occupation of the Sand Canyon locality in southwestern Colorado (Figures 1.1 and 1.2) during the Pueblo III period (A.D. 1150–1300). Project fieldwork began in 1983 and will continue through 1994. The fieldwork includes environmental studies, intensive and sample-based surface surveys, oral history, small-scale test excavations at a number of sites, and intensive excavations at portions of a few sites, including Sand Canyon Pueblo (5MT765) and the Green Lizard site (5MT3901). Sand Canyon Pueblo is the largest thirteenth-century settlement in the locality (see Bradley, this volume). This apparent single-component, walled site has approximately 420 surface rooms, 90 kivas, 14 towers, a D-shaped bi-walled structure, and a great kiva.

The long-term research goals of the Sand Canyon Archaeological Project are (1) to define the community or communities that occupied the Sand Canyon locality during the period A.D. 1150–1300 and to characterize their sociocultural organization and sustaining environments; (2) to identify social, cultural, and environmental changes that took place in the Sand Canyon locality during the period A.D. 1150–1300, with a special focus on the abandonment of the locality in the late 1200s; and (3) to relate the locality's patterns of organization and change to larger patterns in the Pueblo Southwest, as well as to theoretical frameworks that promote understanding and interpretation of both locality and area-wide configurations. The project also includes (4) instrumental studies, such as chronology building and analysis of assemblage-formation processes, that provide necessary foundations for the inferences required to address the three primary problem domains.

This monograph provides a progress report on research through the 1990 field season. It focuses on fieldwork

results; the interpretations offered in this volume are generally limited to preliminary statements about specific subprojects (e.g., Sand Canyon Pueblo excavations, survey, testing program) and are often quite tentative. A number of comparative studies designed to address higher-order questions in the research domains are underway or are planned for the near future. A synthesis of project results addressing the problem domains and incorporating these studies is planned for 1995.

Annual reports have been prepared for all field operations and have been given limited circulation. In addition, a number of meeting papers, several journal articles, and several M.A. theses and Ph.D. dissertations have been produced so far during the Sand Canyon Archaeological Project. Many of these are cited in the "History of Research" section below, and others are cited in the various chapters. In addition, full descriptive reports of the excavations at Sand Canyon Pueblo and at the tested sites are being prepared for publication as Crow Canyon Center Occasional Papers, by Bruce Bradley and Mark Varien, respectively (see also Chapters 5 and 7 of this volume). Results of the upland survey have been presented by Michael Adler in his dissertation (Adler 1990; see also Adler, this volume).

In the remainder of this chapter, the project research design is briefly summarized, as are the history of the research program at the Crow Canyon Center and the history of the Sand Canyon Archaeological Project itself. Chapters 2 and 3 review the results of site survey in the Sand Canyon locality, and Chapter 4 presents some of the findings of an oral history study that focused on historic-period settlement, farming, and treatment of archaeological sites in the upland portion of the project area. Chapter 5 reports test excavations at a number of small sites, while Chapters 6 and 7 deal with intensive excavations at a small

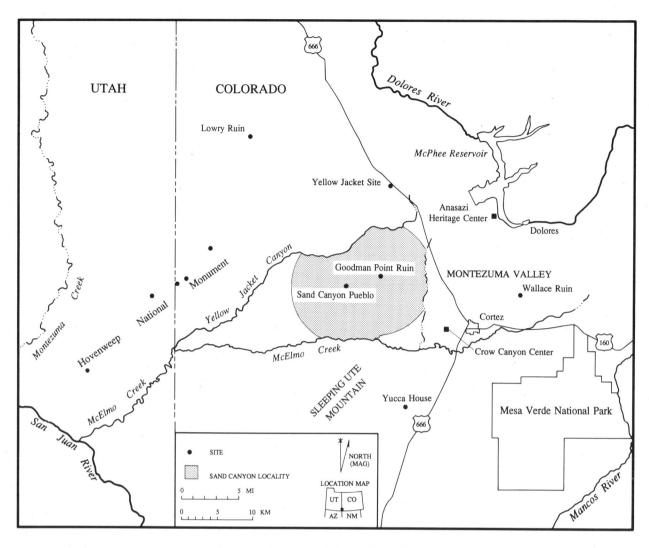

Figure 1.2. Central portion of the northern San Juan area.

site (Green Lizard) and a large site (Sand Canyon Pueblo), respectively. Chapter 8 summarizes the work and plans of the Environmental Archaeology Program—a relatively new component of the Sand Canyon Project. In Chapter 9, results of an attempt to model prehistoric climate, agricultural production, and population in southwestern Colorado are presented. Chapter 10 concludes the volume with a commentary on our current state of knowledge regarding the research domains.

Structure of the Research

The Sand Canyon locality is part of the McElmo drainage unit (Figure 1.2) of the Northern San Juan or Mesa Verde branch of the Anasazi tradition (Eddy et al. 1984). The Sand Canyon locality refers to a study area of approximately 200 km^2 that was defined in 1986 by Crow Canyon researchers (Lipe and Bradley 1986, 1988). It is bounded by McElmo Creek on the south and Yellow Jacket Canyon on the north. The remaining boundaries are defined by an arc with a 7.5-km radius drawn to the west from Sand Canyon Pueblo and a similar arc drawn to the east from Goodman Point Ruin, except where it intersects and follows Alkali Canyon (Figure 1.2).

As defined by Willey and Phillips (1958), a *locality* is a spatial unit larger than a settlement and smaller than a region; here, it is intended to approximate the basic sustaining area for at least one Pueblo III period Anasazi community. It is also possible that more than one face-to-face, or "first-order," community might have occupied or used the space at some time (see also Kane [1983] and Lipe and Kohler [1984] for similar applications of the concept in the Dolores Archaeological Project research). In the context of the Sand Canyon Project, "locality" is a heuristic construct, designed to ensure that the research is conducted at a scale appropriate to investigating one or a few multisite communities.

The Sand Canyon locality was defined in a way that seemed likely to include the community directly associated with Sand Canyon Pueblo and its agricultural sustaining area. The locality's boundaries, although they follow natural features as much as possible, were set at approximately 7.5 km from its two largest Pueblo III sites—Sand Canyon Pueblo and Goodman Point Ruin—because 7.5 km is half the average distance between the six large Pueblo III aggregates that are nearest to Sand Canyon and Goodman Point pueblos. The underlying assumption was that these large sites are community or supracommunity centers and that the boundaries of their social and economic sustaining areas are likely to have been located approximately halfway between neighboring centers.

The period A.D. 1150–1300 was chosen as the temporal frame for the research. This period is also referred to as Pueblo III (and is sometimes dated at A.D. 1100–1300). The Pueblo III period was established as part of the Pecos Classification (Kidder 1927) and today is used as a temporal subdivision of the Anasazi tradition, with no particular implications as to specific cultural content or "developmental stage."

Pueblo III (A.D. 1150–1300) appeared to be a good period on which to focus our research because (1) by A.D. 1150, Chacoan influence in the northern Southwest had waned, but it is not clear what kinds of regional and local-level social or ideological systems had replaced it; (2) debates regarding sociopolitical complexity (or lack of it) in late prehistoric Pueblo communities had erupted in the early 1980s, and an intensive locality-level study investigating both large and small settlements promised to make a valuable empirical contribution to these debates; (3) explanations for the abandonment of the northern Southwest by the Anasazi must lie in the period A.D. 1150–1300, yet these reasons remain obscure; (4) very little modern-era research had been done on this period in the McElmo district, despite evidence for large Pueblo III populations there; (5) a substantial amount of useful comparative data was available on the Pueblo III period occupation of Mesa Verde National Park, located just southeast of the McElmo drainage unit; and (6) many of the Pueblo III sites in the Sand Canyon locality appeared to have relatively brief, single-component occupations; hence, some of the problems of temporal control and of understanding site-formation processes would be eased.

Community is a basic structuring concept in the Sand Canyon research program. Following Murdock (1949), a community is considered to be the maximal group of people who reside close to one another and who interact regularly on a face-to-face basis. In settlement pattern terms, a "first-order" community of this sort could consist of a single village or a cluster of dispersed hamlets or household compounds. Whether there are organizational and functional relationships among such first-order communities, and what the archaeological expression might be for

higher-order organizations, are the obvious next questions. The Sand Canyon Project is attempting to investigate supracommunity organization at the locality level and, by reference to data and theoretical constructs from the literature, to place the Sand Canyon locality in a broader regional context.

Research Domains

Community Organization

The locality's pattern of numerous hamlet-size settlements clustered around larger pueblos appears to be one of considerable frequency and persistence in the more populous parts of the Mesa Verde Anasazi area (Rohn 1983, 1989), as well as in other parts of the Southwest (e.g., Reid 1989). At the outset of the project, it was expected that Sand Canyon Pueblo was contemporaneous with a large number of the small sites in the locality and that it probably served as a ceremonial, political, or economic center for a relatively large, dispersed population. It was also proposed that the site was predominantly nonresidential, or perhaps only seasonally occupied (Adams 1985b). Our research has shown, however, that Sand Canyon Pueblo did have a substantial residential population and that many of the Pueblo III sites in the cluster of small settlements near the head of Sand Canyon were abandoned before the construction of the large pueblo began about A.D. 1250. During the occupation of Sand Canyon Pueblo, the number of small sites occupied in and around upper Sand Canyon appears to have continued to decrease.

Whether or not Goodman Point Pueblo served as a community center in the locality prior to 1250, or whether it was partly or entirely contemporaneous with Sand Canyon Pueblo has not been determined. Castle Rock Pueblo, a "medium-size" settlement located in the McElmo valley at the mouth of Sand Canyon, does appear to have been at least partially contemporaneous with Sand Canyon Pueblo. In any case, defining the temporal and functional relationships between these large sites, and between the small and large sites occupied during the Pueblo III period, is a major aspect of this research domain.

The emphasis on community definition and community organization in the locality was chosen because (1) understanding these basic aspects of Anasazi social organization is essential for understanding many aspects of Anasazi prehistory in this area; (2) much of the current debate about the nature of prehistoric Pueblo social organization revolves around the degree of functional differentiation and hierarchy within and between social units defined at a community or locality scale, yet the organization of few Pueblo II or III period communities or localities has been intensively studied; and (3) the Pueblo III period settlements of the Sand Canyon locality provide an excellent opportunity for such a case study of organization. The research requirements in this problem domain are to infer population size and distribution, community boundaries and organizational structure, and intercommunity relationships within the locality.

Change and Abandonment

The emphasis on change and abandonment was chosen because the locality clearly displays a number of demographic, and possibly organizational, changes during the Pueblo III period. The area also participated in the large-scale abandonment of the region in the late 1200s. In the locality during the Pueblo III period, settlement patterns show a trend to increasing aggregation of the population in large pueblos, and also for settlements to move to the heads and sides of entrenched canyons, close to reliable sources of water. New forms of architecture appear, including some forms of "public architecture" that probably played a role in community or supracommunity integration. Examples of these are the D-shaped biwalled structure at Sand Canyon Pueblo; a poorly understood circular structure subdivided into four quadrants at the Goodman Point Ruin; isolated towers or tower-kiva complexes; masonry walls enclosing all or parts of aggregated pueblos; and possible plaza areas within some of the larger sites. In addition, great kivas and unroofed, circular enclosures appear at some sites. Architectural forms and site locations interpretable as defensive are also present, though they are far from ubiquitous.

The locality's population appears to have grown during the Pueblo III period, perhaps reaching its peak in the mid-1200s, only a few decades before the evidently rapid and complete abandonment of the locality, the northern San Juan region, and the Four Corners area in general. The Sand Canyon locality provides an ideal opportunity for a detailed case study that may reveal new insights into Pueblo III social, demographic, environmental, and adaptive change and eventual abandonment. Models of Pueblo change and abandonment developed outside the Sand Canyon locality can be tested there, and vice versa. Eddy et al. (1984) recognized that the lower McElmo drainage was an appropriate arena for the study of Pueblo II and Pueblo III developments in Southwestern Colorado. In summarizing research problems in the McElmo drainage unit, Eddy et al. (1984:43) note that

> the emergence, growth, and decline of an aggregated settlement system during the late PII–PIII stages . . . and the role/influence of Chaco culture . . . is probably the most important problem, both from a practical and scientific sense, and yet, the most difficult because of the scale of the problem and the inaccessibility of some of the resource.

The scale and long-term commitment of the Crow Canyon Center's research program are addressing the difficulties that Eddy et al. (1984) recognized.

Regional and Theoretical Contexts

The third research domain—placing the Pueblo III occupation of the Sand Canyon locality in broader cultural and theoretical contexts—is essential if we are to use what other archaeologists have learned and if our results are to be meaningful outside our small study area. From the standpoint of placing the locality in regional cultural context, we need to know whether the patterns and trends we see in the Sand Canyon locality are repeated elsewhere in the northern Southwest and, if so, whether this is due to the operation of supracommunity social, political, or religious organizations, to diffusion operating through network-type relationships among individuals or small groups, or to common environmental or demographic pressures.

In the spring of 1990, the Crow Canyon Center began to actively address this need by hosting a working conference entitled "Pueblo Cultures in Transition: A.D. 1150–1350 in the American Southwest." This conference* brought together a number of scholars working throughout the Southwest to summarize what is known about population distribution and sociocultural dynamics in their areas and to compare notes regarding regional and subregional trends and patterns (Lipe and Lekson 1990). A volume incorporating their papers is being edited by Michael Adler, Stephen Lekson, and William Lipe and will be published as an Occasional Paper of the Crow Canyon Archaeological Center.

The focus on community and supracommunity social organization and change plunges the Sand Canyon Project researchers into current debates over the complexity and scale of organization in prehistoric Southwestern Pueblo societies (e.g., Cordell and Plog 1979; Wilcox 1981; Ellis 1981; Upham 1982, 1985, 1989; Reid 1985, 1989; Lightfoot and Upham 1989a, 1989b; Orcutt et al. 1990). Comparative studies and synthesis of Sand Canyon Project data will be oriented toward general dimensions of organizational variation (Blanton et al. 1981) that are theoretically appropriate to characterizing community and supracommunity organization and their degree of complexity.

These dimensions of organizational variation are scale, differentiation, integration, and intensity. *Scale* (Barth 1978; Schwartz 1978) refers to the size of the geographic area occupied by a community or other organization and to its population size. Another aspect of scale is the "reach" of the organization, as indicated by the distance traveled by imported or exported goods. *Differentiation* has two aspects—horizontal differentiation, or the "functional specialization among parts of equivalent rank within a system," and vertical differentiation, or "rank differences among functionally diverse parts" (Blanton et al. 1981:21; see also Plog 1974 and Blau 1975). Vertical differentiation

* The conference was supported in part by Grant 48–32, Wenner-Gren Foundation for Anthropological Research.

implies inequality of access to economic, ideological, or military sources of power (Mann 1986). *Integration* refers to the interdependence of structural units within a society. This can be accomplished in various ways—through common ideology and cultural norms, reinforced through ritual; through flows of information, material, energy, or people among units (Blanton et al. 1981:20); through organizations, such as sodalities, that crosscut local segments (Service 1962); through structures, such as sequential hierarchies (Johnson 1982), that extend consensual decision-making beyond the small-group level; or through centralized managerial control (Lightfoot 1984; Flannery 1972), referred to by Johnson (1982) as "simultaneous hierarchy." *Intensity* refers to the amounts of population, material, information, or energy use per unit area or per capita. The per-unit-area formulations of subsistence intensification have been employed in numerous theories of sociocultural evolution (e.g., Boserup 1965; Plog 1974; Earle 1980; Johnson and Earle 1987). The per capita formulation has had less use in characterizing organizations, but it underlies White's (1949, 1959) "energy capture" evolutionary scheme and has been extensively used to document the unequal access to resources characteristic of vertical differentiation (e.g., Johnson 1989).

The dimensional approach to characterizing organizational complexity and change does not require the assumption that all four dimensions are always highly correlated (cf. Netting 1987; Feinman and Neitzel 1984; Leonard and Jones 1987) but provides the opportunity to determine how covariation does occur—e.g., whether aspects of scale are closely related to aspects of differentiation or intensity. The approach also facilitates comparison across time and space by focusing on general properties of organizations rather than on specific culture-historical configurations or on gross organizational types that are presumed to be cross-culturally recurrent, such as tribe or chiefdom. Comparative statements—regarding greater or lesser degrees of scale or differentiation, for example—are generally more demonstrable in archaeology than are statements that particular thresholds have been crossed or that a particular type of organization is present. Therefore, we hope to examine whether or not aspects of organizational complexity increased or decreased through time in the Sand Canyon locality and to make some general comparisons with community and supracommunity organizations elsewhere—e.g., with Chaco Canyon or the Grasshopper site cluster. We believe that this approach will provide a solid perspective from which to relate our findings in the Sand Canyon locality to the specific models of prehistoric Pueblo organization that have been proposed over the past decade.

Instrumental Studies

A number of instrumental studies must be done in order to pursue the problem domains described above, especially

the first two, which require new field and laboratory data to identify and interpret patterns of community organization and of sociocultural change and abandonment for the Sand Canyon locality. These instrumental studies include reconstructing past environments, building chronologies, identifying processes of assemblage and deposit formation, inferring the character of abandonment of structures and settlements, and estimating the length and continuity of occupation of structures and settlements.

In Chapter 8, Adams provides an overview of the approaches to environmental reconstruction being taken on the Sand Canyon Project, and Van West and Lipe (Chapter 9) summarize the results of an attempt to model past climate and agricultural productivity. Hegmon (1991) has recently completed an attribute-based study of Pueblo III pottery from the project area that promises to improve significantly the resolution of dating assignments based on ceramic assemblages. The use of tree-ring dates and architectural and sediment stratigraphy to establish fine-grained chronology is alluded to in several of the chapters that follow, especially those by Varien et al., Huber and Lipe, and Bradley. Assessments of the longevity of site occupation are one outcome of this chronological work, but considerable effort is also going into rate-of-accumulation approaches to this problem (Kohler and Blinman 1987; Varien 1990a; Lightfoot 1990; see also Varien et al., this volume).

Much work is also going into assessment of processes of assemblage formation. In addition to the increasingly voluminous literature on this subject, these assessments are guided by the work of Lightfoot (1990, 1992) at the Duckfoot site (another Crow Canyon project). A related topic is the abandonment of structures and settlements; chapters by Varien et al., Huber and Lipe, and Bradley provide some examples of how stratigraphy, evidence of the disposition of roof materials, and the composition of floor assemblages in structures are being used to characterize modes of abandonment. Related work at the Duckfoot site (Varien and Lightfoot 1989; Lightfoot 1990, 1992) is also providing helpful perspectives on assemblage-formation processes.

The Research Program

The Sand Canyon Project started in 1983, the same year that the Crow Canyon Center opened its doors as a private, nonprofit organization devoted to research and education in American archaeology. Before moving ahead to describe the history of research on the Sand Canyon Project, a brief discussion of the nature of research at the Center and of the development of its research infrastructure is in order. It is expected that this background information will give the reader a better understanding of how the Sand Canyon Project has developed.

One of the unique characteristics of archaeological research at the Crow Canyon Center is that virtually all of the fieldwork and much of the initial laboratory work involve participation by members of the public who are enrolled in educational programs designed to introduce them to Southwestern prehistory and to the nature of archaeological research. These educational programs are not designed to train participants to be professional archaeologists; rather, they utilize research involvement to provide a "hands-on" educational experience. Quite often the participants have had no previous archaeological experience and spend a total of less than a week in the field and lab during their stay at the Crow Canyon Center. Yet virtually all of the actual excavation at the sites is done by these participants, although the majority of the recording is done by the professional staff. Consequently, the data-gathering part of the research goes quite slowly and requires a high ratio of trained supervisors to educational-program participants.

Student interns also contribute to the research program, both in the field and in the laboratory. These are students who have had previous academic and research experience in archaeology and who spend a 10-week term at the Center, assisting the professional staff in excavations and laboratory operations. Interns also made up the majority of the field crews for the upland surveys reported by Adler in this volume.

The research program at the Crow Canyon Center began in 1983; in that year and 1984, the major focus of field research was the Duckfoot site (Varien and Lightfoot 1989; Lightfoot 1992), but work in the Sand Canyon area was assigned equal importance in 1985 through 1987. After the completion of excavations at Duckfoot in 1987, all field operations were shifted to the Sand Canyon locality.

The program started small and was built one element at a time, as funds became available and as the trajectory of the research demanded it. The initial focus—in 1983 and 1984—was fieldwork. The first full-time research staff members—E. Charles Adams and Bruce Bradley—spent approximately half the year in fieldwork and related educational programs and the remainder doing laboratory work and reports. In 1985, a laboratory director (Angela Schwab) was hired—in a seasonal position, but one that was converted to full time by the end of the year. Additional laboratory staff were added in succeeding years—first as part-time, then as full-time employees. There are now two full-time laboratory staff members, in addition to the lab director. Because the laboratory was understaffed in the early years of the program, it was not until 1990 that the backlog of unanalyzed materials was overcome. Currently, basic processing and analysis of materials obtained in one field season can be completed by the following spring, before the start of the next field season.

Laboratory and office facilities were initially in unheated trailers, so that laboratory work and writing had to be moved to the Center's dining hall during the winter. By the end of 1987, a new office/laboratory/classroom building provided a "home" for the research staff. A third full-time field archaeologist was also hired in 1987, and two assistants were added in subsequent years—first as seasonal staff, and then as full-time employees in 1991. Development of a computer database was planned in 1988, and basic computer equipment was purchased that year. In 1989, development of the database began, and two part-time staff members with expertise in computer applications were employed in 1990. By the end of that year, the computer database was operational. The year 1990 also saw the initiation of the Environmental Archaeology section of the research program. This brought together and coordinated the efforts that were already underway in this area and provided the staffing to do additional work that was needed.

Although descriptive reports of fieldwork were prepared each year from the beginning of the research program, these were photocopied rather than printed and had a limited distribution. In 1988, it was decided that the Crow Canyon Center should start its own research publication series, so that technical monographs reporting the results of its research could be produced. The series was entitled "Occasional Papers of the Crow Canyon Archaeological Center." The first volume was completed in 1989 (Lipe and Hegmon 1989) and made available for sale early in 1990.

Occasional Paper No. 1 was edited and formatted in camera-ready form by staff members working outside their primary jobs, and often after hours. In 1991, it was possible to establish a Publications section within the research program, with additional equipment and a small staff devoted to publications support. With the current level of staffing, the Center expects to be able to publish two or three book-length monographs a year. This progress report on the Sand Canyon Project is Occasional Paper No. 2, and several other works of similar or greater length are "in the pipeline," in various stages of editing.

Preparation of a synthesis of research results from the Sand Canyon Project is planned for 1995. Although a number of special analyses and comparative studies employing data from multiple sites have been done or are underway by staff and affiliated researchers and graduate students, additional studies will be required. A focus on these studies is planned for 1992 through 1994.

History of Sand Canyon Project Research

The Sand Canyon Archaeological Project had its beginnings in a decision by Crow Canyon Center archaeologists in 1983 to investigate Sand Canyon Pueblo, a very large, late Pueblo III site located near the head of Sand Canyon about 19 km (12 miles) west of the Crow Canyon campus.

The decision was based on several considerations, including the relative lack of work done on late Pueblo III settlements outside the Mesa Verde since the 1940s, and especially on the very poor level of knowledge about the very large, late settlements in the greater Montezuma Valley, such as Sand Canyon Pueblo, the Yellow Jacket Ruin, the Goodman Point Ruin, etc. (Adams 1983). Another consideration was that Sand Canyon Pueblo appeared to have been occupied relatively briefly, so that assemblages found there could be related to a single component, without the complexities found in sites having multiple occupations.

Sand Canyon Pueblo was mapped in 1983, and excavations were begun on a small scale in 1984, under the direction of E. Charles Adams and Bruce Bradley. Bradley took over direction of the work in 1985 and spent a full field season there that year. The research design for Sand Canyon Pueblo proposed excavation of a sample of *kiva units*—a kiva and all directly associated rooms, other structures, midden deposits, etc. The kiva units that were excavated were selected judgmentally to sample three categories of architectural complexes, or *blocks,* at Sand Canyon Pueblo, distinguished on the basis of their overall room-to-kiva ratios (see Bradley, this volume, for a fuller discussion of the sampling design). This strategy was maintained through 1989, resulting in the complete excavation of six kiva units in as many architectural blocks (Adams 1985a, 1986; Bradley 1986, 1987, 1988a, 1990, 1991b; Kleidon and Bradley 1989). At the close of the 1989 season, Bradley began work on a comprehensive report on the six seasons of excavations that had been conducted to that date at Sand Canyon Pueblo. No fieldwork was done at the site in 1990, but Bradley returned to the field in 1991 for a 12-week season, to focus on excavations of elements of "public architecture" at the site (Bradley and Lipe 1990).

Although the original research design for the Sand Canyon Archaeological Project (Adams 1983) envisioned systematic survey and site testing to place Sand Canyon Pueblo in a broader locality and community context, it was not possible to begin systematic survey until 1985 and 1986. During the summers of those years, Carla Van West directed surveys on lands surrounding Sand Canyon Pueblo (Van West 1986; Van West et al. 1987) (Figure 1.3).

In late 1986, Bill Lipe and Bruce Bradley prepared a National Science Foundation (NSF) proposal (Lipe and Bradley 1986) that represented an updated research design for the Sand Canyon Project, replacing Adams's 1983 document. In the 1986 design, the Sand Canyon study area was expanded to approximately 200 km², and was referred to as the Goodman Point-Sand Canyon locality (the "Goodman Point" label quickly dropped away, but "locality" stuck). The central research problem stated in the 1986 document was understanding the social organization of the Anasazi community that was centered on Sand Canyon Pueblo. A secondary objective was to understand the extent to which Sand Canyon Pueblo and the Sand Canyon community had social and cultural connections and influence at a regional level. Expansion of the intensive survey was proposed, as was excavation in small sites contemporaneous with Sand Canyon Pueblo, to obtain data that would permit assessment of the scale and organization of the Sand Canyon community.

The 1986 NSF proposal also identified the need for "instrumental" studies—those studies that are necessary to support the more direct attacks on the problem of locality social organization. Funds were awarded by NSF in mid-1987 (grant BNS-8706532). That summer, two survey teams carried out intensive survey under the direction of Michael Adler (Adler, this volume; Adler 1988, 1990), and intensive excavations at the Green Lizard site were begun by Edgar Huber. This site, which has two kivas and an associated roomblock, is located in Sand Canyon about 1 km below Sand Canyon Pueblo. Huber fully excavated the western half of the site in 1987 and 1988 (Huber and Lipe, this volume; Huber and Bloomer 1988; Huber 1989), acquiring data on a kiva unit comparable to those being intensively excavated at Sand Canyon Pueblo by Bradley. Another NSF proposal was submitted early in 1988 (Lipe and Bradley 1988). Although it was not funded, it served the Sand Canyon Project as an updated research design.

In the spring of 1988, the Crow Canyon Center organized a symposium at the Society for American Archaeology meetings in Phoenix on the topic of architectural evidence for integrative rituals in prehistoric Southwestern pueblos. The symposium participants agreed to revise their papers and submit them for publication by the Crow Canyon Center, with Bill Lipe and Michelle Hegmon as editors. Most of the original papers were extensively rewritten, several new ones were added, and the resulting book went to press late in 1989, entitled *The Architecture of Social Integration in Prehistoric Pueblos* (Lipe and Hegmon 1989). In addition to case studies, the book (1) provided some theoretical bases for using architecture as a basis for inferring social integration; (2) concluded that most PI–PIII Mesa Verde kivas probably had domestic as well as ritual functions; (3) identified public architecture as indicative of community level integration; and (4) posited a major change in Anasazi patterns of ritual and social integration about A.D. 1300, immediately after the abandonment of the San Juan drainage.

A project related to the "architecture of social integration" was begun in 1990 by Susan Kenzle, a graduate student at the University of Calgary. Her study concerns "Architecture With Unknown Function" (AWUF). These remains consist of low walls, isolated heaps of stone, and other features that occur on and around some of the larger thirteenth-century sites. It appears that at least some of these features may have to do with defining settlement boundaries, delineating symbolically important connections between parts of the site, and perhaps providing some

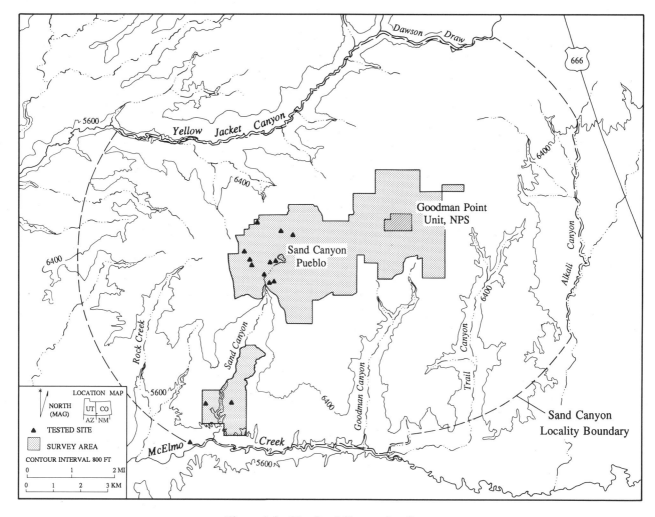

Figure 1.3. The Sand Canyon locality.

type of visible ritual or symbolic mapping of the space in and around the settlement (Thompson et al. 1991).

In the summer of 1988, Peter Gleichman surveyed a portion of lower Sand Canyon (Figure 1.3) for the Bureau of Land Management (Gleichman and Gleichman, this volume; Gleichman and Gleichman 1989). In this survey, the Gleichmans used recording forms and survey procedures compatible with those developed for the earlier Crow Canyon surveys directed by Van West (Van West et al. 1987) and Adler (Adler 1988). In 1990, under its cooperative management agreement with the Bureau of Land Management, Crow Canyon received funds to conduct additional survey in Lower Sand and East Rock canyons. This work was directed by Michael Adler (Adler and Metcalf 1991) and is not reported in this volume.

In 1988, Mark Varien began a testing program focused on the smaller Pueblo III sites located in the central part of the Sand Canyon locality (Figure 1.3). This program has continued through 1991 under his direction (Varien 1990b, Kuckelman et al. 1991). As with the Green Lizard excavations, the purpose of this work is to obtain comparative data

from smaller sites that were contemporary with Sand Canyon Pueblo or that date to the 50–100 years preceding its construction in about A.D. 1250. Unlike the Green Lizard work, in which a kiva unit was intensively excavated, the site testing program relies on stratified random samples of test pits at each site. Through the 1991 field season, 13 sites had been tested in this way. Reports of the 1988–1990 fieldwork are summarized by Varien et al. in this volume.

Sites tested in the 1988 and 1989 seasons were located within 2 km of Sand Canyon Pueblo. In 1990, crews directed by Ricky Lightfoot and Jim Kleidon extended the site testing program to several sites in lower Sand Canyon and the adjacent McElmo valley. One of these—Castle Rock Pueblo—may have as many as 75–100 rooms and is by far the largest site tested so far. Testing at this site continued in 1991, and additional judgmentally selected portions of the site will be excavated in 1992.

The testing program is geared to obtaining comparable samples of assemblages from each site, as well as comparable information about features and architecture. Additional objectives are to understand the chronology of each site and to infer its continuity and longevity of occupation. More information about the objectives and methods of the testing program are presented in Chapter 5 (Varien et al.).

Next to Sand Canyon Pueblo, the largest post–A.D. 1150 site in the Sand Canyon locality is the Goodman Point Ruin. Since the development of the 1986 research proposal and design (Lipe and Bradley 1986), it had been recognized that information from the Goodman Point site would play a key role in understanding community organization in the locality. In particular, whether Goodman Point was contemporaneous with Sand Canyon Pueblo or just preceded it would have a major bearing on our interpretations of community organization. If Goodman Point and Sand Canyon pueblos were contemporaneous, there would be two "community centers" of approximately equal size within 5 km of each other. But if Goodman Point was the earlier, it might indicate that the whole locality had a single central site that moved from the head of Goodman Canyon to the head of Sand Canyon in the mid-1200s.

Adler mapped the Goodman Point site in 1987 (Adler 1988), and Lightfoot (1989) presented a proposal to the National Park Service for testing the site under an Archaeological Resources Protection Act permit. The testing proposed for Goodman Point required excavating substantially less than 1 percent of the site by area and was designed to acquire data that would be comparable to those being obtained by the small (and medium) site testing program. The application was turned down by the National Park Service because its current draft management plan for the site places it in indefinite "reserve" from excavation or other surface-altering modes of research, so that it may be kept intact for archaeological research and interpretation at some unspecified time in the future. Discussions of the possibilities for permissible types of research at the Goodman Point site are continuing between Crow Canyon Center and National Park Service personnel.

In January of 1989, the Crow Canyon research staff assembled at the Recapture Lodge in Bluff for a "research retreat" to consider goals and future directions for the research program. Stephen Lekson and David Braun were invited to the meeting as outside participants and discussants, to provide professional perspectives from outside the Crow Canyon staff. The principal new direction established at the meeting was to make the understanding of the abandonment of Sand Canyon Pueblo, the Sand Canyon locality, and the northern San Juan area a primary research goal, equivalent to the previous primary focus on community organization. This new goal has subsequently been restated as an attempt to understand social, cultural, and environmental change in the period A.D. 1150 to 1300 for the Sand Canyon locality and, to the extent possible, for the northern San Juan area. In this perspective, the late thirteenth-century abandonments remain important foci, but it is recognized that understanding them will require tracking change in the immediately preceding periods as well.

A significant conclusion reached at the 1989 research retreat was that important changes, such as abandonment, that affected the Sand Canyon locality could not be understood without considering a much broader cultural and environmental context. This was not to deny the importance of gaining a good understanding of the pattern and dynamics of change in the Sand Canyon locality. Rather, it was meant to recognize that broader patterns had to be considered as well, including what opportunities existed elsewhere in the Southwest that might have made abandonment of the locality and the northern San Juan seem more attractive to Anasazi populations than staying in the area.

To develop a larger context for the Sand Canyon Project work, Lekson and Lipe planned a conference to bring together researchers from the entire Pueblo Southwest to discuss the pattern and processes of change in the period A.D. 1150–1350. A small grant was received from the Wenner-Gren Foundation, and the conference was held in March 1990. The Crow Canyon research group prepared a paper on "what happened" in the Mesa Verde area during the targeted period (Varien et al. 1990), and Lipe and Lekson summarized the results of the conference at the Society for American Archaeology meetings in April 1990 (Lipe and Lekson 1990). There was general agreement among the Crow Canyon archaeologists and the other conference participants that the conference had been very successful in raising consciousness about the degree to which demographic and social change was integrated over a huge area during the A.D. 1150–1350 period.

Another conclusion reached by the attendees at the original research retreat in 1989 was that a serious attack on the problem of abandonment would require a more intensive and systematic investigation of environmental data—both for a better understanding of prehistoric subsistence and natural resource economies and for a reconstruction of natural and anthropogenic environmental change that may have affected Anasazi adaptations in the study area in the twelfth and thirteenth centuries. Consequently, in mid-1989, Dr. Karen Adams was engaged to plan a comprehensive program of environmental archaeology, to be carried out under her direction (see Adams, this volume). Adams was already quite familiar with aspects of the Sand Canyon Project, having been the Center's primary consultant on macrobotanical remains for several years. The Environmental Archaeology section was designed to have a public educational component, as did other aspects of the research program. Mark Hovezak joined the staff as an assistant to Adams in early 1990, and the new program became fully functional by mid-1990.

In 1989, Marjorie Connolly initiated an oral history project focused on settlement and agriculture in the Goodman Point area, which lies within the Sand Canyon locality. Although the historic Goodman Point community is of interest in its own right, it was also thought that documenting early twentieth-century patterns of land use and farming would prove valuable for understanding prehistoric Anasazi settlement and farming strategies in the same area. A secondary objective was to document changes in the archaeological record that were due to farming activities, so that survey data from cultivated fields could be better evaluated. Connolly's findings are summarized in this volume and in an earlier report (Connolly 1990).

From 1987 through 1990, Carla Van West designed and completed a basic environmental study: a model of potential agricultural productivity in Southwestern Colorado, as conditioned by soil moisture availability (Van West and Lipe, this volume; Van West 1990). The model utilizes Geographic Information Systems computer technology and data on precipitation derived from tree-ring sequences to plot Palmer Drought Severity Indices for soils in an approximately 1800 km^2 area that includes the Sand Canyon locality. The data set and model promise to be extremely useful in studying the effect of climatic and locational variability on Anasazi farming adaptations in the Sand Canyon locality and surrounding areas.

In 1991, Michelle Hegmon completed an attribute-based study of stylistic change in Pueblo III white wares (Hegmon 1991). Working with selected assemblages that were well dated by dendrochronology, Hegmon was able to identify distinctive attribute frequency profiles for the late A.D. 1100s and the early, middle, and late 1200s. This represents a considerable advance over previous levels of stylistic discrimination among Pueblo III ceramic assemblages and promises to improve our understanding of settlement pattern change and composition of community clusters at various points in time during the Pueblo III period.

Fieldwork focused on the Pueblo III occupation of the Sand Canyon locality is expected to continue through 1994. A synthesis of research results, addressing the problem domains outlined above, will be prepared in 1995. Publication of full descriptive reports of archaeological contexts at excavated and tested sites is also planned. The Crow Canyon Center's research program will continue after the conclusion of planned work on the Pueblo III occupation of the Sand Canyon locality. A final decision has not been made, but an attractive research direction would be to focus on the A.D. 1000–1150 period in the greater Montezuma Valley, including a consideration of the nature of the "Chacoan" presence in the area.

2

The Upland Survey

Michael A. Adler

Introduction

Archaeological survey plays an integral role in the Sand Canyon Archaeological Project. Survey data are essential for estimates of prehistoric population and population change, as well as for the documentation of settlement patterns. Aspects of settlement pattern emphasized in the survey research design include: (1) community spatial structure—e.g., dispersed, nucleated, or aggregated—and the extent to which spatial distributions indicate community boundaries; (2) distribution of possible community integrative features such as great kivas; and (3) distribution of site sizes and types with respect to environmental variables such as soil type and water sources.

The Crow Canyon Archaeological Center began systematic archaeological survey in the Sand Canyon locality in 1985 under the direction of Carla Van West (Van West 1986). Surveys continued in 1986 and 1987, led by Van West and Michael Adler, respectively (Van West et al. 1987; Adler 1988, 1990). During these three seasons, a total of approximately 650 person-days was expended, resulting in the survey of a contiguous area of approximately 2600 ha (6400 acres) around Sand Canyon Pueblo and the Goodman Point Ruin (Figure 1.3). Survey coverage included both federal lands (Bureau of Land Management and the National Park Service) and private lands.

The 1985-through-1987 surveys focused on the rolling uplands in the center of the Sand Canyon locality but also extended into the upper portions of some of the canyons that drain this area. In the summer of 1988, the Bureau of Land Management (BLM) contracted with Carol and Peter Gleichman of Native Cultural Services to survey portions of lower Sand Canyon (Gleichman and Gleichman, this volume; Gleichman and Gleichman 1989); in 1990, Adler surveyed additional portions of lower Sand Canyon and

adjacent parts of the McElmo valley for the Crow Canyon Center, under a cooperative agreement with the BLM (Adler and Metcalf 1991). Only the 1985–1987 upland surveys are discussed in this chapter; Gleichman and Gleichman summarize the results of the 1988 lower Sand Canyon survey in Chapter 3. The final report on the 1990 survey (Adler and Metcalf 1991) is still in the process of revision in response to agency review.

The upland survey recorded 429 archaeological sites, representing a minimum of 696 cultural components. To the extent possible, components were classified by functional type and by chronological period (Table 2.1). Estimates of resident population were made for sites considered likely to have been permanent habitations. The methodologies used to make chronological and functional assignments, and to estimate population, are briefly discussed below (more detailed treatments are found in Adler 1990).

Chronological placement of sites and components depended on assessments of surface artifacts and architectural evidence. Pottery styles generally provided the most useful indicators, but lithic artifacts (e.g., metate and projectile point forms) and temporally sensitive aspects of architecture (e.g., presence or absence of pecked-block masonry) were useful in some cases. Components dating prior to A.D. 930 were assigned to either a broad Basketmaker III or Pueblo I period, as data permitted. For the A.D. 930–1300 occupation, a somewhat finer chronological subdivision was attempted. The Pueblo II period was subdivided into early, middle, and late subphases. For the Pueblo III period, the first entry in both Tables 2.1 and 2.2 is for all Pueblo III habitation components. The second entry (late Pueblo III) is for those components confidently believed to postdate A.D. 1225.

The pottery dating scheme used for these periods relied primarily on work by Blinman (1986) and Breternitz et al.

Table 2.1. Distribution of Components in the Upland Survey Area by Functional Type and Time Period

Site Type	Basketmaker/ Pueblo I Pre–930	Early Pueblo II 930–980	Middle Pueblo II 980–1060	Late Pueblo II 1060–1150	Pueblo III[a] 1150–1300	Late Pueblo III[b] 1225–1300	Unknown	Protohistoric/ Historic
Indeterminate							7	2
Habitation	108	20	75	96	109	97	6	2
Limited-activity[c]	18	2	6	7	27	24	73	5
Tower					2	2		
Great kiva		1?	1	2	2	2		
TOTAL	126	23	82	105	140	125	86	9

[a] General Pueblo III, including both early and late components.
[b] Sites with evidence of post-A.D. 1225 occupation. Not all Pueblo III sites show this evidence.
[c] See Table 2.2 for breakdown of limited-activity site types.

(1974), but with assistance from other archaeologists working in the area (Fuller 1984; Dykeman 1986; Morris 1991; Wilson 1991) and from Crow Canyon Center staff members. Based on these sources, we distinguished "core" as well as "extended" date ranges for a number of key pottery types (Adler 1990). The core dates provided a time range within which the type was most likely to occur in abundance. The boundaries of the time periods we used in summarizing the survey data (e.g., Table 2.1) are based largely on the appearance and disappearance of key pottery types and type complexes—i.e., on our ability to make temporal distinctions among assemblages. In dating site components, we also found it useful to distinguish core and extended dates, with the former representing our best estimate of the actual range of dates within which the occupation occurred. Core dates were assigned to occupations only when over 50 sherds had been tallied on the surface and when the tally included a sufficient number of temporally diagnostic sherds to provide some confidence in the assignment (Van West et al. 1987: Appendix A).

The use of several pottery dating schemes to analyze our survey data reflects the scarcity of well-dated pottery assemblages in the McElmo dome area itself. Such assemblages are rare in relation to the large number of dated contexts analyzed in the nearby Dolores Project area, most of which deal with the pre–A.D. 900 occupation of that area. The pottery chronology developed for the Sand Canyon locality upland survey depends heavily on Blinman's (1986) Dolores Project dating scheme for the pre–A.D. 930 periods. As noted, a variety of sources was used for the Pueblo II and III periods to formulate idealized pottery-type and attribute profiles for points in time that could be anchored to chronological dates; the pottery characteristics of intervening times were extrapolated on the assumption of gradual, monotonic change in pottery styles.

During field recording, considerable effort was made to record evidence and inferences about site function. Indications of domestic activity or lack of it, types of structures and features present, and evidence of the intensity of occupation were all factored into the assessment of site

function. Two main functional classes—limited-activity sites and habitations—were recognized, with definitions largely following those of Schlanger and Orcutt (1986). Habitations were differentiated from limited-activity sites largely on the basis of presence/absence of evidence of multiple activities and of domestic activities. Artifact scatters that did not appear to have had significant post-depositional disturbance and that exhibited a low diversity of artifact types, low numbers of artifacts, and small areal extent were classified as limited-activity loci. To the extent that it could be justified, an attempt was also made to assign a more specific functional subtype to limited-activity loci (Table 2.2).

Two other nonhabitation-site classes that also did not seem to fit the limited-activity rubric were recognized—isolated great kivas and isolated towers or tower complexes (Table 2.1). These two types of site are not thought to have been used as permanent habitations; instead, they may have functioned at the community level, or at least have been used by groups larger than the coresidential unit (Adler 1990).

Population estimates (Table 2.3) were made only for the period A.D. 930–1300 and are based on estimates of rooms at habitation sites. When actual wall outlines were not observed, room counts were based on interpolation from rubble area, assuming that each room was represented by 10 m² of rubble. This assumption was based on average surface-room sizes in the Mesa Verde area (Lipe 1989), with additional area allowed for wall fall.

The step from room count to resident population requires further assumptions. The two primary methods of estimating site population from architectural evidence have been based on (1) ethnographic data on average household size across cultures (Cook 1972; Hill 1970; Longacre 1970), which requires that room counts be converted to household counts, or (2) averages of domestic space used per person (Brown 1987; Casselberry 1974; Naroll 1962). A combination of both approaches was used to arrive at an estimate of 1.5 persons per surface room. Brown (1987), after reevaluating Naroll's (1962) data, concluded that 6

Table 2.2. Limited-Activity Sites in the Upland Survey Area by Site Subtype and Time Period

Site Subtype	Basketmaker/ Pueblo I Pre–930	Early Pueblo II 930–980	Middle Pueblo II 980–1060	Late Pueblo II 1060–1150	Pueblo III[a] 1150–1300	Late Pueblo III[b] 1225–1300	Unknown	Protohistoric/ Historic
Indeterminate	10	1	2	3	1		7	
Storage room					4	2	24	
Field house	3		2	2	9	9	1	
Hearth	4	1	1	1			5	1
Stone circle					3	3	1	
Stone rectangle					5	5		2
Cairn/shrine							2	
Lithic scatter							17	
Water control					3	3	9	1
Kiln			1				1	
Petroglyph							3	
Reservoir				1	2	2		1
Storage cist	1						2	
Processing							1	
TOTAL	18	2	6	7	27	24	73	5

[a] General Pueblo III, including both early and late components.

[b] Sites with evidence of post-A.D. 1225 occupation. Not all Pueblo III sites show this evidence.

Table 2.3. Population Size and Density Estimates for Pueblo II and Pueblo III Periods in the Upland Survey Area

	Early Pueblo II 930–980	Middle Pueblo II[a] 980–1060	Late Pueblo II[a] 1060–1150	Pueblo III[b] 1150–1300	Pueblo III[c] 1150–1300
Number of habitation components[d]	20	75	96	107	109
Estimated number of dwelling rooms per habitation	6?	6	8	13	20
Average momentary number of habitations[e]					
20-year site use life	8	18	21	14	15
50-year site use life	20	46	53	36	37
Average momentary population[f]					
20-year site use life	72	162	252	273	450
50-year site use life	180	414	636	702	1110
Average momentary population density (per km^2)[g]					
20-year site use life	2.8	6.4	9.9	10.7	17.6
50-year site use life	7.1	16.2	24.9	27.5	43.5

[a] Average room count does not include the Casa Negra site because of the difficulty of (a) identifying habitation use from surface evidence and (b) the possibility that there were additions to the site in the Pueblo III period.

[b] This estimate is based on a room count that excludes the rooms at Sand Canyon Pueblo (400) and Goodman Point Ruin (400).

[c] This estimate includes 800 total rooms at Sand Canyon Pueblo and Goodman Point Ruin.

[d] The number of habitation sites occupied during the period.

[e] The average number of habitation sites estimated to be occupied at any one point in time during the period.

[f] The estimated average number of inhabitants in the survey area at any one point in time during the period.

[g] The average number of inhabitants per km^2 at any one point in time during the period.

m^2 of room space per person is a reasonable cross-cultural constant. For the Sand Canyon upland survey, I estimated that each 10 m^2 of roomblock rubble indicated one room, and that approximately 1.5 persons occupied the room space indicated by that area of rubble.

Finally, population estimates for chronological periods also. involve an assumption of site use life in order to calculate the number of settlements, rooms, and people present, on average, at any one time during the period in question. These estimates are expressed as *average momentary population* (Table 2.3). In this study, two estimates of site use life are employed—20 and 50 years. The first figure is consistent with recent work on use lives of Basketmaker II and Pueblo I pithouses, which tend to be coterminous with the use lives of at least the smaller sites of these periods (Gilman 1983; Schlanger 1985; Cameron 1990). The second estimate recognizes that by late Pueblo II times the common use of load-bearing masonry walls had at least potentially lengthened the use lives of Anasazi domestic surface structures. Also, to the extent multiple-household settlements are increasingly represented in the Pueblo II and III archaeological record, potential site longevity—and hence the potential for maintaining houses longer—may have increased. Larger settlements would appear to be less vulnerable than smaller ones to population flux due to the effects of the domestic cycle or of variations in rates of reproduction and mortality.

Despite these theoretical considerations, it is not at all clear that the "typical" Pueblo II and III settlement, which remains quite small, actually displayed an increased longevity. Results of the Crow Canyon Site Testing Program so far (Varien et al., this volume; also see Ahlstrom 1985) suggest that site use life may typically be closer to 20 than to 50 years, although much remains to be done to test this. One of the objectives of the Site Testing Program—not yet achieved—is to use rate-of-accumulation studies (Kohler and Blinman 1987), along with other data sources, to investigate variability in settlement longevity during the Pueblo III period.

In Table 2.3, two sets of population estimates are given for the Pueblo III period. The first excludes the populations living at the two largest sites in the survey area—Sand Canyon Pueblo and Goodman Point Ruin. The second includes these populations, based on an estimated 400 domestic surface rooms at each site. This allows the reader to evaluate the effect of these two very large sites on population density in the survey area. No other sites even a third this size are known from the Sand Canyon locality. If Pueblo III occupation were extensive over the area, which it appears to be until at least the early 1200s, the estimated population density for this area would decrease if the surveyed area were expanded, even with the inclusion of Sand Canyon Pueblo and Goodman Point Ruin.

It must also be kept in mind that the population estimates given refer to the average momentary population for the period. In any of the periods, population undoubtedly varied above and below this average during the period. For the Pueblo III period in the upper Sand Canyon area, the results to date of the Site Testing Program (Varien et al., this volume) indicate that many Pueblo III small sites were abandoned by sometime in the early 1200s, and that population was increasingly concentrated in and around Sand Canyon Pueblo. Because settlement longevity is taken into account in calculating average momentary population, it is quite possible that population in the survey area changed relatively little during the period, but that people moved from a more dispersed to a more aggregated settlement pattern.

Estimates of site size and layout could not be made at a number of sites because their surface expression had been substantially altered by historic-period land use—primarily agricultural practices. Digging by artifact collectors had also made some sites difficult to evaluate. Of the 429 sites

recorded, 161 (37 percent) were heavily disturbed by agricultural plowing, road building, or some form of modern land modification. While inferences of site function, extent of artifactual scatter, and site occupation date were still made for these disturbed sites, estimates of room counts and of types of structures present often were not possible.

Even after disturbance by agriculture, the larger habitation sites generally still exhibit identifiable architectural remains. The surface information potential of the smaller, limited-activity sites such as field houses has been relatively much more affected, leading to many of these sites being placed in "indeterminate" categories (Table 2.2).

In analyzing the survey data, we attempted to evaluate the extent to which settlements tended to cluster, as a rough indicator of degree of dispersion or aggregation of communities. Table 2.4 provides summary statistics for average distance to nearest neighbor among habitation sites, by period. Average distance to nearest neighbor does not in itself distinguish changes in site spacing due to overall increased density of sites in the survey area from changes due to increased clustering of sites. However, the standard deviation and coefficient of variation do provide some insights to whether spacing is regular or not, as do the actual site-location maps (Figure 2.1b–d; Figure 2.2a–c).

The relationship between settlement location and soil type was also explored in a preliminary way during analysis of the survey data. Two measures of the spatial association of habitation sites with arable land were used (Table 2.5). The first measure is the average arability score of the 4-ha area immediately surrounding the site. If this contained a predominance of nonarable soil (or rock), it received a score of 1; a score of 2 indicates that the primary soil type is sometimes arable, but only under optimal conditions of moisture and temperature. A score of 3 indicates that the site is located on soils that fall into the most consistently arable and potentially productive soil types in the study area. Information on soil quality was provided by Carla Van West, whose research on modeling prehistoric agricultural

Table 2.4. Nearest-Neighbor Distances between Habitation Sites in the Upland Survey Area

Period	Number of Sites	Average Distance (m)	S.D.	C.V.
Basketmaker III	82	243	176	73
Pueblo I	26	397	296	74
Early Pueblo II	20	427	335	78
Middle Pueblo II	75	289	300	103
Late Pueblo II	96	252	191	75
Pueblo III, total	109	230	164	71
Late Pueblo III	97	252	197	78

S.D. = Standard deviation.

C.V. = Coefficient of variation.

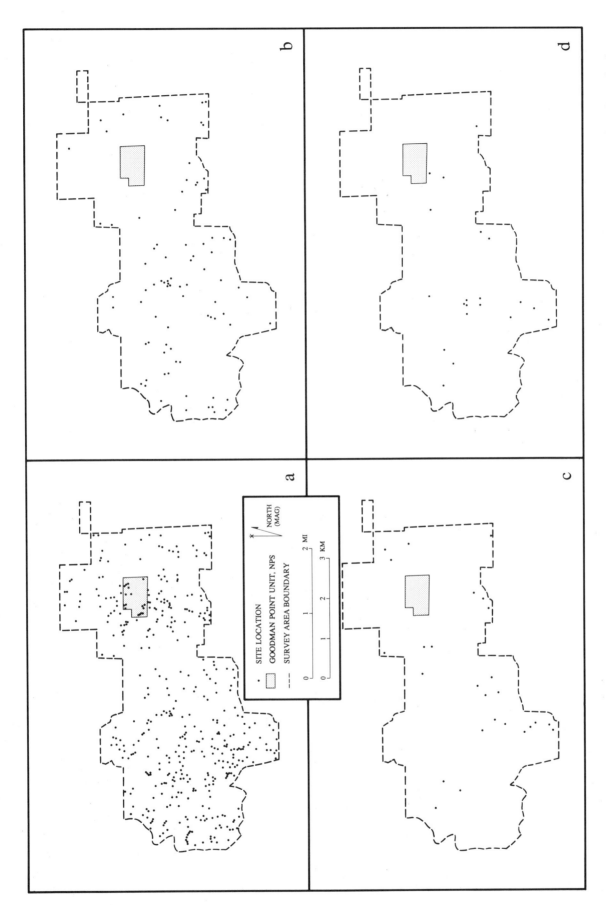

Figure 2.1. Sites recorded in the upland survey area: *a*, distribution of all recorded sites; *b*, distribution of Basketmaker III (A.D. 450–750) habitation components; *c*, distribution of Pueblo I (A.D. 750–930) habitation components; *d*, distribution of early Pueblo II (A.D. 930–980) habitation components.

Legend:

• SITE LOCATION

▢ GOODMAN POINT UNIT, NPS

--- SURVEY AREA BOUNDARY

NORTH (MAG)

2 MI

3 KM

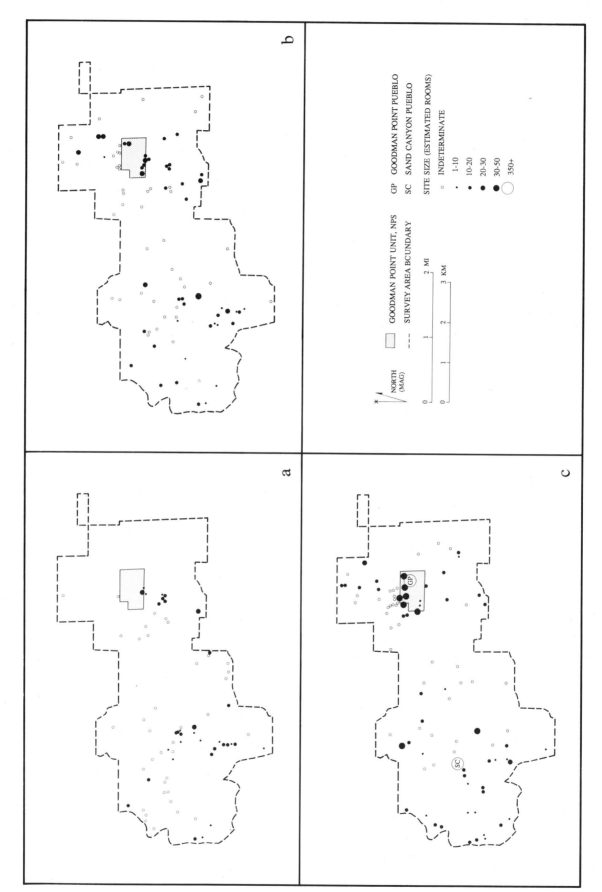

Figure 2.2. Sites recorded in the upland survey area: *a*, distribution of middle Pueblo II (A.D. 980–1060) habitation components; *b*, distribution of late Pueblo II (A.D. 1060–1150) habitation components; *c*, distribution of Pueblo III (A.D. 1150–1300) habitation components.

Table 2.5. Association of Soil Classes with Habitation Sites in the Upland Survey Area

Period	Number of Components	Site Soils[a]			Catchment Soils[b]		
		Average	S.D.	C.V.	Average	S.D.	C.V.
Basketmaker III	82	2.84	.45	15.8	21.80	2.66	12.2
Pueblo I	26	2.95	.20	6.7	22.50	2.32	10.3
Early Pueblo II	20	2.85	.49	17.1	22.20	2.50	11.2
Middle Pueblo II	75	2.81	.53	18.8	21.10	3.36	15.9
Late Pueblo II	96	2.81	.54	19.2	20.79	4.24	20.3
Pueblo III, total	109	2.69	.63	23.4	20.90	3.85	18.4
Late Pueblo III	97	2.65	.66	24.9	20.80	3.95	18.9

S.D. = Standard deviation. C.V. = Coefficient of variation.
[a] Average soil classification score for 4-ha quadrat in which the site is located. Maximum score = 3.
[b] Average soil classification score for 32-ha catchment surrounding the 4-ha quadrat in which the site is located. Maximum score = 24.

productivity is reported in this volume (Van West and Lipe; see also Van West 1990).

The second measure is an approximation of the agricultural quality of the "catchment" of soils surrounding each site. This measure considers the eight 4-ha quadrats (total of 32 ha) surrounding the quadrat in which the habitation site is located. The same scores used in the first measure are added, so that the minimum catchment quality score is 8, meaning that each of the eight surrounding quadrats contains a predominance of nonarable soils or bedrock. The maximum score is 24, meaning that all eight surrounding quadrats are dominated by Class 3 soils, the most desirable for agricultural production.

Basketmaker III (A.D. 450–750)

Although the primary focus of this research is on the A.D. 930–1300 period, survey personnel recorded all sites encountered in the study area. Those pre–A.D. 930 sites to which dates could be assigned were lumped into two extended time periods, either Basketmaker III (A.D. 450–750) or Pueblo I (A.D. 750–930). A finer chronology for late Basketmaker III and Pueblo I was developed by archaeologists on the nearby Dolores Archaeological Project (Kane 1986; Blinman 1986), but we did not feel that our pottery samples and architectural evidence from these periods in our study area were sufficient to allow us to apply this scheme.

A total of 82 habitation components dating to the Basketmaker III period were recorded within the survey area (Figure 2.1b). Information on size and architectural layout of these habitations is poor, because 65 (79 percent) have been significantly disturbed by cultivation. Most undisturbed sites consist of a thin scatter of sheet trash on the surface, and have at least one shallow pit structure depression. They also often display upright slab features that probably served as extramural hearths or storage cists.

Most Basketmaker III habitation sites are located in loose clusters on deep, arable, mesa-top soils, frequently

along the tops of well-drained ridges. These clusters often contain several concentrations of cultural material. Limited-activity sites from this time period appear as light scatters of gray wares and lithics, often associated with isolated hearth or slab-lined cist features.

The pattern of loose clustering of pit structures may indicate the existence of dispersed communities, assuming that a majority of the structures in each cluster are contemporaneous. However, recent data (Lipe and Breternitz 1980; Schlanger 1985; Cameron 1990) indicate that average pithouse life may be as short as 10 to 15 years. Thus, some of the Basketmaker III site clusters may be the remains of successive episodes of pit structure construction in one general vicinity.

The association between Basketmaker habitations and arable lands is similar to that for later habitation sites (Table 2.5). The nearest-neighbor data for the Basketmaker III sites (Table 2.4) indicate a fairly irregular pattern of spacing, with a relatively low nearest-neighbor average (243 m [S.D. 176]) and a coefficient of variation (73) that is moderately low compared to the other periods. Some of the irregularity in spacing can probably be attributed to the dendritic pattern of ridges and drainages on the mesa top. Location of sites on these ridges creates a sinuous, discontinuous settlement pattern.

Assuming 250 years for this period and three nuclear-family households occupying each habitation site for 25 years, the average momentary population of the entire survey area would have been approximately 25 families, or about 125 people.

Pueblo I (A.D. 750–930)

The McElmo dome area did serve as the home for some Anasazi groups during the Pueblo I period (Figure 2.1c), but most of the regional occupation was elsewhere, to the north and east, especially in and around the Dolores valley (see Breternitz et al. 1986). Habitation sites from this time period generally contain evidence of pit structures and slab-based surface rooms. White ware pottery profiles on the sites are expected to contain a predominance of Piedra Black-on-white, with declining evidence of Chapin Black-on-white as the period progresses. Gray ware vessels frequently are neckbanded, with Moccasin Gray present during most of the period, and Mancos Gray showing up in the terminal portion of the period.

In the Sand Canyon locality upland survey, as in other surveys from the McElmo dome and Montezuma Valley, Pueblo I sites are scarce relative to the number of sites inhabited during the preceding and following periods. In the Sand Canyon area, 26 sites were assigned to the Pueblo I period, 24 of which were judged to be habitation sites. Of the habitation sites, only four were sufficiently undisturbed to allow a site size estimate. Average site size is small, with 5.5 surface rooms and 1 to 2 pit structures, but this is a conservative estimate.

Site spacing exhibits a high level of dispersal, with an average nearest-neighbor distance of 397 m and a standard deviation of 296 m (Table 2.4). The coefficient of variation is approximately the same as in the Basketmaker III period, however. The data indicate a fairly wide spacing among habitations, a high degree of variation in the spacing (but with some clustering occurring), and wide spaces between the clusters (also see Figure 2.1c).

The relative scarcity of Pueblo I occupants in the study area is no surprise, given the population immigration and aggregation in the Dolores valley during this period (Schlanger 1985, 1988). The large settlements that formed in and around the Dolores valley near Dolores, Colorado, in the A.D. 800s (Kane 1986, 1989) represent early, and relatively short-lived, experiments in population aggregation in the northern San Juan region. Similar, but slightly earlier, aggregations occurred at Alkali Ridge, near Blanding in southeastern Utah (Brew 1946), and in the Ridges Basin area near Durango, Colorado (Fuller 1989).

The relatively small sample of Pueblo I habitation sites does exhibit an interesting pattern of association with the best arable soils. Though there is always a relatively high degree of association between Anasazi habitation sites and arable soils in the survey area (Table 2.5), the Pueblo I sites have the highest degree of association and lowest variation for any time period. All but one of the habitation sites are located on the most desirable soils for agricultural production. This is not solely an artifact of the low site density, as evidenced by the lower soil association index for the early Pueblo II period, which has a smaller total number of habitation sites.

Early Pueblo II (A.D. 930–980)

Early Pueblo II, shortest of the four Pueblo II–III phases defined for the survey, represents the initial part of the Pueblo II period. The Anasazi of the Pueblo II period have traditionally been thought to have made more use of surface architecture than those who lived in previous periods. However, archaeological excavations in the region show a continued reliance on pit structures, some of which have begun to take on the characteristics of the later Anasazi kiva (Gillespie 1976; Dykeman 1986; Hayes and Lancaster 1975). Dykeman's recent review of excavated early Pueblo II sites (1986:159) leads him to conclude that pit structures may be the norm, rather than exception, for Pueblo II domestic architecture. Since sites where the primary residential architecture is a pithouse generally have a poorer surface expression than do sites with surface habitation rooms, the early Pueblo II survey data may underrepresent the actual number of habitations in the study area during this phase.

Only 20 early Pueblo II habitation sites were recorded in the survey area (Figure 2.1d). Of these habitation components, only seven (35 percent) escaped modern agricultural disturbance. The undisturbed components did have rubble mounds, which averaged 70 m^2, indicating an average of approximately six to seven masonry surface rooms on these habitation sites. The population estimates for the phase follow the low-density trend set during the Pueblo I period. The 20-year site use life may be the more reasonable estimate for this phase (Table 2.3), given the probable continued use of pithouses, the jacal/masonry construction techniques associated with surface rooms of the period (Hayes and Lancaster 1975; Kent 1986), and the possibility that settlements were relocated when structures became deteriorated.

The settlement pattern for this phase is characterized by wide dispersal of permanent habitation sites, with the highest average nearest-neighbor distance (427 m [S.D. 335]) and the second highest coefficient of variation (78) of any phase of Anasazi occupation (Table 2.4). Also of note is the slight decrease in the association of habitation sites with the best arable soils (Table 2.5). This decrease may initiate a gradual trend toward use of less favorable soils that continues through the Pueblo II and III periods.

Middle Pueblo II (A.D. 980–1060)

Environmentally, middle Pueblo II appears to have been a period of mild temperatures and a codominant summer and winter precipitation pattern (Petersen 1986, 1988). The rise and initial spread of the Chaco Phenomenon within the San Juan Basin, as well as the increased use of previously more marginal ecological zones by the Anasazi, are both hallmarks of this period in the northern Southwest.

The number of cultural components recorded for this phase (Table 2.1) shows a marked increase over the A.D. 930–980 phase—an increase too great to be accounted for by the somewhat greater length of the middle Pueblo II period. Of the total number of middle Pueblo II sites of all types (n = 82), 75 (84 percent) are identified as habitation sites. Two potential field houses, one isolated hearth, one possible pottery kiln, and one indeterminate site make up the sample of limited-activity sites.

If the estimates of average momentary population (Table 2.3) are taken at face value, there is a significant increase in local population during this phase, on the order of 230 percent. This is not an unreasonable growth rate for the entire period (.0136, an annual increase of 1.36 percent, or 14 persons per thousand); although high, it falls within the range of intrinsic growth rates observed in preindustrial societies (Schlanger 1985:149).

Settlement patterns begin to show some definite clustering of habitation sites in three locales during middle Pueblo II (Figure 2.2a). The first cluster is in the vicinity of the Casa Negra site, south and east of what later became Sand Canyon Pueblo. The probable Chaco-style great house and associated roomblocks at Casa Negra may have contained between 40 and 60 rooms at the height of its occupation, which appears to have occurred largely during the second half of the eleventh century A.D. However, during the A.D. 980–1060 phase, there were between 6 and 10 smaller sites (each with between 6 and 10 rooms) in the vicinity. Although surface sherd tallies at the associated great kiva may be misleading, there is pottery evidence that cultural materials were being deposited at the great kiva during this phase as well.

The two other areas of increased settlement clustering are south of Casa Negra near the east rim of Sand Canyon and farther west, just south of Goodman Lake. In the Goodman Lake site cluster, at least five separate roomblocks ring the lake. The lake is actually a reservoir with a prehistoric retaining dam (Gould 1982).

The association between habitation sites and the best agricultural lands continues to weaken during this time phase (Table 2.5), but only slightly. The increase in the coefficient of variation is related to this same trend, indicating that relatively more sites are becoming spatially associated with relatively poorer agricultural lands.

Late Pueblo II (A.D. 1060–1150)

Although the late Pueblo II phase marked the heyday of the Chaco Phenomenon in the northern Southwest, it was also a time of gradually decreasing effective moisture and of increasing climatic variability (Dean et al. 1985). A major drought affecting the region began during the early twelfth century. Changes are evident not only in environment but in Anasazi culture history and material culture during this phase.

In the upland survey area, the late Pueblo II phase has 96 habitation components, 48 (50 percent) of which had not been disturbed by historic land development. The intact roomblocks that were free of later occupations averaged

eight surface rooms. However, the standard deviation surrounding this average is plus or minus seven rooms. This represents the beginnings of a trend not only toward larger habitation site size but toward greater variability in the range of habitation site sizes.

The increase in population indicated (Table 2.3) is not a dramatic one. However, potential complications in the use of these comparative data may rest with the dating scheme used for the survey. The main problem is that 43 sites were assigned to both the A.D. 980–1060 and the A.D. 1060–1150 periods, largely because of similarities in the expected profiles of chronologically sensitive pottery for both time periods. In both the middle and late Pueblo II phases, a predominance of Mancos Black-on-white is expected. In the latter phase, however, McElmo Black-on-white is expected in some frequency. The inability of local researchers, myself included, to come to a decision about the diagnostic characteristics of McElmo Black-on-white contributes to this problem of differentiating the middle and terminal portions of the Pueblo II period. A relatively large number of carbon-painted sherds were placed in "indeterminate" categories, perhaps weakening the usefulness of the sherd tallies as guides to chronology.

The spatial data for late Pueblo II habitation sites are mixed in comparison to earlier trends (Figure 2.2b and Tables 2.4 and 2.5). Direct access to the best agricultural lands is identical to that seen in the preceding period, but there is a slight decrease in the quality of the catchment zone soils for the late Pueblo II sites (Table 2.5). This indicates that habitation sites are still located on very productive lands, but that the surrounding catchment is slightly patchier in soil quality than was the case for the preceding phases.

Of interest in the site distribution (Figure 2.2b) is that both site clustering and large gaps between site clusters are evident. Multisettlement clusters continue to develop in the same areas as in the previous phase, and two probable great kivas do seem to be associated with the site clusters.

Even though the occupation of the lands immediately surrounding the upper portion of Sand Canyon continued during late Pueblo II, complete with various forms of probable community-level integrative facilities, the primary occupation cluster in the surveyed area was on the lands surrounding the eventual site of Goodman Point Pueblo. Excavation and survey data underscore this Anasazi florescence of the Goodman Point locale during the eleventh and twelfth centuries. This eventually culminated in the construction of Goodman Point Pueblo, probably in the early Pueblo III period.

Pueblo III (A.D. 1150–1300)

In the northern Southwest, the traditional dating of the Pecos Classification periods has put the start of Pueblo III at A.D. 1100. The later date of 1150 is used here to take both local cultural patterns and regional dynamics into account. By A.D. 1150 we see the weakening and demise of the unique, and still somewhat poorly understood, pan-regional influence of the Chaco Phenomenon (Judge 1989). By the late twelfth century, there are higher population levels and larger settlements in the area north of Chaco Canyon. The florescence of areas such as the Montezuma Valley, the Mesa Verde, and the San Juan River valley (including reoccupations at Salmon Ruin and Aztec Ruin) in the late twelfth and thirteenth centuries contrasts sharply with declining occupation in Chaco Canyon during the same time period.

The late twelfth and thirteenth centuries are known best for the Pueblo III occupation on Mesa Verde and the surrounding area. A great deal of archaeological interest focuses on this period, which not only begins with the decline of intensive occupation in Chaco Canyon but ends with the "Great Drought" and the end of the Anasazi occupation in the San Juan drainage and most of the southern Colorado Plateau by A.D. 1300. The upland survey data document significant changes within the survey area during this period.

Because of present ambiguities in the dating of Pueblo III habitation sites, two different strategies were employed in estimating population pattern statistics. The first strategy is the more conservative and pools the settlement data for sites that appear to have been occupied at some point after A.D. 1150, the start of the Pueblo III period as used here. The second strategy attempts to isolate those settlements in the survey area that appear most likely to have been inhabited after A.D. 1225.

This second strategy assumes that an internal chronology can be developed for the Pueblo III period. Similar divisions of the Pueblo III period have been proposed several times in the past (Rohn 1977; Reed 1958; Brew 1946; Fetterman and Honeycutt 1987). For the present research, the distinction is considered analytically defensible, but still tentative.

Relative to Pueblo II, both the pooled and the late Pueblo III settlement data exhibit an increase in settlement size and decrease in the spacing between settlements (Figure 2.2c; Tables 2.3 and 2.4). The average site size of 13 rooms is derived from relatively undisturbed habitation sites. As in the preceding period, however, the standard deviation for site size also increases, in this case to 10 rooms. These measurements do not include either Sand Canyon Pueblo or Goodman Point Ruin, both statistical outliers in every category of site measurement used here.

This high level of variation in average site size is due largely to the early Pueblo III introduction of "multi-roomblock habitation sites" (Figure 2.3). These are sites that contain from two to four separate roomblocks, usually placed one after another, 10–30 m apart, on ridge crests. Four such sites exist within or close to the boundaries of the Goodman Point unit. Another late Pueblo II/early Pueblo III multi-roomblock site, partially disturbed by a road, is located 400 m east of Sand Canyon Pueblo. And at least two sites that date to the same time period also may have had this type of site structure. One, recently destroyed by agricultural practices, appears in a 1973 aerial photograph as having four distinct rubble mounds. Sherd tallies on the middens associated with each of the roomblocks within the multi-roomblock sites show a high level of similarity, indicating occupational contemporaneity for all of the architectural units within each site.

Site spacing decreases from the Pueblo II to Pueblo III periods (Table 2.4). The pooled data for the entire Pueblo III period exhibit a decrease in average nearest-neighbor distance to 230 m (S.D. 164 m). This is a conservative average. Had the various architectural blocks in the multi-roomblock sites been recorded as separate settlements, the nearest-neighbor average would have shown an even greater decrease.

As might be expected with increasing population density and more crowding within the productive landscape, the locations of habitation sites during the Pueblo III period show a relatively weak association with the best arable soils (Table 2.5). On the other hand, the catchment scores are slightly higher than those recorded for the late Pueblo II period, but the amount of difference is negligible. Based on the conservative data derived from pooling early and late Pueblo III settlement locations, it is clear that by the thirteenth century we have the highest proportion of settlements located on soils that are potentially poorer for agriculture.

This trend away from living directly on the most desirable soils is most marked if we consider the smaller data set comprising just those settlements with late Pueblo III temporal affiliations (Table 2.5). This movement into the patchy soil conditions of the canyon benches and escarpments during the early thirteenth century is responsible for a decrease in the association of habitation site locations with the best arable soils.

Overall, the larger Pueblo III sites reflect the trend toward population aggregation that reaches its apogee with Sand Canyon and Goodman Point pueblos. While these two pueblos certainly had the capacity to house large numbers of Anasazi, it appears that an equally large population aggregation took place in the habitations just to the north of Goodman Point Pueblo. At least 25 large habitation sites were recorded within 1 km of the main ruin during the 1987 field season. Several sites exceed 30 rooms, resulting in a conservative estimate of 500 rooms surrounding the location of Goodman Point Ruin. Because there are relatively few surface sherds at the Goodman Point Ruin, our dating of this site is weak. It appears likely that it dates to the very late A.D. 1100s or to the first half of the A.D. 1200s, but it could be somewhat earlier or later. It seems likely that the population housed in the above-referenced cluster of hab-

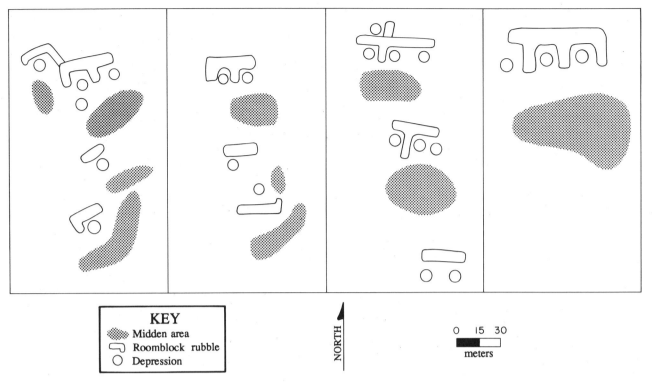

KEY
Midden area
Roomblock rubble
Depression

NORTH

0 15 30
meters

Figure 2.3. Examples of multi-roomblock sites.

itation sites moved from these sites into Goodman Point Pueblo. However, we are currently not able to test this proposition. Likewise, the precise chronological relationships between Goodman Point Pueblo and Sand Canyon Pueblo remain unclear. It seems likely that Sand Canyon Pueblo is the later, but, based on present evidence, we cannot exclude the possibility that the occupation of the Goodman Point aggregate overlapped with that of Sand Canyon Pueblo, or even that the two were fully contemporaneous.

There is a noticeable decrease in habitation sites in the vicinity of Sand Canyon Pueblo during the Pueblo III period. It is tenuous at this point to say whether Sand Canyon Pueblo represents a pulling in of the surrounding population, but available survey evidence hints at a late population aggregation at Sand Canyon Pueblo. Data from the Site Testing Program (Varien et al., this volume) give support to this idea.

Post-Anasazi Sites (Post–A.D. 1300)

A single, probable Shoshonean campsite was located a few hundred meters to the east of Sand Canyon Pueblo. The small site consists of two hearth areas, a scatter of bone and teeth of a large mammal, and several sherds of the distinctive micaceous pottery that serves as the basis for the temporal assignment of the site. No diagnostic lithic artifacts were associated with the site.

In addition to the Shoshonean site, several archaeological components assignable to the historic Anglo settlement of the area were recorded. These range from the locations of homestead cabins to various limited-activity sites such as hearths and a reservoir.

Indeterminate Sites

The classification "indeterminate site" was used by field personnel when they could not confidently assign a site to any site-use category because of a lack of diagnostic artifacts or architectural patterns. Ninety-nine such sites were recorded in 1987. Overall, this is a catchall for small, problematic sites that often occur as ephemeral scatters in cultivated fields. The scatters often contain a few nondiagnostic sherds or flakes. It is likely that these sites were formerly limited-activity sites, such as field houses, isolated hearths, and temporary camps, but have been disturbed by natural or cultural postoccupational modifications of the land surface.

Sites were also assigned to an unknown status for temporal placement if not enough temporally sensitive artifacts were found to permit estimation of the range of occupation dates. Among the types of sites often assigned to this category were water and soil control features (checkdams, terraces), small storage rooms tucked into small rock shelters, lithic and pottery scatters, isolated petroglyph sites, and ambiguous rubble scatters.

Conclusions

This analysis of the survey results highlights several patterns. First, the study area was utilized as far back as the Archaic period (7000–2000 B.P.). Though not indicated in Table 2.1, two probable Archaic-period campsites were located within the survey area. Due to the small amount of evidence available, however, there is little that can be said about land-use patterns in the upland study area prior to the Anasazi period (but see Fetterman and Honeycutt 1987 for evidence from a nearby locality).

Second, there does appear to have been a sustained, and at times dense, Anasazi occupation of the lands within the upland survey area. The bulk of the recorded sites fall in the Basketmaker III through Pueblo III periods, approximately A.D. 500 to 1300.

Third, the size and spatial structure of the prehistoric population seem to have undergone steady change throughout the Anasazi occupation. Estimates of population density range from 3 to 7 persons/km^2 in the mid–A.D. 900s to as many as 18 to 44 persons/km^2 in the Pueblo III period, before abandonment of the region in the late A.D. 1200s. The increase in population is associated with an overall increase in site size. Excluding for the moment the two obvious statistical outliers, Sand Canyon Pueblo and Goodman Point Ruin, settlements often grow to include multiple roomblocks of over 100 rooms by early in the Pueblo III occupation of the area. Because these settlements are composed of spatially separate roomblocks, they often are recorded as a cluster of separate "sites," so that site-based room-count averages reflect roomblock size more directly than actual settlement size. By the late 1200s, however, a high proportion—perhaps the majority—of the survey area population was living in village-size aggregates, and the residential community had become more nearly coterminous with the settlement.

From a land-tenure point of view, a relatively mobile agricultural strategy can result in the creation of a much greater number of residential sites per unit of time than would be seen in a more sedentary form of settlement. This has serious implications for societies in which retention of land rights is defined in part by residential or special purpose structures. I believe the Anasazi were one such society. The Pueblo II tactics of domestic mobility, extensive use of the landscape, and community investment in land access created a regional situation in which the landscape became increasingly crowded, not just with people but with actual rights to land use and access, as well as with visible signs of the land use (i.e., field houses, field boundaries). As population grew, these tactics may have contributed to "filling up" the productive landscape with people, communities, and the material evidence of land use and land rights. This would have restricted the overall degree of mobility possible within and between communities.

It seems likely that the approximate doubling in site size observed between A.D. 1050 and the late 1100s is an expression of reduced residential mobility, as is the increase in agriculturally related limited-activity sites in the late 1100s. This increase in site size and in use of agricultural facilities away from the residence is most probably linked to decreasing potential for household fissioning and movement.

The decreasing potential for mobility, increased size of coresidential units, and continued "packing" of communities in the Mesa Verde region all contributed to the eventual large-scale residential aggregations we see at Sand Canyon and Goodman Point pueblos and other large late Pueblo III settlements. We really can't know at this point what historical processes conspired to bring the first large aggregations together. But it appears clear from recent reviews of aggregated sites in the Mesa Verde region (Varien et al. 1990, 1991; Adler 1990) that, prior to A.D. 1150, the consistently largest sites were Chacoan-style great houses, most of which contain no more than 50 to 100 rooms. By A.D. 1175, the largest residential aggregates in the region contain in excess of 300 rooms. In the thirteenth century, we see settlements such as the Yellow Jacket site (Lange et al. 1986) with more than 600 rooms, as well as Goodman Point Ruin and Sand Canyon Pueblo in our survey area with 400 or more rooms. It is at this point that we are probably seeing entire Anasazi communities aggregating into single settlements.

While the "look" of the Anasazi settlement pattern changed, there are social organizational continuities that tie together the dispersed Pueblo II and the aggregated Pueblo III communities. First, within the residential architecture of the later aggregated sites, it is clear that the Anasazi generally preserved the architectural integrity of smaller, previously dispersed, coresidential units. Groups of associated rooms and kivas are discernible as distinct spatial units within the later aggregated sites. These architectural complexes are similar in size and composition to the "units" (Prudden 1903) in the earlier dispersed communities.

Second, within the Mesa Verde core area, there is a marked spatial continuity in the use of community integrative facilities and in the overall location of residential settlement. In the upland survey area, at least one and possibly two great kivas were in use during the tenth and eleventh centuries, and two great houses were constructed, both probably during the early twelfth century. These facilities occur in two very compact site clusters, one in the vicinity of what later becomes Goodman Point Pueblo, and the other near the eventual site of Sand Canyon Pueblo. In addition, a prehistoric road (possibly constructed during the late eleventh or early twelfth century?) links these two central areas (Adler 1988, 1990; Hayes 1981:63). In the thirteenth century, architecturally distinctive integrative facilities are embedded within the larger, primarily residential, aggregates—Sand Canyon Pueblo and the Goodman Point Ruin. Sand Canyon Pueblo has a great kiva, a D-shaped structure enclosing two kivas, an informally bounded plaza, an enclosing wall, and several isolated tower complexes. The Goodman Point Ruin has a great kiva, an above-ground circular structure that appears to enclose four kivas, a partial site-enclosing wall, a possible informal plaza, and at least one isolated architectural complex dominated by a large tower.

This spatial clustering of both residential and integrative facilities was not by chance. A succession of integrative facilities served as the foci for two distinct communities during at least three centuries of Anasazi occupation in the study area. These integrative facilities were constructed, used, and replaced in two fairly limited areas, both of which are close to the two most dependable water supplies in the study area—the springs near the head of Goodman Canyon and those in the head of Sand Canyon. I believe that each series of integrative facilities marks the location of a first-order, or face-to-face, community that persisted in place for a number of generations, and probably for several centuries. The settlement pattern and architectural expression of these communities changed in form during Pueblo II and III. When the residential and integrative structures are viewed functionally, however, they document community coherence and continuity through time and in space.

3

The Lower Sand Canyon Survey

Carol L. Gleichman and Peter J. Gleichman

Introduction

A Class III archaeological survey of approximately 364 ha (900 acres) of public land in lower Sand Canyon (Figure 1.3) was conducted by Native Cultural Services (NCS) for the Bureau of Land Management (BLM) in October and November of 1988 (Gleichman and Gleichman 1989). The work was authorized under BLM Contract Number CO-910-CT8-034 and was done to obtain information necessary for managing cultural resources that would potentially be affected by recent and projected increases in public recreational use of Sand Canyon.

As a result of the field inventory, 37 new archaeological sites and 16 previously recorded sites were located in the inventory area. In addition, 135 limited occurrences of artifacts were also recorded. These were either loci having one or a few artifacts or dispersed, low-density artifact scatters. Six of the limited occurrences were isolated projectile points; these were collected and the loci were assigned site numbers.

The distribution of sites in the project area, including 52 prehistoric and 1 historic sites, is indicated in Figure 3.1. The historic site consisted of two segments of an abandoned road following approximately the same route as the existing Sand Canyon road—itself an unimproved dirt track that provides access to several carbon dioxide wells in the central and lower parts of Sand Canyon.

Prehistoric sites were classified into 11 types (Table 3.1) on the basis of observable archaeological attributes. Although the first three types are interpreted as habitation sites, assignment of the other site types does not imply site function. This descriptive typology was chosen over a more thoroughly functional one because the authors felt that there was too little evidence on which to base functional inferences for limited-activity sites.

To examine demographic and settlement-pattern changes within the lower Sand Canyon area, the sites were divided into two broad groups: habitations and limited-activity sites. Habitation sites show evidence that a wide range of domestic/economic activities were carried out by their occupants, including storage, preparation, and consumption of food; manufacture, storage, use, and repair of artifacts; and discard of the waste products of these activities (Lindsay and Dean 1971:111). Domestic structures, and often storage and ceremonial structures, are present.

Limited-activity, or special-use, sites are more limited in scope: loci where specific exploitative activities occurred, such as wild-resource gathering or processing. The use of these sites is believed to have occurred primarily in association with nearby habitation sites. In the lower Sand Canyon project area, specific activities indicated at limited-activity sites include hunting, lithic reduction for tool manufacture, biotic resource processing (plant or animal), storage, water control, construction and use of temporary structures (perhaps field houses), and possibly communications and pottery firing.

Sites were assigned to temporal periods based mainly on the occurrence of temporally diagnostic artifacts—primarily pottery and projectile points. In some cases architecture was also helpful, although the dating of architectural style is less precise than for pottery. Several sites recorded in the lower Sand Canyon survey area could not be assigned to either a temporal or a cultural affiliation. These sites include three lithic scatters and an upright slab feature. For the post-Archaic sites, these time periods are equated with the developmental stages of the familiar Pecos Classification: Basketmaker II through Pueblo III (Kidder 1927). Here we use these familiar labels to indicate time periods and do not mean to imply that the sites assigned to these periods always conform to the original characteriza-

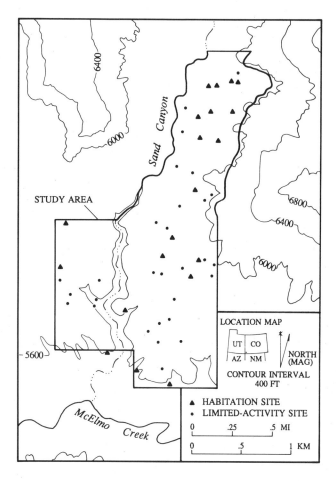

Figure 3.1. Sites recorded in the lower Sand Canyon survey area.

tion of these developmental stages. The time boundaries of the periods are the ones most commonly assigned to the Pecos stages; they depart somewhat from the time boundaries Adler (this volume) assigned to his Anasazi periods. In the following section, the general characteristics of sites from each period are described, including site types, features, functional interpretations, site density, site distribution, and estimated population figures.

Archaic Stage (6000 B.C.–A.D. 1)

The Archaic stage is represented in the project area by one site and four isolated finds. Site density for this stage is .3 site per km². Although seven sites in the project area contained only chipped-stone material, and numerous isolated chipped-stone artifacts were recorded, only those sites or isolates containing projectile points identified as Archaic types were assigned to this period. Although some or all of the lithic scatters may actually precede the Formative stage, without further investigation there was no way to determine if they are prepottery sites or merely special-use sites at which pottery vessels were not used or were used but not broken.

At only one site was an Archaic point associated with other cultural materials. Located on the first terrace of Sand Canyon, this lithic scatter occurs on a low hummock in a fairly open area of pinyon-juniper forest. Surface finds at this site included a projectile point, debitage flakes of quartzite and obsidian, a small end scraper, and a core/hammerstone. The complete projectile point is of light gray, very fine grained quartzite and has a long, triangular blade; it is corner notched and has

Table 3.1. Prehistoric Site Types in the Lower Sand Canyon Survey Area

Site Type/Subtype	No.[a]	Unknown	Archaic	Unknown Anasazi	Basketmaker II–III	Pueblo I	Pueblo II	Pueblo III
					1–725	725–900	900–1100	1100–1300
Habitation								
Cliff dwelling	11							11
Cliff-base structure	2						1	1
Open site	7			1	3		1	2
Limited-Activity								
Temporary structure	2			1				1
Overhang with nonpermanent structure	1			1				
Isolated masonry wall	1			1				
Large circular dry-wall structure	1			1				
Upright-slab feature	5	1		4				
Burned-rock-and-soil feature	9			2			1	6
Lithic scatter	9	3	1	1	4			
Sherd and lithic scatter	7	1		5			1	
TOTAL	55	5	1	17	7	0	4	21

[a] Number of components.

Table 3.2. Lower Sand Canyon Survey Area Population Estimates by Time Period

	Basketmaker III	Pueblo I	Pueblo II	Pueblo III
	600–725	725–900	900–1100	1100–1300
Number of habitation components[a]	3	0	2	14
Estimated number of dwelling rooms per habitation	6		6	51
Average momentary number of habitations[b]				
15-year site use life	0.4		0.2	1.1
50-year site use life	1.2		0.5	3.5
Average momentary number of households[c]				
15-year site use life	0.7		0.5	3.8
50-year site use life	2.4		1.5	12.8
Average momentary population[d]				
15-year site use life	3.6		2.3	19.2
50-year site use life	12.0		7.5	63.8
Average momentary population density (per km^2)[e]				
15-year site use life	1.0		0.6	5.3
50-year site use life	3.3		2.1	17.5

[a] The number of habitation sites occupied during the period.

[b] The average number of habitation sites estimated to be occupied at any one point in time during the period.

[c] The average number of households estimated to exist at any one point in time during the period.

[d] The estimated average number of inhabitants in the survey area at any one point in time during the period.

[e] The average number of inhabitants per km^2 at any one point in time during the period.

a short, rounded stem. This is an apparent limited-activity site where tool manufacture and some resource processing may have occurred. The projectile point is similar to those of the En Medio phase, dated ca. 800 B.C. to A.D. 400 (Irwin-Williams 1973).

Anasazi Tradition (A.D. 1–1300)

The great majority of sites recorded within the project area are affiliated with the Anasazi cultural tradition. In the northern San Juan drainage area, this tradition began around A.D. 1 and continued until about A.D. 1300 (Eddy et al. 1984). Of the 53 sites (and 56 cultural components) recorded, 46 sites (and 49 components) were determined to be Anasazi. Most were assignable to a specific temporal period. Seven components were assignable only to the Anasazi tradition (A.D. 1–1300), and ten others to either the "early" or "late" Anasazi because of the limited dating resolution of the diagnostic materials obtained. Thirty sites (32 components) were assignable to more specific temporal periods within the Anasazi cultural tradition. Because of the small sample size involved and the sparseness of diagnostic pottery on sites in the project area, sites can be described most efficiently in the context of the broad temporal units noted above.

Momentary population estimates were calculated for each Anasazi time period represented in the project area (Table 3.2). For all periods, population estimates were based on the number of habitation sites recorded within the project area boundaries and the estimated numbers of

pithouses or living rooms present at each site. It is assumed that each pithouse or surface dwelling room indicates the presence of a single nuclear family household with an average family size of five. [Editor's note: These assumptions are slightly different from the ones used by Adler in Chapter 2.] Momentary population was calculated on the basis of a minimum site life of 15 years and again for a maximum 50-year site life. Obviously, these figures are somewhat conjectural and provide only a rough estimate of population size to give an idea of relative changes in the population utilizing the project area from one period to another.

Basketmaker II and III (A.D. 1–725)

Seven sites within the project area contained materials datable to the period A.D. 1–725, encompassing the Basketmaker II and Basketmaker III developmental stages. Three of the seven are habitations; the others are limited-activity loci. The habitation sites all appear to date to the Basketmaker III period. Of the three habitation sites dated A.D. 600–725, one contained an estimated three or four pithouses, and the other two were estimated to have one or two pithouses each, for a total of approximately six houses. When site longevity is taken into account, this suggests that, on the average, from A.D. 600 to 725 only one occupied site and one to three households were present in the study area at any one time and that the average momentary population was between 3 and 12 individuals.

Pueblo I (A.D. 725–900)

No sites dating to this period were identified within the project area. Although some of the five site components identified as "early" Anasazi (A.D. 600–900) may in fact be from this period, pottery specifically associated with the A.D. 725–900 time frame (e.g., Piedra Black-on-white) were not found. It appears, therefore, that use of the area was extremely limited, if any use occurred at all. Climatically, the region was relatively drier than during the previous period, with areas of lower elevation, such as Sand Canyon, probably receiving inadequate rainfall for dry farming (Petersen 1986:316). The unsuitability of the climate for crop production appears a likely factor in the absence of sites within our project area.

Pueblo II (A.D. 900–1100)

The A.D. 900–1100 period is represented by four sites in the project area, two of which are portions of multicomponent sites. Two of the sites are small habitations (Table 3.2). Although this may indicate an increase in the ratio of habitations to limited-activity sites within the project area, the very small size of the sample renders this speculative.

Site density during this period is 1.1 sites per km², with a habitation site density of .55 sites per km². With two habitation sites and an estimated three dwelling rooms at each, it appears that there must have been times during the period when no sites were occupied in the study area. Even with the assumption of a 50-year use life for habitation sites, an average of only 1.5 households was present during the period. Average momentary population for the period is calculated at roughly two to eight persons, depending on assumptions about settlement longevity. This is an increase over the eighth and ninth centuries, but somewhat lower than site density and population estimates for the A.D. 600–725 period, indicating that although a population recovery was under way, occupation and use of this part of the canyon had not yet recovered to the level of the seventh and early eighth centuries.

Pueblo III (A.D. 1100–1300)

By far the best-represented period of occupation and use in Sand Canyon is A.D. 1100–1300, during which at least 21 sites were utilized. This was the final period of Anasazi (and prehistoric) occupation evidenced within the project area. Although we were able to place nine of the sites into either the first half (A.D. 1100–1200) or second half (A.D. 1200–1300) of the period (Gleichman and Gleichman 1989), most lacked surface assemblages sufficiently diagnostic for this purpose. Largely because of the heavy visitation to these sites, particularly the cliff dwellings,

artifact assemblages are currently quite meager. Collections made at some of the cliff dwellings during 1965 by the University of Colorado contained more decorated pottery than what remains at the sites today and allowed us to date more precisely five of the cliff dwellings to the A.D. 1200–1300 period. No cliff dwelling was specifically dated to A.D. 1100–1200 (although six were dated A.D. 1100–1300). It is likely, however, that at least some of them were used during the twelfth century, with architecture and artifact assemblages obscured by later reuse of the overhangs.

Sites from A.D. 1100–1300 are concentrated in the central and northern portions of the project area, on the upper terraces of Sand Canyon. Habitation sites take full advantage of cliff alcoves in exposures of the Entrada and Navajo formations. The concentration of habitations in the northern portion of the study unit reflects the locations of these alcoves and overhangs. Two surface habitations with towers, two cliff dwellings with associated towers, and an unusual habitation site with large circular dry-wall structures are all located within the southern half of the project area. These include all the sites with tower remains, and their locations in the broader, lower part of the canyon, near its mouth, may possibly indicate that the towers played a role in a communication network during the thirteenth century.

With 14 habitation sites and 7 limited-activity sites, site density during this period is 5.8 sites per km², with a habitation site density of 3.9 sites per km². This is a substantial increase over all previous periods. This is also the first period during which the number of habitation sites exceeds that of limited-activity sites, with 67 percent of the sites from this period being habitations.

Momentary population estimates for this period were based on actual room counts in the cliff dwellings and on the length of rubble mounds for surface habitations (assuming an average room width of 2 m and a single row of single-story living rooms). Use of these assumptions assures that the A.D. 1100–1300 estimates of the number of living rooms are conservative, since standing walls in cliff dwellings represent a minimum number of the rooms present originally, and rooms without clear surface expression may exist at both cliff and open sites. Assuming a 15-year site life, an average of three to four households resided in lower Sand Canyon during this period, indicating an average momentary population of about 19 people. Based on a 50-year site life, there was an average of 13 households residing at three to four sites, and an average momentary population of 64 individuals (Table 3.2).

Summary and Conclusions

The inventory of lower Sand Canyon has provided us with some insight into prehistoric aboriginal use and occupation of the area. For the Archaic stage, an extremely low site density (.3 site per km²) and evidence for only limited activity were noted in the lower Sand Canyon project area. With only one site and four isolated finds dated to this period, it appears that the project area was used to a limited extent for hunting and wild floral (and perhaps faunal) resource processing during the middle-through-late Archaic (3000 B.C.-A.D. 1), but that the base camps or habitation sites of these people were located elsewhere. Substantial evidence for Archaic use and occupation is found in northwestern New Mexico south of the San Juan River (Reher 1977; Simmons 1981). Findings in lower Sand Canyon are similar to other nearby areas of southwestern Colorado (cf. Fetterman and Honeycutt 1987; Adler 1988). In fact, throughout the northern San Juan region in southwestern Colorado, there is only scant evidence of Archaic use, represented by stray projectile points and sparsely distributed sites (Eddy et al. 1984:29).

Human use of the lower Sand Canyon project area increased after the Archaic stage, so that by the Basketmaker II-III periods, site density was 2.75 sites per km². No sites in lower Sand Canyon could be specifically dated to the Basketmaker II period (A.D. 1-450), but based on projectile point styles, three sites are considered to be either Basketmaker II or Basketmaker III in age. Substantial evidence for a Basketmaker II occupation is found in other portions of the northern San Juan drainage, such as the Animas drainage near Durango (Morris and Burgh 1954; Reed and Kainer 1978; Fuller 1988), the Navajo Reservoir District (Eddy 1966), and Cedar Mesa in southeastern Utah (Matson and Lipe 1978; Matson et al. 1988). However, areas near Sand Canyon, such as the Hovenweep–Cajon Mesa locality (Winter 1976), Mockingbird Mesa (Fetterman and Honeycutt 1987), the Dolores River drainage (Kane 1986:362–363), and Mesa Verde (Hayes 1964; Rohn 1977), have been found to contain only very limited evidence of a Basketmaker II occupation.

By A.D. 600-725, the first habitation sites were occupied in the lower Sand Canyon project area. This time period correlates with the Pecos Classification Basketmaker III stage and is well represented in other drainages near Sand Canyon (cf. Fetterman and Honeycutt 1987; Winter 1976; Kuckelman and Morris 1988; Kane 1986:363), as well as on Mesa Verde (Hayes 1964) and in the Animas and La Plata drainages (Morris 1939; Carlson 1963; Gooding 1980).

In the study area, Basketmaker III sites are located on the broad upper terraces and benches of the canyon. Within the McElmo drainage area (Fetterman and Honeycutt 1987; Winter 1976), the Dolores drainage area (Kane 1986:363), and on Mesa Verde (Hayes and Lancaster 1975; Rohn 1977), sites of this period tend to occur as dispersed, single-household hamlets located on mesa tops where deep, cultivable soils are available. The sites in lower Sand Canyon appear to fit this pattern, except that they are located on the broad upper terraces and benches of the canyon, where soils are considered generally unsuited to cultivation. Nevertheless, small pockets of land, such as alluvial fans, may have been cultivated, as well as the McElmo floodplain just south of the project area. This area could have reasonably supported the estimated average momentary population of one site with one or two households. If the Basketmaker III sites in the study area were part of a larger community pattern, it must have been a very dispersed one.

No sites in lower Sand Canyon were specifically assignable to the period A.D. 725-900. Other nearby areas, such as Hovenweep (Winter 1976:286), the mesa top in the vicinity of Sand Canyon Pueblo (Adler 1988), and Mockingbird Mesa (Fetterman and Honeycutt 1987:58), experienced only limited occupation during the eighth and ninth centuries. This seemingly dramatic decline of population in the lower elevations along the numerous canyons draining into McElmo Creek is in contrast with a marked population increase and aggregation into larger communities or villages to the north, in the Ackmen-Lowry locality and the Dolores River valley (cf. Martin 1936, 1938; Kane 1986; Schlanger 1985, 1988). Petersen's (1986:316) climatic reconstruction indicates that relatively drier conditions during this period may have resulted in the lower canyon areas receiving inadequate rainfall for dry farming. As a result, groups appear to have aggregated in areas of higher elevation, such as the Dolores River valley, where more successful dry land farming could be practiced. Further from Sand Canyon, areas of higher elevation such as Mesa Verde (Hayes 1964), the Navajo Reservoir District (Dittert et al. 1961; Eddy 1966), and the Durango area (Fuller 1988) were also intensively occupied. However, some areas of intermediate elevation were also occupied during this period. The Duckfoot site (Lightfoot and Varien 1988; Varien and Lightfoot 1989) dates to the late A.D. 800s and is located at approximately 1921 m (6300 ft) elevation. Other late Pueblo I sites occur in the vicinity.

After A.D. 900, lower Sand Canyon appears to have experienced a slight population recovery. Four sites, two of which are habitations, date to the period A.D. 900-1100. These habitation sites contain surface masonry architecture and associated pit structures or kivas characteristic of this period (Hayes 1964; Kuckelman and Morris 1988; Fetterman and Honeycutt 1987). Although towers are noted elsewhere in the region (Hayes 1964:94), none in lower Sand Canyon are dated to this period. Sites in lower Sand Canyon are more numerous than during the previous period. This is consistent with findings in upper Sand Canyon (Adler 1988), the Hovenweep–Cajon Mesa locality (Winter 1976), and Mockingbird Mesa (Fetterman and Honeycutt 1987). In all these nearby areas, an increased use of the mesa margins was observed, especially after A.D. 1000. Unfortunately, the lower Sand Canyon project area is too small to make any similar assertion. Pueblo II cliff dwellings, such as those occupied during the Mancos phase on Wetherill Mesa (Hayes 1964:95), were not found in lower Sand Canyon. Their presence may, however, be obscured by later occupations of the larger alcoves. The two A.D. 900–1100 habitations in lower Sand Canyon are built in areas of sandstone outcrops; one of these sites has structures abutted to a cliff face.

In the Dolores River valley, both site size and density dropped after A.D. 1000 (Kane 1986:382). Other areas of the northern San Juan, including the upper Animas and La Plata drainages, also saw greatly reduced site densities during this time. Anasazi populations apparently shifted to areas of lower elevation. Petersen (1986:316) notes that increased summer precipitation after A.D. 1000 accounted for a higher amount of annual rainfall during the eleventh century. This, along with mild temperatures (Van West et al. 1987:97), may be an important factor in the reoccupation of the lower elevations in Sand Canyon and the surrounding drainages.

During the final period of Anasazi occupation, A.D. 1100-1300, site density within lower Sand Canyon jumped dramatically. Twenty-one sites, including 14 habitations, were dated to this period. Habitation site density increased from .55 per km^2 during A.D. 900–1100 to 3.87 per km^2 during A.D. 1100–1300, and the average number of dwelling rooms per site also increased. This period represents the final and maximum level of Anasazi occupation in the project area, as well as on nearby Mockingbird Mesa (Fetterman and Honeycutt 1987), the upper Sand Canyon research area (Adler, this volume; Adler 1990, 1988:42), and Chapin Mesa (Rohn 1977). In contrast, Anasazi use of the Dolores River valley was very limited after A.D. 1100, with permanent habitation represented at only a few sites, such as Escalante Village and the Reservoir Ruin (Eddy et al. 1984:52). Kane (1986:385) argues that most, if not all occupation at the Reservoir Ruin complex had ended by A.D. 1100.

During the A.D. 1100–1300 period, sites of all types were concentrated on the upper terraces of Sand Canyon, in the central and northern portion of the lower Sand Canyon project area. Habitations took full advantage of the cliff alcoves within this portion of the project area. In other areas of the northern San Juan region where cliff alcoves were available, they were heavily used (Hayes 1964; Nickens 1981). In areas where cliff alcoves are not available, mesa margins, cliff-face locations, and canyon heads were heavily utilized during this period (Winter 1976; Fetterman and Honeycutt 1987).

Large cliff dwellings such as those found at Mesa Verde National Park and in the Ute Mountain Ute Tribal Park just south of it are not present in lower Sand Canyon. The relatively small size of the available cliff alcoves does place constraints on the size of site that could be built in them. Nevertheless, both cliff dwellings and open habitation sites in lower Sand Canyon are relatively small, averaging three

to four dwelling rooms. Judging from Martin's (1976) stabilization inventory, this pattern is also found in the canyon country both east and west of Sand Canyon. Even at Mesa Verde National Park, Hayes (1964) found that the average cliff dwelling on Wetherill Mesa was quite small.

The most reliable water sources for these sites appear to have been the various natural seeps emitting from sandstone exposures. Soils in the vicinity of the 1988 survey area are shallow and not considered suitable for cultivation today by the Soil Conservation Service. The newly arrived Pueblo III population of lower Sand Canyon most certainly brought with it an economy based on agriculture. Exactly where they farmed is therefore left open to question. There are a few patches of land on the broader southern portion of the first terrace which are suitable for crop production. It is likely that small plots of land within the northern portion of the project area and in the southern portion of the inner gorge of Sand Canyon also contained soils sufficient for cultivation, although perhaps not for long periods of time. The McElmo floodplain, which contains substantial areas of arable soil, is another likely location for Anasazi farmland and is easily accessible from the project area.

Two surface pueblos and two cliff dwellings in the southern portion of the project area were constructed in association with circular towers. A fifth habitation site is located high on the talus slope at the mouth of Sand Canyon and contains three unusual dry-laid structures. The presence of these towers and the unusual dry-laid structures in this portion of the project area suggests that communication and/or defensive considerations were very important near the mouth of the canyon during the twelfth and/or thirteenth centuries. Further to the north where the cliff dwellings (and therefore population) are concentrated, one possible communication structure was recorded. This is 5MT2796, a large dry-wall structure. Another A.D. 1100–1300 habitation with a tower (5MT135) is located just west of the northern sites, outside of the project area (Martin 1976).

Site density in the project area, without regard to specific time periods, is low when compared to other nearby localities, such as the uplands near the heads of Sand and Goodman canyons or Mockingbird Mesa. This is especially true for habitation site densities. It is not surprising, however, that higher site densities are found in these other areas, because they are at higher elevations and therefore receive somewhat greater precipitation than does lower Sand Canyon (Iorns et al. 1964). Furthermore, the mesa-top soils of those areas were more suited to cultivation.

Throughout the Anasazi era, lower Sand Canyon was limited in the basic resources needed to sustain dry farming: groundwater, precipitation, and arable soil. Until sometime after A.D. 1100, occupation and use of lower Sand Canyon was extremely limited, with likely no more than a single habitation site of one or two households in use at any one time. These earlier residences may not even have been year-round occupations, and it is suspected that they were in fact used only seasonally.

A population expansion occurred throughout the McElmo Canyon system during the 1100s and 1200s. Just outside of the project area, Pueblo III cliff dwellings are found in East Rock Canyon and along the smaller canyons to the east of Sand Canyon (Martin 1976). The Castle Rock Pueblo, 5MT1825, is a large habitation located a little less than 1 km west of the southwest corner of the project area. This site contains between 5 and 10 kiva depressions and at least 50 rooms (Michael Adler: personal communication). As one of the largest settlements in the lower Sand Canyon area, it undoubtedly would have had some influence on land use and demographic patterns in lower Sand Canyon during the A.D. 1100–1300 period.

The increased use of lower Sand Canyon no doubt was also affected by population pressure in areas to the north, where Sand Canyon Pueblo and Goodman Point Ruin were in use and population density was considerably higher. Adler (this volume; Adler 1988:ii) notes that the area around Goodman Point Ruin in the late twelfth and early thirteenth centuries was one of the densest centers of prehistoric population in the McElmo dome area. The limited productivity of lower Sand Canyon makes it questionable whether the Anasazi who lived there during this time were able to fully support themselves through farming, hunting, and gathering. Economic and social ties, which may have been based on expanded social networks and alliances with other localities, such as the community around Sand Canyon and Goodman Point pueblos, may have helped these groups make it through difficult periods.

This kind of alliance formation has been suggested for fourteenth century Puebloan groups farther south (Upham 1982), and the Crow Canyon Archaeological Center is currently involved in research focused on defining changes in the structure and size of the local settlement system surrounding Sand Canyon Pueblo (Lipe, this volume: Introduction). Findings during the investigation of lower Sand Canyon suggest that the population of this area may at times have depended on exchange or on social networks for basic subsistence needs. At any rate, the population peak experienced in the twelfth to thirteenth centuries was relatively short-lived, and the project area was ultimately abandoned along with the rest of the Sand Canyon locality and the northern San Juan area.

4

The Goodman Point Historic Land-Use Study

Marjorie R. Connolly

Introduction

The Goodman Point community, located approximately 16 km (10 mi) west of Cortez, Colorado, consists of the residents of a number of widely dispersed homes and farms. Homesteading in the Goodman Point area began in 1911 and continued into the 1960s, though at a decreasing rate after 1925. Between 1911 and 1925, Goodman Point developed into a farming community supporting over 160 people. These settlers cleared the sagebrush, pinyon, and juniper and supported their families with dry-land crops.

On U.S. Geological Survey (USGS) topographic maps, the label "Goodman Point" is applied only to the area between Sand and Goodman canyons, but residents of the area apply the term somewhat more broadly. Locally, the Goodman Point area is defined on the south by the rims of McElmo Canyon and lower Sand and Goodman canyons, and on the north by Yellow Jacket Canyon and Dawson Draw (Figure 4.1). The eastern boundary begins at the western rim of Trail Canyon, and the western boundary is located past Sand Canyon, where private lands give way to lands administered by the Bureau of Land Management. Thus defined, the Goodman Point area encompasses approximately 75 km² (29 mi²).

The Goodman Point study area ranges in elevation from approximately 1750 m (5750 ft) in the bottom of Goodman Canyon at the southern edge of the study area to approximately 2180 m (7160 ft) on the divide between Sand and Goodman canyons, near the McElmo Canyon rim. The study area is centered on the McElmo dome, a structural uplift with a north-northeast dipping axis. The surface of this feature is formed on the Lower Cretaceous Dakota Sandstone, which is locally overlain by eolian-deposited silts and dissected by canyons draining south to McElmo Creek or northeast to Yellow Jacket Canyon. Elevations on the McElmo dome are highest on Goodman Point proper—the divide between Goodman and Sand canyons, just north of where the uplifted rocks are truncated by McElmo Canyon. From this point, the surface of the dome slopes both east and west, and more gradually along its axis to the north-northeast.

Deep, rich eolian soils and an average annual precipitation exceeding 14 in per year make the Goodman Point area one of the most productive farming locations in Montezuma County. When Anglo settlement began, it was an area of open sage parks on the deeper upland soils, surrounded by stands of pinyon and juniper trees occupying the canyon rims as well as some of the deep soil areas.

In 1983, the Crow Canyon Archaeological Center began a long-term archaeological research program that focused on the Sand Canyon locality, an approximately 200 km² area around Sand Canyon and Goodman Point pueblos (Figure 1.2). The Sand Canyon locality includes the Goodman Point study area defined for this report (Figure 4.1). Prehistoric Anasazi communities occupied the Goodman Point area for at least 700 years (Adler, this volume)—from the A.D. 500s or 600s through most of the 1200s. Surveys by Crow Canyon Center archaeologists and other researchers in the study area have revealed abundant evidence of habitation and limited-activity sites, as well as prehistoric reservoirs, agricultural features such as checkdams, and traces of a road that appears to have extended from near the head of Sand Canyon to the area just north of the Goodman Point Ruin (Adler, this volume; Adler 1988, 1990). These sites are located on privately owned farms and on public lands administered by the Bureau of Land Management and the National Park Service.

In 1989, the Crow Canyon Archaeological Center initiated an oral history project involving older residents of Goodman Point. It was expected that these residents'

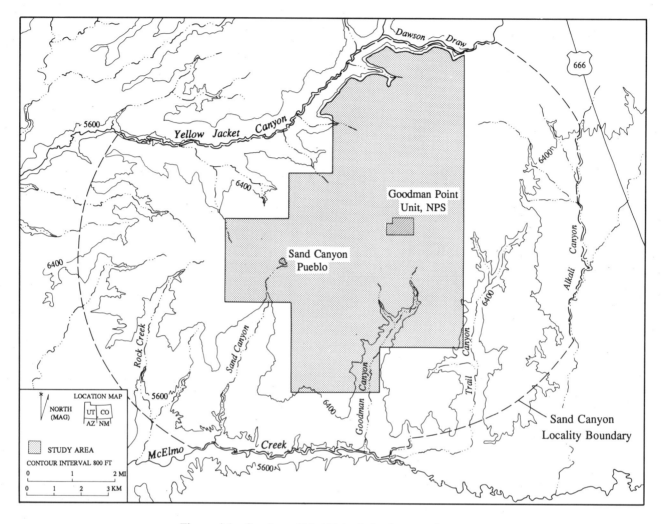

Figure 4.1. Goodman Point historic land-use study area.

recollections of homesteading and dry farming in the area would be helpful in understanding the earlier response of Anasazi farmers to the same challenges—finding suitable soil, farming in a semiarid region with a highly variable climate, and finding reliable domestic water sources. Furthermore, since 1911, historic land use has significantly altered the archaeological resources of the area. No one knows more about this transformation than the residents of Goodman Point. The older residents gained an intimate understanding of the archaeological resources when they cleared the lands for agricultural use. Through informal meetings, questionnaires, and taped interviews, the Center hoped to accomplish the following goals:

- Understand the criteria and techniques farmers used in selecting their land for homesteading and for farming
- Document the location of early homesteads and the identities of the families that settled them
- Learn about crop selection and successes and failures in farming

- Identify local water sources
- Document the impact of farming on archaeological sites
- Record current residents' perceptions of archaeology

Methods

The Goodman Point oral history project was carried out during 1989 and early 1990, under the direction of the author (Connolly 1990). Funding assistance was provided by the Colorado Endowment for the Humanities, the Ballantine Family Charitable Fund, and the Crow Canyon Archaeological Center. An initial search for literature on Anglo settlement in the Goodman Point area provided few sources of information. No reference to early farming practices on Goodman Point was found. Documents at the Cortez office of the Soil Conservation Service and at the Center for Southwest Studies at Fort Lewis College in Durango contained no specific reference to the immediate study area. However, climate and crop production records for Montezuma County as a whole were located at the Soil Conservation Service office, and these records served as reliable cross-checks for information obtained from the informants.

The fieldwork for this study was conducted from December 1989 through February 1990. A questionnaire (Connolly 1990: Appendix A) was developed by the project director and reviewed by the Crow Canyon staff. The questionnaire was designed to gain insight into three areas: early homesteading, farming practices, and land use effects on archaeological sites.

The project director conducted all interviews in the informants' homes. For each interview, USGS topographic maps were used to record the location of homesteads, springs, and ruins. Every individual from the Goodman Point community who could recall the early days in the study area and who was still living in Montezuma County was contacted. Everyone who was contacted agreed to be interviewed and was friendly and helpful. Fifteen people were interviewed: Leslie Black, Steve Chappell, Lucile Everett, Edith Flanagan, Laura Fulks, Marie Graves, Lois Hearne, Alex Martin, Oscar Martin, Birney Seitz, Luther Shields, Catherine Stanley, Ford Stanley, Theron Story, and Dorothy Willbanks. Eight of these individuals are children of the first homesteaders. Six others moved to Goodman Point in the late 1920s with their parents, who had purchased land from the original homesteaders. One respondent was born in the 1940s. Although the people interviewed represent only a small number of the families who lived on Goodman Point prior to 1930, they were able to contribute a great deal of information about the early years of settlement, farming, and community formation. In the material that follows, these informants are often referred to collectively as "residents." This implies that they represent the larger group of early-day (pre-1930) residents of the Goodman Point community, many of whom are now deceased or have moved away.

Interviews with nine of the informants were tape-recorded. The tapes and transcriptions are permanently stored at the Montezuma Valley Historical Society, the Crow Canyon Archaeological Center, and the Cortez Public Library. A file was established for each person interviewed. The file includes a biographical data sheet, an interview release form, and a map.

After each interview, the responses to the questions were recorded in numerical order on a chart. The chart organized the data so that responses could more easily be compared. Below, responses to the questions are summarized in a descriptive manner, although occasionally direct quotes from individuals are provided. The chart and field notes are archived at the Crow Canyon Archaeological Center. The interview results are reported here by subject category: homesteading, farming practices, and archaeological sites.

Homesteading

From the late 1870s to 1900, a large portion of the land in Montezuma County was used for grazing. The earliest land applications on Goodman Point were made by cattlemen. Goodman Point was named after Henry Goodman, a rancher from Dolores who lived in the area in the late 1800s. Although Goodman never legally applied for any land, his name appears on the first surveyors' maps of Goodman Point in 1889. James P. Gallaway, a prominent rancher from Paradox Valley, applied for land north of Sand Canyon in 1892. By 1910, the cattle industry had been restricted to private and federally approved public lands, and new areas were opened to homesteading in Montezuma County.

The Homestead Act of 1862 allowed anyone who was 21 years of age or the head of a household to homestead up to 160 acres of public land. The Rio Grande Southern Railroad and the irrigation projects sponsored by the Montezuma Valley Water Supply Company attracted new settlers to Montezuma Valley. Between 1911 and 1925, over 62 people filed for land on Goodman Point. The dry-farming successes of the initial settlers encouraged their friends and relatives to settle in the area as well. The community grew quickly; by 1920 the population was approximately 160 people. Figure 4.2 shows the locations of homesteads settled in the period 1911–1925. This map is adapted from one kindly prepared for the oral history project by Ford Stanley, a resident of the Goodman Point community. The names of the homesteading families are given in Table 4.1.

The Goodman Point Archaeological Reserve (Figure 4.2) was a full section of land that had been set aside in 1889 to preserve the Goodman Point Ruin and other sites located close to it (National Park Service 1990). Consequently, it was not available for homesteading in the early period of settlement in the Goodman Point area. This was one of the first instances of archaeological preservation by the U.S. government. Approximately 143 acres of the original 640-acre Reserve were designated as a unit of Hovenweep National Monument in 1951 and 1952 (National Park Service 1990). Of the nearly 500 acres removed from the Reserve at that time, the majority was retained in public ownership under the Bureau of Land Management, but approximately 160 acres located just south and west of the monument unit were released for acquisition by private landowners.

As land in the Goodman Point area was settled, families arrived from Arkansas, California, Kansas, Michigan, Oklahoma, Texas, Washington, and West Virginia. The first priorities of the homesteaders were to construct a home, cistern, and root cellar and to plant a garden. Ten to 20 acres were quickly cleared to meet the requirements of the Homestead Act. The approximate locations of the earliest houses are shown in Figure 4.2.

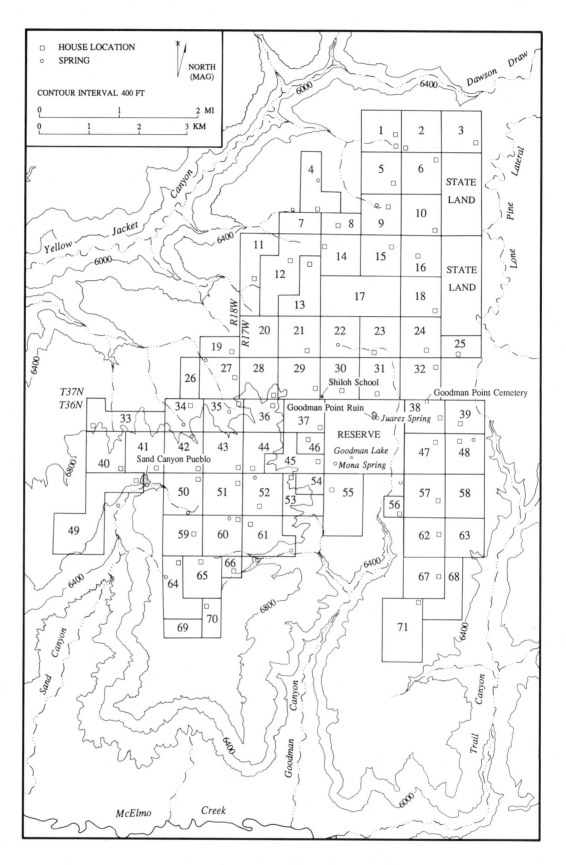

Figure 4.2. Homesteads of Goodman Point, 1911–1925. See Table 4.1 for the names of homesteading families.

Table 4.1. Homesteading Families of Goodman Point

Homestead[a]	Homesteading Family	Offspring
1	Bill and Viola Ferguson	Dorothy
2	Walker	
3	Carl Hinman	
4	Theodore and Lilly Belle Walton	Pearl, Max, Noble, Flossie, Earl, Sallie
5	Max Walton	
6	Dunn	
7	Kenneth Rowley	
8	Rowley	
9	Tom Tyghe	Sydney, Anne, Harry, Tommy
10	Hoyt	
11	Cook	
12	Thomas and Margaret Martin	May, Lenard, Lela, Alex, Oscar (O.J.), Elbert, Claude, Edith
13	Lovell and Annie Chastain	Hugh
14	Earl Walton	
15	Clark	
16	Scot	
17	Zane	
18	Scot	
19	Cook	
20	Annie Chastain	
21	Jake and Sally Plemons	Basil, Zelma, Ernest, Cicero, Lewie, Joe
22	Elmer and Madia Mays	Kenneth, Ivan
23	Rena Cook	
24	Robert and Ida North	Niles, Ruth
25	Carraway Rice	
26	George and Earl Cook	Rena, Jim, Goff, Betty
27	McEwen	
28	Washington Fulks	
29	Ray Rowley	
30	William and Ethel McGechie	Bill, Onis
31	John and Liberty Fulks	Ione, Jim, Lyod, John, Joe
32	Thomas and Isabelle Rice	Carraway, Minnie
33	Harles	
34	Shelby and Ava Harles	
35	Gus Lightfoot	
36	Seitz	
37	Eldarado and Nellie Seitz	Merle, Mona, Eva, Ralph, Birney
38	Lige and Linnie Phillips	Opal, Clyde, Royal, Johnny
39	Samuel Stone	
40	Jim and Dot Johnson	
41	Don and Blanche Johnson	Paul, Lucile
42	Dacus Wallace	
43	Emma Berryman	
44	Comisky	
45	Charlie Flagg	
46	Shelby and Ava Harles	
47	Minnie Rice	
48	John and Leona Gregory	Marie, Johnny, Gladys, Norma Jean, Ermadine, Uyla Belle
49	Everett and Mary Williams	Wilbert
50	Rayford Berryman	
51	Pearl and Mina Black	Mary, Marshall, Clyde, Ruth
52	Eagen	
53	Conoley	
54	Flagg	
55	Jim and Fannie Layman	Mollie, Linnie, Dole, Cole, Gole, Clyde, Harvey, Bessie
56	Lewis Matson	
57	William and Donye Conoley	Eloise, Malcom, Orrel, Lois
58	Thurogh North	
59	J.H. Farmer	
60	Effie Berryman	
61	Alcy Baker	
62	Glen Fields	John
63	Elsie Finley	
64	John and Audra Stanley	Omar, Harry, Ollis, Ford, Leslie, Dean
65	Straton and Sally Hutchinson	
66	Lawrence Mahon	
67	Joe and Mollie Phillips	
68	Frederick Schnaufer	
69	Howard Hutchinson	
70	Lewis and Edith Hutchinson	
71	James and Frances Finley	Lela, Mildred, Virgil, Bessie

[a] See Figure 4.2 for the location of each homestead.

By 1913, the first schoolhouse was constructed on land donated by the McGechie family. It was named the Shiloh School (Figure 4.2). Forty-six students attended classes the first year. The schoolhouse also functioned as a Baptist church and as a community center for such activities as Ladies' Club meetings and school programs. The Goodman Point Baseball Team games were played at Goodman Lake. Although dances were not common on Goodman Point, residents often met to play music and sing songs at neighbors' homes. A post office was established in 1915 at Bud Fulks's home. It was named the Renaraye Post Office in honor of Rena Cook and Raye Rowley, two Goodman Point residents.

Informants were asked six questions about homesteading. The goals of the questions were to develop a chronology of the homesteads, to understand where the people came from, to learn how they heard of Goodman Point and why they moved there, and to record the criteria used in selecting a homestead.

1. When did your family first move to Goodman Point?
The Seitz family arrived in 1911. The Terrys, Fulkses, and Blacks came in 1912. The Conoleys, Gregorys, and Martins homesteaded in 1913. The Stanleys and Hutchinsons arrived in 1914. The Johnson family homesteaded in 1915. The Shieldses and Storys settled in 1926, buying land from previous homesteaders.

2. What was your family's background?
The Fulks, Terry, and Gregory families moved from Texas. The Martin, Story, and Shields families came from Arkansas, and the Seitzes from Oklahoma. The Stanley family came from West Virginia via Kansas. The Johnsons moved from Kansas and the Blacks from Missouri.

Through the course of the interviews, information was noted concerning the origins of other families whose relatives could not be located. The Chastains and Walkers came from Arkansas. The Finleys and Hutchinsons moved from Kansas. Lewis Matson arrived from Michigan. The Harles and Zane families moved from Oklahoma. From Texas came the Baker, Berryman, Conoley, Cook, Field, Lightfoot, Phillips, and Plemons families. The Waltons moved from Washington, and the Rowleys from West Virginia.

3. How and why did your family pick Goodman Point as a place to live?
Three of the individuals responding to this question had no recollection of why their families moved. The remaining twelve said that their families moved to Goodman Point at the suggestion of a relative. News spread quickly of the good soil and the opportunity for a more prosperous life. The county records show that by 1915 the Black, Chastain, Comisky, Eagen, Gregory, Rowley, Stone, and Seitz men had all filed on the land.

Eldarado Seitz moved his family to Colorado in 1908, looking for a better climate for his children's health. They first homesteaded south of Cortez, but in 1911, after noting the storm clouds building up on Ute Mountain and the rain falling on Goodman Point, Seitz became one of the first men to homestead on Goodman Point.

The Johnson family was inspired to move to Colorado by an uncle, who was a prospector. He visited Montezuma County and wrote home to his relatives, encouraging them to come out.

4. Why did your family pick its homesite?
The earliest homesites were chosen to receive protection from the north wind and for their proximity to water. The families who arrived after 1915 chose homesteads wherever the land wasn't already claimed.

5. What were the dependable water sources in the early days?
Informants located 20 springs in the study area (Figure 4.2). All the early residents hauled water from Goodman Lake or the Lone Pine Lateral. Goodman Lake, located south of the Goodman Point Ruin, was a good source for livestock water. Residents drove their teams into the lake and filled water barrels. No one could recall a time when Goodman Lake dried up.

Flowing from Narraguinnep Reservoir in a westerly direction and then south to Trail Canyon, the Lone Pine Lateral was the most reliable drinking water source. This canal was built about 1907 by the Montezuma Valley Water Supply Company. Other water sources frequently cited were Mona Spring, close to Goodman Lake, and Juarez Spring, located at Goodman Pueblo. Other springs located at the heads of small canyons were used throughout the year by families. One example is the spring located within the confines of Sand Canyon Pueblo, used by the Johnson family, which homesteaded the land just north of the site.

At most homes, cisterns were built in order to store rainwater and melted winter snows. The Martin and Shields families, on homesteads located close to Dawson Draw, dug wells by hand. They hit water between 10 and 30 ft below the surface.

6. Was the land altered significantly before 1920 by the cattlemen?
This question drew the least response. Some of the residents could recall sheep and cattle roaming freely, but their first impression of the land was that it was almost all sagebrush with scattered pinyon and juniper trees. Luther Shields said, "Years ago, I talked to the old-timers who lived out in this country. They brought in herds of cattle from Texas and overgrazed the grassland. It was nearly all sagebrush when we came in."

Summary

Between 1911 and 1925, 62 people filed for land in the Goodman Point area, and a dry-land farming community rapidly developed that supported over 160 people, a school, a church, and a post office. People moved to this area from their previous homes for economic reasons. The factors that made Goodman Point their destination were generally social, usually word-of-mouth recommendations from one relative to another.

Once in the Goodman Point area, both economic and social factors were considered in choosing a homestead location, along with the availability of land, proximity to water, and protection from the weather. Goodman Lake and the Lone Pine Lateral were the most dependable water sources. In addition, residents identified 20 springs. At most homes, cisterns were used to store rainwater and melted winter snow.

Farming Practices, 1911–1930

Early farms on Goodman Point were small, self-sufficient family operations. The land was cleared by hand, using a grubbing hoe and an axe. After some land had been cleared, a large garden, fruit trees, and a small amount of corn were planted. The corn was for livestock feed. Although the family farms were self-sufficient, it was common for a family member to work in town or out of state for wages.

From 1910 through 1930, corn, cane, potatoes, and pinto beans were grown for sale or trade. Corn was the most abundant crop in the early years. Two varieties, Swadely Yellow Dent and Australian White Flint, were successful. In 1918, the county agricultural agent located a market for pinto beans and arranged for a carload of beans to be shipped to the East by train. Gradually, pinto beans became established as the main cash crop.

By the end of the 1920s, the Goodman Point farmers began using tractors, and the amount of land under cultivation again increased. As people turned to tractors, corn production declined because there were fewer farm animals to feed. In the 1930s, modern farm machinery was introduced, including large threshers, combines, and tractors.

Today the land is prepared in the same manner as in the early days of farm machinery. After fall harvest the ground is tilled 8 in deep. In the following spring, when the ground is dry enough to work, the farmers prepare the soil by disking it twice before planting. This works the soil to a depth of 4 to 5 in and breaks it up into clods. The thin layer of dust and small lumps of soil that are left on top help preserve the moisture in the soil. This process creates what is referred to as a clod mulch. Corn is planted between May 1 and 15. Beans are planted in early June because they are less resistant to frost. Corn and bean seeds are planted 3 to 4 in deep. The land is cultivated and harrowed to keep it loose and free of weeds. A good yield for beans is 10 to 12 sacks per acre. A sack is equal to 100 pounds. During a poor year, each acre will produce only ½ to 3 sacks of beans. Forty bushels of corn per acre is considered a good yield.

1. What were the best lands for farming? Pinyon and juniper? Sagebrush? What were the best locations?

All but 3 of the 15 informants believed that sage and timber lands produce equal yields. The three who disagreed believed that the organic matter deposited by the trees makes the timber land soil more productive than the sage land. Corn and potatoes were always planted on the newest ground cleared. Beans need "cleaner" ground that has been tilled longer. Residents believe that north-sloping fields and land at the bottom of hollows produce the greatest yields.

2. When Goodman Point was first settled, how was the land cleared? With tools? Fire? How long did it take?

In the 1910s, the land was cleared with a grubbing hoe and a shovel. The roots of the sagebrush, pinyon, and juniper were dug out. The children would help the farmers by piling the sagebrush and timber, which then was burned. The Stanley brothers dug up 600 trees in two months. A good hard worker could grub an acre a day. Only three men, Lewis Matson, Ken Rowley, and Shelby Harles, were known for that type of stamina. More commonly, it would take two people to clear an acre of land in one day.

Teams of horses were also employed. A drag, such as a railroad tie, would scrape the vegetation. The material that didn't loosen would be grubbed out and burned.

3. If you had your choice, what lands would you clear?

Everyone questioned felt that the sage-covered land was the best choice because it was easiest to dig out the roots.

4. What were the first crops that were planted on a new homestead?

The first crops planted were in the family garden. They included cabbage, corn, carrots, green beans, onions, radishes, rhubarb, squash, turnips, and potatoes. These vegetables all stored well in a root cellar.

5. What were the early sources for seeds?

The most common seed source was the Henry Fields Company in Shenandoah, Iowa. Seeds were ordered from this company from the 1910s to the present. Harry Rogers's store in Arriola also was a seed source. Additionally, many people saved corn, bean, and watermelon seeds from their own crops. Two people had samples of beans that they have been growing since their families moved out on the Point. One bean was an "Arkansas" bean and the other a brightly colored "Anasazi" bean.

6. What are the requirements for a good crop? Can it ever be too wet?

The overwhelming response to the first question was that adequate winter snow and summer rain are required for a good crop. Moisture is considered the most important element in dry-land farming. Rain in the fall can hurt a crop because it delays the harvest. In 1957, it rained all spring and summer. The beans were not planted until the middle of June. The crop is usually cut in early to middle September and left to "cure," or dry, for a week before the beans are threshed. In 1957, several of the farmers were three to four weeks late cutting the crop, because of the wet weather. The vines were so heavy that it took twice as long for the beans to cure out. When they finally could be harvested, the farmers reaped 12 sacks to the acre, but many could not finish harvesting before the snow came. In January of 1958, they returned to the fields during a dry spell. The unharvested beans had to be removed for the next season. The farmers plowed the beans up onto the top of the snow and harvested them. They averaged 6 sacks to the acre. The beans had swelled as big as a person's thumb and sold for only about half the normal price.

7. How were the crops protected? Did your family use scarecrows? Pesticides? Fertilizers?

Three people recalled the use of scarecrows in gardens. Only one early use of pesticides was noted. Strychnine mixed with flour was employed to kill pinyon jays. The birds were a problem because they ate the tops of the corn husks. No one used fertilizers in the early days. In later years when combines came into use, the bean hulls were placed back into the soil. Chemical fertilizers have been used with wheat, but haven't proven to be cost effective.

8. What types of insect and animal problems were there? What wild animals were seen in the early days?

In the early years, problems with insects were minimal. Since the 1950s, people have had problems with grasshoppers and cutworms. The animals most commonly seen in the early days were coyote, mountain lion, bobcat, fox, jackrabbit, and porcupine. Of all the animals mentioned, porcupines caused the most damage, as they would eat the blossoms off the beans closest to the edges of the fields. Porcupines were frequently shot. Jackrabbits also caused crop damage, and in the 1930s a few communal jackrabbit drives were organized. The farmers would spread out across the country, drive the rabbits into a designated area, and then shoot them. Other pest animals included deer, prairie dogs, owls, and hawks. The large birds would eat the chickens.

9. How did dry beans become established as a major crop?

Helen Martin (Alex's wife) grew up in the Yellow Jacket area. She says her father, Floyd Cummings, was the first person to plant pinto beans in the Montezuma Valley. In the early 1910s, he ordered garden beans from Henry Fields, but they were out of that particular variety so the company substituted the order with pinto beans. They produced so well that he planted a larger patch the next year.

Pearl Black is credited as the first person to grow pinto beans on Goodman Point. The Blacks homesteaded in 1912. The Stanleys planted ½ acre of pinto beans in 1916, and by 1922 they had enlarged their plot to 10 acres. In 1927, Eldarado Seitz planted 70 acres of beans. The first bean planted was called a San Juan pinto or a Mexican bean. It had spots on it and a definite stripe up the side. It was the predominant bean planted until a few years ago, when the farmers switched to the Cahone variety. They always save seed to be planted for the following year's crop.

Red, white, and black beans were also grown on Goodman Point. Half of the informants recalled their parents growing a variety now referred to as "Anasazi beans" in the family garden. They were brighter than the present-day Anasazi beans. Leslie Black has been growing a bean of this type all her life. [Author's note: What has recently come to be called the "Anasazi bean" in Montezuma County appears to be the same as a variety called "Jacob's pole bean" elsewhere.] Yearly, Edith Flanagan plants an "Arkansas bean" that her parents brought out with them. It looks like a small pinto bean.

10. What were the best and worst years for farming?

Oscar Martin summed up the best years for farming by stating, "The best years were the sevens. It started in 1927, and it followed through every [tenth] year until 1977. [The years] 1927, 1937, 1947, 1957, and 1967 were all good years."

The years 1927 and 1947 were cited as the best ones for farming. The beans produced 10 to 12 sacks per acre. The women interviewed could easily recall 1947 because it was the year that they could afford to buy extra household items.

The years 1934 and 1951 were the driest years anyone could remember. Birney Seitz said, "In 1934, we had to sell our livestock except our work animals. It was so dry, we didn't raise anything. It was worse than last summer [1989]. All the springs—everything went dry. You could walk across the Dolores River without getting your feet wet. It didn't rain or snow."

For all those questioned, 1951 was a year of almost total crop failure. The fall of 1950 was dry and the winter produced little snow. By spring, only 1½ in of moisture had been received since the beginning of the previous fall. Beans came up, but they never produced. When harvest came, in most areas the farmers didn't even make back their seed. Oscar Martin recalls harvesting a total of 10 sacks of beans from 30 acres.

11. How and when were new farm machines introduced?

A team of one to three horses pulling a walking/turning plow could plow 3 acres a day. The land was harrowed 6 to 8 in deep. The seeds (beans and corn) were planted 3 to 4 in deep.

Luther Shields recalled the first time he ever saw a bean harvest. It was in 1925 at Pearl Black's house. "I can remember how they tried to cut the beans with an old horse cutter. It drug them down. So, the farmers jumped in and pulled them by hand [about 30 acres]. Then, they hauled the beans up to a big spot of hard ground by the original Black place. They hooked an old disk to the horse team. They drove round and round over those beans. Next, they took pitchforks and tossed the hulls up in the air. That's how they winnowed those beans! They sacked them up, and it ended up to be 300 sacks. That was my first experience in the bean business!"

A few families had purchased tractors and brought them to Goodman Point by the late 1920s. The first tractor on the Point was an International Farm-All Regular with spade lugs. At the same time, small Wade threshing machines arrived. They were powered by automobiles. The rear wheel of the car was removed, and a pulley was attached to the axle so the car powered the threshing machine. The beans were scooped into the threshing machine by hand and then sacked.

By the mid-1930s, almost all the farmers had tractors. The International Farm-All F-20 Row Crop tractor and the John Deere Row Crop tractor were the most popular models. These tractors had rubber tires and two-row planters. Although several families moved off Goodman Point during the Great Depression, it is interesting to note that all the remaining families purchased tractors in the 1930s.

The Universal Thresher, a larger machine, was used in the early 1930s. The beans were shocked (cut) and left to dry in the field. They were then loaded onto wagons pulled by teams or a tractor and taken to the threshing machine, which separated the beans from the hulls.

At threshing time, approximately 20 neighbors and relatives worked together. The work party was organized by the landowner and machine operator. When they were finished at one farm, they would move on together to the next field. In the early days, beans were threshed, sacked, and loaded all at the same time by the work party. Today, the beans are sacked by the warehouses.

The combine came into use in the 1930s. The earliest one on the Point was the International Combine Model #42. The threshing machine continued to be used into the early 1950s. It was preferred by farmers who used the bean hulls for cattle feed.

12. What clues to the weather were used?

All the people interviewed looked to the Ute Mountain as a weather guide. "Mom said you couldn't plant corn until all the snow was off Ute Mountain." It was time to plant beans when there was "a warm feeling in the air." One farmer said he waits until the deerbrush (cliffrose, *Purshia stansburiana* [Torrey] Henrickson) starts to bloom on the McElmo Canyon rim, then he knows it's time to plant beans.

Three of the project participants said their parents were "moon planters." Birney Seitz said that his dad wouldn't plant anything that grew below the ground unless it was by the dark of the moon (new moon).

13. Does the length of time a field is in use affect crop production?

Everyone replied yes. Some responses included:
"The land gets sorrier over time."
"This land has worn out."
"The land goes downhill."
"Yes, that's why I switched to alfalfa."
"If I ever wanted a piece of land, I'd rather have the new land than any other. It would raise better crops, and it was weed-free."
"If you grow beans on the same land year after year, it wears out in about 25–30 years."

The early farmers didn't rotate their crops or rest their fields often. Today farmers rotate their fields, and some have placed their land in the Federal Land Bank Program.

14. What do you consider the most important factors for successful farming? Winter snows? Rainfall? Depth of soils? Timing of frosts?

Everyone responded that winter snows and summer rainfall were the most critical factors.

15. Annually, what affected crop production levels the most?

Again, the answer was winter snows and summer rain. Good farming practices, such as knowing when and how to prepare the soils, were also mentioned.

Summary

In historic times, portions of the Goodman Point area have been farmed since 1911. The amount of land cleared for farming grew rapidly in the initial period of settlement, and more slowly thereafter, though some new lands continue to be brought into cultivation. For example, pinyon-juniper forest on the edges of fields is still being cleared today as fields are expanded. The questions asked of residents dealt with some of the important details of dry-land farming and focused on the production of corn and beans because these crops were also grown in prehistoric times.

Early settlers preferred sagebrush-covered lands because they were easiest to clear, though most informants did not think they were necessarily more productive than the pinyon/juniper-covered lands. The most productive lands were thought to be those on north-facing slopes or in hollows, presumably because of greater retention of soil moisture in these locations.

When a homestead was established, family vegetable gardens were planted first. The crops grown by the first homesteaders included corn and potatoes, in addition to the vegetables grown in family gardens. Corn was necessary for livestock feed, potatoes were grown for food or trade, and the family vegetable garden provided food to live on. Problems with insects, disease, and animal pests were minimal on the newly cleared lands.

During the early 1910s, pinto beans were introduced into the area. Gradually, with the establishment of eastern markets for the beans and the advent of tractors, pinto beans became the principal cash crop.

Although crop yields have varied over the years, it is significant that 1951 was the only year of virtually total crop failure. Residents agree that the land is being exhausted by repeated seasons of growing beans. New farming techniques, which include rotating crops and resting fields, are now employed. There is general agreement that moisture is the most important factor in crop success, and that both winter and summer moisture are essential.

Archaeological Sites

The questions in this section were designed with two goals in mind. The first was to acquire specific data from the Goodman Point residents regarding site locations and the clearing of prehistoric sites from agricultural land. The second goal was to better understand attitudes toward the archaeological sites and to determine how these attitudes may have changed over time in the Goodman Point community.

1. Where are the archaeological sites on your land?

Residents were able to mark the locations of 100 sites on USGS 7.5 minute quad maps of the study area (Connolly 1990: Figure 5). Everyone identified the location of the sites by the presence of rubble mounds. From residents' descriptions, these sites date to the Pueblo II and III (A.D. 900 through 1300) time periods. Isolated finds that were mentioned included arrowheads, axeheads, whole pots, canteens, mugs, manos, and metates.

2. Have you ever seen any evidence of prehistoric roads, lakes, or farms?

All the residents knew of the prehistoric road (Connolly 1990: Figure 6) which ran from "the large site above Sand Canyon" (5MT3925—named the Casa Negra site by Crow Canyon archaeologists [Adler, this volume; Adler 1988, 1990]) to the "ruins east of the schoolhouse" (and just north of the present Goodman Point Unit of the National Park Service; see Adler 1988, 1990). It is possible that this road

had a branch. Two residents said that the road ended at Goodman Point Ruin (5MT604) itself rather than in the cluster of sites north of it. One resident mentioned that the prehistoric road ended at Goodman Lake.

Of the main road Ford Stanley said, "It's probably 12 to 14 feet wide by about 1½ to 2 feet deep." Birney Seitz noted, "It was a big scooped-out place as wide as this room [about 12 ft wide]. It went right across from that big ruin south of Fulks's old homestead [Goodman Point Ruin, 5MT604]. It went right across from that ruin, just as straight as you could go. Across our place and up across Stanley's, Marshall Black's, and up to that big ruin over there [Casa Negra, 5MT3925]."

Leslie Black said that the road goes right under her house. Her son Stanley, a former employee of the Soil Conservation Service, generously shared his October 27, 1954, aerial photo of the Black farm. The photo clearly depicts the prehistoric road running northeast from Casa Negra across the Black and Seitz properties toward the ruins east of the schoolhouse (5MT3807).

The possible existence of two other prehistoric roads was noted. The first is a road that may run from a spring south of Casa Negra to the McElmo Canyon rim. The second possible road runs in a northwesterly direction from Goodman Point toward Dawson Draw (Yellow Jacket Canyon).

Two prehistoric lakes were mentioned. Goodman Lake is believed by many, but not all, residents to have been constructed prehistorically. It consists of an earthen dam that floods approximately 1 acre and holds water year around. Moqui Lake (5MT1736), located 5 mi west of Sand Canyon, consisted of a low rock and earthen dam. Residents stated that the reservoir was largely destroyed by Bureau of Land Management chaining in the 1960s. Everyone who responded to this question believed that Moqui Lake was a prehistoric reservoir.

Birney Seitz said you could see the remains of an Anasazi ruin and farm terraces in the SW ¼ of the NE ¼ of Section 6, Township 37N, Range 17W. Birney said, "There was a ruin up there in the southwest corner. I never did clear it up. There was a place that was terraced, about an acre squared. When we cleared it up, you could see the terraces where they had put them, about an acre square—kind of like they do with contouring. They had this little garden spot on the northeast slope where they raised their corn."

These farm terraces were located on top of the mesa and were identified by lines of stone. Steve Chappell, the current landowner, does not recall seeing any of these terraces.

3. How were the sites cleared? When? Where is the masonry?

Residents recalled removing 25 sites from their property (Connolly 1990: Figure 7). In the early days, the farmers would plow around the sites. Five people remembered removing a total of seven sites by hand. They would pick up the rocks and haul them off in a wagon. The rocks were used for fences, foundations, dams, and dikes to prevent erosion.

Beginning in the 1940s, bulldozers were used to clear sites. Eighteen sites were identified by residents as having been moved by bulldozers. The rocks were either used in dam construction or pushed off the edge of a field. Two residents recalled burying sites with a bulldozer. They dug a hole and placed all the rocks from the site in the hole.

The ruin located east of the schoolhouse and north of Goodman Point Ruin (5MT3807, now owned by Colorado Mountain College) was bulldozed in the 1960s. Prior to bulldozing, it was described as a large rubble mound measuring 5 to 6 ft in height. Residents said that a large amount of pottery was found at the ruin.

4. What types of artifacts did people find?

From talking with residents and viewing private collections, it was learned that people dug most often in the midden areas and masonry-lined pit structures. Shovels and probes were used to examine the ruins. Residents kindly showed their collections, which included Pueblo I through Pueblo III (A.D. 750–1300) gray ware and white ware vessels, arrowheads, other projectile points, pendants, beads, sandals, corn, beans, axes, manos, metates, and bone tools. Arrowheads were found and collected more frequently than any other type of artifact.

Artifacts were frequently unearthed in fields during plowing. Stone axes were the most commonly collected artifacts from the fields. Five private collections consisted of wooden crates filled with axes and manos. Three of the five collections had between 70 and 100 of these artifacts. (In the Mesa Verde area, ground-stone axes are most common in the Pueblo III period [Mills 1987].) The remaining two collections consisted of approximately 30 to 50 axes and manos. Sherds, arrowheads, and an occasional whole pot were also noted in the personal collections. One present-day farmer says he often plows up burnt corn from clay-lined firepits.

Five residents interviewed were particularly knowledgeable about Anasazi prehistory, architecture, artifacts, and pottery types. These residents had whole vessels in their collections and could identify the locations from which they were recovered. The residents all knew and remembered Cliff Chappell, who had often excavated on Goodman Point. He amassed a large collection of artifacts, known as the Chappell Collection, which is now housed at the Anasazi Heritage Center (Olsen 1988). A large percentage of his collection appears to have come from ruins in the Goodman Point area.

5. What were the first homesteaders' attitudes toward the sites?

People felt that their parents had a great respect for the ruins. In the beginning years on the farm, people worked so hard clearing the land and planting crops that they really didn't pay much attention to the ruins.

Ford Stanley said, "You know, way back then, when we homesteaded, all summer long we had plenty of work to do. We had a baseball team to play on Saturdays. When you grub sagebrush or trees all week, you kind of want to rest on Sundays."

As time passed and homesteads were established, people's interest in the ruins began to grow. This was particularly true for the younger-generation residents of Goodman Point, who explored the cliff dwellings in Yellow Jacket and Sand canyons.

6. What do you think about archaeology now?

No attempt was made to categorize or quantify the responses to this question. The following comments are taken directly from the taped interviews:

"We probably should have preserved more."

"It's okay. I just wasn't interested in it. We didn't know anything about it in those days. It's just new to me now, the digging and the studying."

"I like to go and watch it. Talk to them [the archaeologists]."

"There's a whole lot they're doing nowadays. So much of it is guesswork, but that doesn't keep them from being interested."

"I respect it. I think to a degree we're getting carried away with it, but on the other hand, it's part of history. Now this Sand Canyon deal is supposed to go on for 10 years. It's all right because it's not hurting anybody. The land already belongs to the government. What I object to a lot is what's on an individual's land should be that individual's business. If he wants to turn it over or let the archaeologists dig it, then that's his business. I don't feel he should be harmed by what he does on his own land."

"It's fine for people who like it."

"The Park Service and the oil companies talked about putting a road in Sand Canyon in 1923. That was the last I ever heard about it. I guess that would have been too expensive, because they would have had to protect the ruins and have a guide. I feel sorry that they haven't protected those ruins over the years."

Summary

Archaeological sites were recognized by residents by the presence of rubble mounds. From the descriptions of these sites, it appears that most if not all date to the Pueblo II and Pueblo III periods. Residents identified 100 sites in the study area. Among the sites recalled by the residents were one prehistoric road, two possible prehistoric roads, one terraced farming area, one prehistoric reservoir, and one possible prehistoric reservoir.

Of the sites identified, residents recalled that 25 were removed by hand or bulldozer in land clearing or farm improvement. The masonry rubble was reused in dams, fences, or foundations or pushed to the edges of fields. Farming has had significant impact on larger, more obvious archaeological sites on Goodman Point. Many smaller or more subtly expressed sites (e.g., limited-activity sites, jacal structures, outdoor hearths) may have been destroyed.

Goodman Point residents have a great deal of respect for the Anasazi culture. Many are knowledgeable about, and interested in, the prehistory of the area. Several people expressed concern over the deterioration of ruins in their lifetimes. These people, and the knowledge they have about dry-land farming and about the area's archaeological sites, represent a human resource that has been underutilized by researchers.

5

The Site Testing Program

Mark D. Varien, Kristin A. Kuckelman, and James H. Kleidon

Introduction

The Site Testing Program was designed as a multiple-year program, including four seasons of fieldwork (1988–1991) and an adequate subsequent period for final report preparation. This will produce comparable data from 13 sites (for locations, see Figure 1.3 in Chapter 1). Preliminary descriptive reports have been completed for the 1988, 1989, and 1990 seasons (Varien 1990b, 1991; Kuckelman et al. 1991). Later in our discussion, we provide summaries of the Site Testing Program research questions and field methods; brief descriptions of the sites tested in 1988, 1989, and 1990; and a preliminary summary of the results of the first three years of the program.

The Site Testing Program is designed to collect selected data on small (and, in one case, medium-size) Pueblo III sites in the central portion of the Sand Canyon locality. Investigation of these smaller sites is essential for understanding demographic and organizational change in the locality during the Pueblo III period. The Testing Program provides a level of investigation intermediate between the site survey component of our research and the intensive excavations. This latter type of excavation has been carried out only in selected portions of one very large site—Sand Canyon Pueblo (see Bradley, this volume)—and at one small site—Green Lizard (see Huber and Lipe, this volume).

Research Questions and Theoretical Orientation

The Site Testing Program addresses a limited set of research questions and employs a sampling strategy designed to obtain the necessary data with minimum impact to the sites. Testing affects less than 1 percent (by area) of each site included in the program, and we estimate that when the program is completed, fewer than 1 percent of the Pueblo III sites in the Sand Canyon locality will have been tested.

Research questions addressed by the Testing Program are derived from the overall Sand Canyon Project research design (Lipe, this volume: Introduction; see also Lipe and Bradley 1986, 1988). The central problem set forth in the general research design is characterizing and understanding Anasazi community organization in the Sand Canyon locality during the Pueblo III period (A.D. 1150–1300). This of course involves investigating changes that occurred during the Pueblo III period, including eventual abandonment of the locality. Lipe and Bradley (1986, 1988) propose that the dimensions of scale, differentiation, integration, and intensity be used as an organizing framework to characterize Sand Canyon Anasazi communities at several points in time; these dimensions provide a basis for comparing community organization through both time and space.

In an overview of the context for archaeological research in southwestern Colorado, Eddy et al. (1984) also focus on community organization. These authors identify the emergence, growth, and decline of aggregated settlement systems in the McElmo drainage unit during the Pueblo II and Pueblo III periods as one of the most important research questions for this area (Eddy et al. 1984:43). They also believe that identifying the mechanisms of abandonment at the end of the Pueblo III period is an essential task for researchers working with Anasazi prehistory in the McElmo drainage unit (Eddy et al. 1984:44). They argue that canyon-head architectural complexes (such as Sand Canyon Pueblo) are unique to the McElmo unit and use these canyon-head systems as diagnostic elements of the late Pueblo III Hovenweep phase (Eddy et al. 1984:43).

The Sand Canyon Project is the most detailed study to date of a Pueblo III Anasazi community centered—at least in the middle and late A.D. 1200s—on a large canyon-head settlement. The project is also designed to investigate the more dispersed early Pueblo III community or communities that preceded the aggregation of settlement in and around Sand Canyon Pueblo.

In the general research design for the Sand Canyon Project (Lipe, this volume: Introduction; Lipe and Bradley 1986, 1988), a set of middle-range instrumental studies is also identified as essential. These studies—chronology, paleoenvironments, settlement continuity and longevity, and site-formation processes—must be carried out to obtain data suitable for addressing the higher-order questions about community organization and change.

The Site Testing Program addresses several aspects of the substantive and instrumental questions identified in the general research design. The program is designed to acquire representative samples of architectural, feature, and assemblage data that are complementary to those collected by the survey and intensive excavation programs. Adequacy of sample size (both the size of the collections from individual sites and the number of sites needed when comparing categories of sites) is an issue that is being addressed by the Site Testing Program.

With respect to the general problem of understanding community organization through time, differentiation is the organizational dimension for which the Testing Program can most directly contribute data. For the late Pueblo III period, data sets from tested sites plus Green Lizard can be used to evaluate the degree of sociopolitical and functional differentiation between Sand Canyon Pueblo and nearby contemporary smaller sites that were part of the same settlement cluster and, presumably, of the same community. Tested sites from the earlier part of the Pueblo III period will also provide data useful for assessing intracommunity differentiation in the more dispersed community that preceded the one dominated by Sand Canyon Pueblo. Together, the intensive and test excavation data sets will provide a basis for comparing earlier and later Pueblo III communities in the same area.

Ecofactual and artifactual data from the Testing Program will also be essential in studying subsistence intensification and resource depletion through time in the locality. Testing Program data can be used to evaluate hypotheses about community scale derived from analysis of survey data—for example, can upper and lower Sand Canyon settlement clusters be considered different first-order communities? Likewise, are models of community integration based on considerations of site size and the distribution of public architecture (Adler, this volume; Adler 1990) supported by the architectural and artifactual evidence gained through both the intensive and test excavations?

The instrumental, or middle-range, research domains addressed directly by the Site Testing Program are chro-nology, continuity and longevity of occupation, site abandonment, and site-formation processes. These are discussed briefly below.

Chronology

The Site Testing Program was designed to obtain tree-ring dates that can be used to refine the chronological relationships between sites in the Sand Canyon locality. A series of well-dated sites will permit the development of a more finely divided pottery style sequence, and this sequence will permit better dating of study area sites where absolute dates are not available. Improved understanding of the chronological relationships between sites is essential for studies of community change, organization, and interaction.

Continuity and Longevity of Occupation

Site testing seeks to improve our understanding of the continuity and longevity of particular sites and site types. This includes determining site use life, the degree to which sites represent seasonal or year-round occupations, and the extent of abandonment and reoccupation of sites. Currently, small sites with one to a few kivas are treated as a single functional category, with the implicit presumption that all were occupied for the same length of time. An important goal of the Site Testing Program is to assess variation in the continuity and longevity of occupation at the smaller sites. This goal will be accomplished through accumulation-rate studies (Varien 1990a).

Site Abandonment

Excavations at Sand Canyon Pueblo have produced abundant data on abandonment processes at individual structures, at blocks of contiguous structures, and at the site as a whole. Although a variety of abandonment strategies occurred within Sand Canyon Pueblo, much of the site seems to have been abandoned at, or very close to, the time when the entire northern San Juan region became depopulated (Bradley, this volume; Bradley 1987, 1988a, 1990, 1991b; Kleidon and Bradley 1989). Comparative data on small-site abandonment will improve our understanding of how large settlements such as Sand Canyon Pueblo formed, the processes by which populations aggregated and dispersed, and how and why the Anasazi abandoned the Mesa Verde region in the late A.D. 1200s. Most of the small sites that have been tested were abandoned in a different manner than much of Sand Canyon Pueblo. In most cases, structure roofs on small sites appear to have been deliberately dismantled and timbers salvaged for use elsewhere. This implies that many of the small Pueblo III sites were abandoned before the depopulation of the Sand Canyon locality and of the Mesa Verde region.

Site-Formation Processes

The sites we test have been formed by both cultural and natural processes. These processes occurred during the occupation of the site and after site abandonment. Cultural processes that took place during the occupation of the site include refuse disposal, reuse processes, and abandonment processes. More then seven centuries have passed since the abandonment of the sites we are testing, and both natural and recent cultural processes have altered the character of these sites in that period. These processes are varied, and relevant studies range from specific geoarchaeological projects that focus on how pit structures were abandoned and filled to studies that evaluate the effect of historic land use on the sites (e.g., see Connolly, this volume). The Site Testing Program will attempt to provide a better understanding of these site-formation processes.

An important goal of the Site Testing Program is to understand the range of variation present in the Sand Canyon area community, at least among habitation and seasonally used sites. This approach contrasts with the normative one, which would examine a single "typical" small site and generalize from that case to the entire community. For example, site testing attempts to document the length of site occupation for each of the 13 sites that have been tested. We are testing unit pueblos (Prudden 1903; Lipe 1989), as well as sites that do not conform to the standard unit-type pueblo layout, and we are testing sites that contain both high and relatively low densities of surface artifacts. We are also attempting to document the range of variation in site location, site layout, and types of surface features present. We are focusing, however, on sites that have significant amounts of architecture and surface artifacts. These sites are most likely to be datable and to provide data comparable to those from the intensive excavations, which have focused on blocks of structures and associated middens. As a result, some types of small limited-activity and seasonal sites are likely to have been excluded from the Testing Program.

Field Methods and Site Selection

Sampling Strategy

To address the general research domains identified by the Site Testing Program, a stratified random sampling technique is employed as the primary data-recovery method. Figures 5.1 through 5.3 illustrate the approach. Figure 5.1 provides an example of the surface evidence of gross site structure at Roy's Ruin (5MT3930), a small, Pueblo III site tested in 1988 (Varien 1990b). The surface evidence indicated that this site had a surface roomblock, a kiva, a tower, and a midden area. Low, linear mounds with moderately high surface artifact densities were also mapped on the east and west sides of the kiva depression. Finally, the boundaries of the surface artifact scatter were mapped. All these surface indications were employed in designing sampling strata for this site. Figure 5.2 shows the stratified random sampling plan of 1-×-1-m test pits that was carried out at this site, as well as the location of several judgmental test pits that were added to the randomly chosen ones during the course of the excavations. Figure 5.3 shows the probable location and characteristics of major cultural features at the site, as identified or inferred on the basis of the surface evidence plus the results of the test excavations.

Stratified random sampling is particularly well suited to the sites selected for testing because the same types of features (surface architecture, pit structures, and middens) are often present in predictable configurations and can be recognized by surface remains. The Sand Canyon locality lies in the heart of the area explored by T. Mitchell Prudden (1903, 1914, 1918), who was the first to recognize and interpret the typical layout of small habitation sites in this area. He coined the term *unit-type pueblo* to describe the small sites in this region (Prudden 1903:12) and to recognize that larger pueblos were generally made up of aggregates of these small "units" (Lipe 1989). Gorman and Childs (1981) criticize the use of the term unit pueblo, arguing that construction details vary significantly from site to site. Construction details may vary, but the general site layout that Prudden emphasized, consisting of a small set of surface rooms, a pit structure, and a trash midden, is standard enough to make it possible for us to apply a consistent stratified random sampling design to most of the sites selected for testing.

Several tested sites, including Roy's Ruin, are typical *Prudden units*. At these sites, the masonry room-block, pit structure, and midden were easily defined on the basis of surface remains. Other types of sites, especially the tower-kiva sites, cliff dwellings, talus-slope sites, and the larger villages, do not conform as well to the standard unit-pueblo layout. However, the surface expression of particular types of features—e.g., pit structures—is similar from site to site, regardless of the configuration of features present. Consequently, the surface remains provide generally reliable guides for defining the sampling strata. In designing the stratified sample at a particular site, rubble from fallen surface structures represents one stratum. At Roy's Ruin (Figure 5.2), for example, this is Stratum 1. Pit structure depressions are used to create another sampling stratum (Stratum 2 at Roy's Ruin). A courtyard sampling stratum (No. 3 in Figure 5.2) surrounds the pit structure stratum on all but the tower-kiva sites. The midden, defined on the basis of the highest density of surface artifacts and the presence of gray-brown, ashy sediments, is another sampling stratum (No. 5). This core area of the site is surrounded by the inner periphery sampling stratum (No. 4). Outer periphery sampling strata (Nos. 6 and 7) surround this portion of the site and extend to the edge of the surface artifact scatter. At Roy's Ruin, the southern portion of the

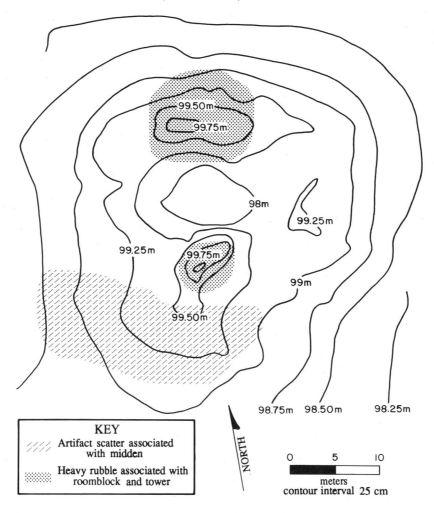

Figure 5.1. Surface remains and topography at Roy's Ruin.

midden and outer periphery extend into a plowed field and consequently had been "smeared" and expanded spatially.

The stratified random sampling design enables us to efficiently obtain the data required to address research questions. Surface architecture and pit structure depressions are separate sampling strata. This ensures that some test pits fall in the contexts most likely to contain the tree-ring specimens essential for establishing site chronology. In addition, examination of the floor assemblages of artifacts, evidence of roof remains and of culturally deposited fills, and evidence of postabandonment fill sequences enable us to gain insights into abandonment and postabandonment processes.

The stratified random sample also allows statistical estimates of the total artifact populations. Total populations of artifacts provide the raw data for accumulation-rate studies; these studies will refine estimates of the length of site occupation (see Kohler and Blinman 1987). The low variance that generally occurs between sampling units within a stratum helps produce the most accurate point estimates of total populations. Thus, by defining relatively

homogeneous sampling strata, we improve the precision of the point estimates for the entire site.

This sampling technique also provides representative samples of artifacts for comparative studies that will help address questions of site function and intracommunity differentiation. We expect to use these samples to determine whether or not there is functional variation among the sites tested. Finally, the stratified random sample minimizes the impact to the site while enabling us to achieve our research objectives.

Site Selection

The research design for the Site Testing Program draws on the information collected by Sand Canyon Project surveys (Adler, this volume; Adler 1988, 1990; Van West et al. 1987) and by the lower Sand Canyon surveys sponsored by the Bureau of Land Management (Gleichman and Gleichman, this volume; Gleichman and Gleichman 1989; Adler and Metcalf 1990, 1991). These surveys indicate that there is a great deal of variation among sites and that a simple

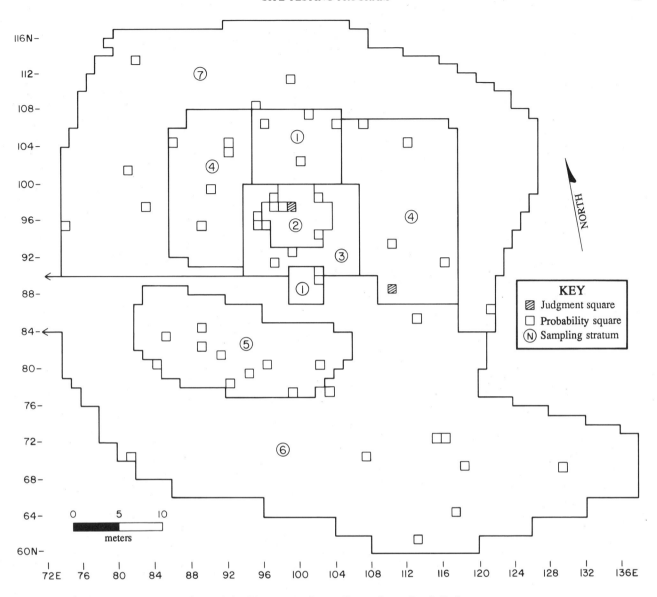

Figure 5.2. Plan map of sampling units at Roy's Ruin.

normative approach (all small sites are equal) would not produce results that could be generalized to the entire community. Variation exists in site location, size, and layout; in period of occupation within the Pueblo III period; and in surface artifact density. The Site Testing Program is designed to sample this diversity and to obtain data useful in evaluating and more fully understanding the variation that is present.

First, the Testing Program is designed to sample two different Pueblo III site clusters. The first—termed the upper Sand Canyon cluster—is a group of Pueblo III sites located near the head of Sand Canyon, close to Sand Canyon Pueblo. The cluster of sites in this general location also includes sites from the Pueblo II to late Pueblo III periods. The second, or lower Sand Canyon, cluster is more diffuse and is located in lower Sand

Canyon and adjacent parts of McElmo Canyon. Castle Rock Pueblo, a medium-size pueblo, is the largest Pueblo III site in this cluster.

Second, sites have been selected to sample diversity in physiographic setting. Four categories have been employed: uplands or mesa tops, cliff shelters and talus slopes within canyons, benches within canyons, and McElmo Canyon. The only site in this last category is Castle Rock Pueblo, which is located around an isolated rock outcrop on the floor of McElmo Canyon. All the sites in the canyon-bench and cliff-talus categories are in Sand Canyon. If Sand Canyon Pueblo had been included in the tested-sites sample, we might have added a fifth physiographic category—canyon head. Sand Canyon Pueblo is built around the head of a small tributary to upper Sand Canyon and surrounds what was probably a running spring

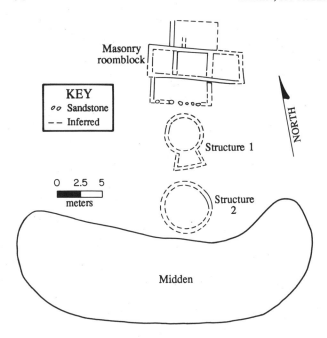

Figure 5.3. Main cultural features at Roy's Ruin.

in prehistoric times. Part of the site is built on the canyon rim, and part on the talus slopes just below the rim.

Third, an attempt was made to sample variation in gross site size. As noted earlier, intensive excavations have focused primarily on a very large site—Sand Canyon Pueblo. The only other similarly large settlement in the area surveyed to date is the Goodman Point Ruin (See Figure 1.3 in Chapter 1). Permission to do limited testing at this site was refused by the National Park Service because the current draft management plan for this property places it indefinitely in "reserved status," with no provision for consumptive research. We also wished to understand the smaller settlements most closely associated with Sand Canyon Pueblo in both time and space. Consequently, our efforts have focused on the Sand Canyon drainage. After Sand Canyon Pueblo, the second-largest site in this drainage is Castle Rock Pueblo (5MT1825), located in McElmo Canyon near the mouth of Sand Canyon. This site, which has 12 to 15 kivas and an estimated 75 other structures, was tested in the 1990 and 1991 field seasons. The remaining Pueblo III habitation sites in the upper and lower Sand Canyon site clusters are smaller; the great majority have only one or two kivas. Consequently, the majority of sites selected for testing are in this size range.

Fourth, gross site layout was considered in selection of sites for testing. Habitation sites are the primary focus of the Testing Program, so the majority of sites tested have at least one kiva, several probable surface habitation rooms, and some amount of midden deposit. In upland or mesa-top settings, the layout of these sites conforms well to the Prudden-unit model (Prudden 1903; Lipe 1989). In cliff-talus and canyon-bench settings, the configuration is much

more variable, although the association of a kiva, a small group of surface rooms, and a midden can ordinarily be recognized. In addition, two tower-kiva units that lacked clear evidence of surface roomblocks were tested (Troy's Tower and Mad Dog Tower). These were selected on the possibility that they were not habitation sites or were habitation sites that functioned differently from the "standard" ones in the settlement system.

Finally, an attempt was made to select sites that varied in date within the Pueblo III period. It was initially thought that most of the small Pueblo III sites in the Sand Canyon drainage were contemporary with Sand Canyon Pueblo. As our understanding of cultural chronology within the Sand Canyon drainage developed, it became clear that the occupation at Sand Canyon Pueblo was largely or entirely after A.D. 1250, and that many, and perhaps most, of the upland Pueblo III Prudden units had been abandoned before that date. Consequently, the selection strategy shifted to one of choosing small sites that were at least partially contemporary with Sand Canyon Pueblo, as well as those that represented the earlier parts of the Pueblo III period. As discussed later in this chapter, we believe we have sampled some small sites that were occupied beyond 1250 and a number that date to the earlier part of the 1200s. In an effort to obtain artifact and ecofact samples from a third period—middle or late 1100s—Kenzie Dawn Hamlet (5MT5152) and G and G Hamlet (5MT11338) were added to the tested sample in 1991. Several of the tested sites may have components that represent light occupation in the late A.D. 1000s or early 1100s, but these have not yielded sufficient quantities of structures or artifacts to permit clear characterization of the component. Exceptions may be G and G and Kenzie Dawn hamlets, tested in 1991, which appear to have more substantial Pueblo II occupations.

To the extent possible, we have tested more than one site in each of the categories listed above. This will allow us to determine if intracategory variation is less than or as great as between-category variation. Ideally, larger numbers would be tested in each category, but limitations of time and funds make that impossible at this stage of the research. Because the Testing Program affects only a small fraction of the potentially eligible sites in the Sand Canyon locality, the results of the 1988–1991 Testing Program could be examined further in the future, either by the Crow Canyon Center or by other researchers.

The characteristics of the sites selected for testing are summarized in Table 5.1. Many of the sites are named after landowners in the Sand Canyon locality. As indicated in Table 5.1, testing at several sites extended over two field seasons. The Green Lizard site (5MT3901) is included in this compilation, even though it was investigated by intensive excavation of its western half rather than by testing (see Huber and Lipe, this volume). This site is included here, however, because it figures into a number of comparisons made among the smaller sites.

Table 5.1. Characteristics of Tested Sites

Name	Number	Location	Field Season	Settlement Cluster	Layout	Number of Kivas
Green Lizard Site	5MT3901	Canyon bench	1987–88	Upper	Unit-type pueblo	2
Shorlene's Site	5MT3918	Mesa top	1988	Upper	Unit-type pueblo	1
Roy's Ruin	5MT3930	Mesa top	1988	Upper	Unit-type pueblo	1
Lillian's Site	5MT3936	Mesa top	1988	Upper	Unit-type pueblo	1
Troy's Tower	5MT3951	Mesa top	1988–89	Upper	Tower-kiva	1
Catherine's Site	5MT3967	Canyon bench	1989	Upper	Unit-type pueblo	2
Stanton's Site	5MT10508	Cliff-talus	1989–90	Upper	Unit-type pueblo	1
Lester's Site	5MT10246	Cliff-talus	1990	Upper	Unit-type pueblo	2
Mad Dog Tower	5MT181	Canyon bench	1990	Lower	Tower-kiva	1
Saddlehorn Hamlet	5MT262	Cliff-talus	1990	Lower	Unit-type pueblo	1
Lookout House	5MT10459	Cliff-talus	1990–91	Upper	Unit-type pueblo	2
Castle Rock Pueblo	5MT1825	McElmo Canyon	1990–91	Lower	Village	12–15
G and G Hamlet	5MT11338	Mesa top	1991	Upper	Unit-type pueblo	1
Kenzie Dawn Hamlet	5MT5152	Mesa top	1991	Upper	Unit-type pueblo	3

The history of tested-site selection and excavation is briefly summarized below, by field season.

1988 Field Season. Three mesa-top sites (Roy's Ruin, Shorlene's site, and Lillian's site) were tested in the 1988 field season (Varien 1990b). Huber also completed intensive excavations at the Green Lizard site, located on a bench within upper Sand Canyon. Work at this site had begun in 1987 (Huber and Lipe, this volume; Huber 1989). The layout of all four sites conformed fairly well to Prudden's unit-type-pueblo model. In 1988, sampling of variation in site layout and surface features began through work at Troy's Tower. This is a mesa-top tower-kiva site that lacks the surface roomblock normally associated with unit-type pueblos. The absence of a roomblock presented the possibility that Troy's Tower was functionally different from the unit-type pueblos.

1989 Field Season. During the 1989 field season, excavation was completed at Troy's Tower, and Catherine's site was tested. The latter is located, like Green Lizard, on a bench within upper Sand Canyon. Work at Stanton's site—in a cliff-talus setting—was also initiated in the 1989 field season.

1990 Field Season. Work at Stanton's site was completed in 1990, and testing was undertaken at two more cliff-talus sites in upper Sand Canyon—Lester's site and Lookout House. Only the former had been completed by the end of the field season. Both Lester's site and Lookout House had much lower densities of surface artifacts than did Stanton's site. Test excavations in 1990 also included, for the first time, sites from the lower Sand Canyon cluster near McElmo Creek. These included Mad Dog Tower, a tower-kiva site with only a single surface room, similar to

Troy's Tower. Another small site tested in the lower Sand Canyon cluster was a cliff dwelling with a kiva and a midden located on the slope in front—Saddlehorn Hamlet. Testing also began at Castle Rock Pueblo. The testing of this site provides us with excavation data for the full range of site sizes in the central part of the locality. As mentioned earlier, Castle Rock Pueblo is located in McElmo Canyon near the mouth of Sand Canyon. Unlike any of the other tested sites, it is very close to an alluvial floodplain, which might have provided agricultural field locations in prehistoric times.

1991 Field Season. In 1991, test excavations at Lookout House and Castle Rock Pueblo were completed. In addition, two upland unit pueblos were tested—G and G Hamlet and Kenzie Dawn Hamlet. Surface pottery at these sites indicated they had substantial occupation in the early part of the Pueblo III period. By testing these sites, data from the middle to late A.D. 1100s could be obtained and compared with data from two other segments of the Pueblo III period—the early 1200s and the middle to late 1200s. Data from the mid- to late 1100s will provide us with the opportunity to study possible adaptive responses to the severe drought of A.D. 1130–1170. This appears to have been the most severe drought during the last 300 years of Anasazi occupation of southwestern Colorado (Van West and Lipe, this volume; Van West 1990).

The sites completed in 1991 are not summarized in the section that follows, and they are not treated systematically in the interpretations and comparisons made later in the chapter. This is because fieldwork at these sites had not been completed at the time that this chapter was drafted. Some information about these sites—especially regarding chronology—was inserted during the editing of the chapter for publication.

Summaries of Sites Tested, 1988–1990

Below are brief summaries of the sites at which test excavations had been completed by the end of the 1990 field season. More detailed accounts of the fieldwork are available in annual preliminary reports (Varien 1990b, 1991; Kuckelman et al. 1991), and a full report on the results of all four seasons of testing is being prepared for publication. The procedures for site definition and sampling have been discussed above and illustrated for one site—Roy's Ruin (Figures 5.1–5.3). The discussion of each of the other sites is accompanied by a map of the main cultural features, including structures, middens, and other major features. These maps are based on inferences from surface evidence, as well as on the results of test excavations. Locations of individual test pits are not shown on these maps but are provided in the preliminary reports and will be included in the published final report on the Site Testing Program.

Lillian's Site (5MT3936)

Lillian's site (Figure 5.4) is located in the uplands at an elevation of 2073 m, approximately 1.7 km to the north-northwest of Sand Canyon Pueblo. It is a multicomponent site, with a strong Pueblo III occupation that overlies a light Pueblo II occupation. The testing was designed to focus on the last occupation. Thirty-six 1-×-1-m sampling units were excavated as a part of the stratified random sample. Five additional, judgmentally located, 1-×-1-m pits were also excavated. The tops of walls were swept and troweled to define the layout of the masonry roomblocks. The presence of surface rooms, a kiva, and a midden with abundant artifacts indicates that this location was used during the Pueblo III period as a habitation site.

Excavation located two masonry roomblock units connected by a single curving wall. The roomblocks date to the Pueblo III period. The presence of two roomblock units may indicate that two households resided at Lillian's site during the Pueblo III occupation.

A single, masonry-lined pit structure—Structure 1—lies in front of the two roomblock units. Internal features, including a southern recess, bench, pilasters, hearth, and deflector, indicate that the structure can be classified as a kiva. Use of this term here does not imply a particular function, only an architectural type (see recent discussions by Lekson 1988; Lipe 1989; Lipe and Hegmon 1989).

A masonry tower, Structure 4, which probably stood at least two stories tall, is located south of Structure 1, so that the southern recess of Structure 1 points at the tower. Structure 4 is also interpreted as a part of the Pueblo III component. This interpretation is based on the masonry construction style and the alignment of Structure 4 relative to the other masonry architectural features.

Low, curving masonry walls abut and extend east from the east side of Structure 4. This construction was built

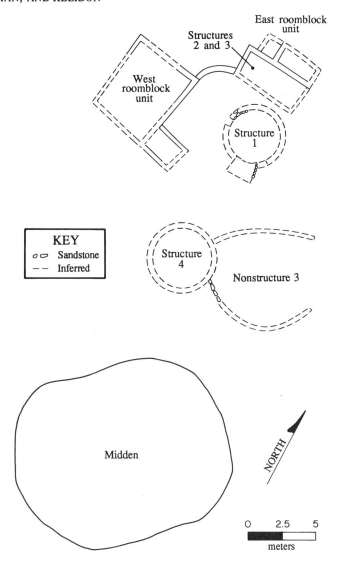

Figure 5.4. Main cultural features at Lillian's site.

after Structure 4, and therefore also dates to the Pueblo III occupation. These low walls do not appear to enclose a structure and may therefore enclose a courtyard or outdoor activity area of some type. The enclosed space is labeled Nonstructure 3. *Nonstructure* is a convention used in the Crow Canyon recording system. It refers to a culturally delimited area that was never a structure—that is, appears not to have had full-height walls or a roof.

South of the tower lies the trash mound, or midden area (Nonstructure 1). This trash mound is aligned with the east roomblock unit, the kiva, and the tower. This alignment suggests that the trash mound accumulated primarily during the Pueblo III occupation at Lillian's site.

Dating the Pueblo III component requires several lines of evidence. Fifty-nine tree-ring samples from the fill of Structure 1 produced dates. A substantial proportion of the dates were in the early A.D. 1200s. The latest cutting date is 1211rB. The latest date is 1214vv. This pattern of dates suggests occupation at the site in the early 1200s, probably extending for some years after A.D. 1214. Although there is evidence that the kiva had burned, it is not clear whether all the dated specimens were from kiva roof timbers or from burned structural material that had originated elsewhere on the site and had been dumped into the kiva.

An archaeomagnetic sample from the hearth of Structure 1 dates between A.D. 1175 and 1250. Painted white ware pottery associated with the Pueblo III occupation includes both McElmo and Mesa Verde black-on-white. Wilson (1991), working with pottery from a well-dated site 30 km north of Lillian's site, dates the beginning of the manufacture of Mesa Verde Black-on-white to after A.D. 1180, and possibly as late as A.D. 1200.

Together, these pieces of evidence indicate that the Pueblo III occupation of Lillian's site was probably between A.D. 1200 and 1250, and possibly between A.D. 1220 and 1250. Abandonment by A.D. 1250 is inferred because it seems unlikely that the kiva roof would have remained intact for more than 30 years without need of substantial repair or replacement. The latest dated wood sample from the site—at A.D. 1214vv—is from the kiva's fill. If the kiva roof had been built or rebuilt after A.D. 1214, it seems likely that when the kiva burned, wood dating later than A.D. 1214 would have been incorporated and that some pieces would have been dated, given the large number of dated samples collected from the structure.

Analysis of the stratigraphy and inclusions in the fill of Structure 1 suggests that at abandonment roof beams were scavenged and that a large portion of the kiva was intentionally filled. Structural material from dismantled surface rooms appears to have been the source of some of the fill deposited in the kiva. The paucity of artifacts on the examined portions of both kiva and surface room floors also suggests an abandonment pattern that may have involved a relatively short-range move, with most usable materials being scavenged at the time of abandonment.

At least one earlier occupation is also present at Lillian's site. Collapsed post-and-adobe rooms lie beneath the masonry roomblock. Tree-ring samples from deposits representing the post-and-adobe roomblock yielded dates in the A.D. 500s and 1070s. Pottery from the same deposits includes small numbers of Mancos Black-on-white, and this supports the later tree-ring dates. We infer that the occupation represented by the post-and-adobe roomblock dates to the late Pueblo II period. Recently excavated sites with post-and-adobe roomblocks located 20 km north of Lillian's site date between A.D. 1000 and 1100 (Kuckelman and Morris 1988).

Small amounts of pottery made in both Pueblo I and Basketmaker III times were also found on Lillian's site. It is possible that occupations dating to these periods are present, but Basketmaker III and Pueblo I architectural features were not identified.

Roy's Ruin (5MT3930)

Roy's Ruin (Figures 5.1 through 5.3) is a multicomponent site with a strong Pueblo III occupation. It is located at 2076 m elevation in the uplands approximately 1 km north-northeast of Sand Canyon Pueblo. Testing was designed to sample the Pueblo III component most heavily, but it was also hoped that the stratified random sample would identify each of the occupations present at the site. Fifty-three probabilistic and three judgmental sampling units were excavated to achieve the goals of the Testing Program. Sweeping and troweling wall tops and excavating four small trenches helped determine the layout of the masonry roomblock.

Site layout during the last occupation in the Pueblo III period conformed to a Prudden-unit pattern. Elements present at this time include a masonry roomblock, a masonry-lined pit structure, a masonry tower, and a midden. The centers of the roomblock, kiva, tower, and midden can be connected by an approximately straight north-to-south line.

The roomblock contains at least three, and possibly five, masonry-walled rooms. Additional nonmasonry rooms, located west of the masonry roomblock and pit structure, may be present as well. The masonry-lined pit structure, Structure 1, is more than 2 m deep and displays the standard features of a Pueblo III kiva in the Mesa Verde area. The tower is located between the kiva and the midden area.

The dating of the Pueblo III component is based on tree-ring and pottery data. The kiva fill yielded 21 dated tree-ring samples. The latest cutting date was 1213r and the latest date was 1223vv. Interpretation of these tree-ring dates is difficult, because the origins of the dated wood are unclear. Patches of ash on the floor and bench indicate that a fire had taken place in the structure, but no burned roof fall stratum was found. The samples from the kiva fill are probably from structural wood rather than from wood used as fuel, but they do not appear to result from the in-place burning of the kiva roof. The bulk of evidence indicates they may have been introduced into the kiva with materials used to partially fill it after its roof had been dismantled. No clear evidence of primary or secondary kiva roof beams was found, in the form of either charred or decayed wood.

The pottery from Roy's Ruin is consistent with the tree-ring dates. The pottery assemblage indicates a predominantly Pueblo III occupation. Mesa Verde Black-on-white is also present, indicating occupation after A.D. 1180 and probably after A.D. 1200 (see Wilson 1991). Our overall estimate of the timing of the Pueblo III occupation is that it falls in the period 1180 to 1250, and probably in the first third of the thirteenth century. The tree-ring dates suggest a construction episode in the early 1200s and indicate that construction or repair of buildings was going on at the site as late as the A.D. 1220s. Hence, occupation must have continued at least until then and perhaps somewhat later.

The pottery assemblage from Roy's Ruin also includes small numbers of decorated white wares assignable to the Pueblo II period. In the excavations, a number of features were encountered in stratigraphic contexts that indicated they probably predated the Pueblo III occupation. However, no architectural units dating to the probable earlier occupation were discovered. Our conclusions at this point are that a pre–Pueblo III occupation or occupations probably exist, but that it is unlikely that there was substantial use of the site as a habitation before the Pueblo III period.

The relative lack of floor artifacts suggests that usable artifacts were removed to another location at the time of abandonment, though this inference must be made cautiously because of the relatively small areas of floors that were exposed. However, evidence that the kiva roof beams were removed at abandonment is consistent with this inference.

Shorlene's Site (5MT3918)

Shorlene's site (Figure 5.5) is a multiple-component site located in the uplands at an elevation of 2115 m, approximately 1 km southwest of Sand Canyon Pueblo. The major architectural units visible on the surface include the rubble from a masonry roomblock, a pit structure depression, and a fallen masonry tower; these conform to the Prudden-unit configuration and date to the Pueblo III occupation of the site. A midden area is also present south-southwest of the Pueblo III architectural features, and it clearly was also used during the Pueblo III period.

Testing was designed to sample this Pueblo III occupation most heavily, and to this end a stratified random sample of 39 1-×-1-m sampling units was excavated. To determine the masonry roomblock size and layout, wall alignments were swept and lightly troweled.

The Pueblo III masonry roomblock contains at least three rooms. There probably was a larger room in front (south) of these rooms, and possibly a smaller back room as well, as indicated by wall rubble north of the well-defined portion of the roomblock. Structure 1, the pit structure located just south of the roomblock, is approximately 2 m deep and is apparently entirely lined with masonry. Sampling units encountered the upper lining wall, a wall of the southern recess, and a portion of the hearth on the main chamber floor. On the basis of this evidence, Structure 1 appears to have the features of a Mesa Verde area kiva from the Pueblo III period.

The masonry tower, Structure 3, was also sampled. This structure was found to have a slab-lined floor and was built on the fill of an earlier occupation. A masonry surface-room wall was found just north of the tower. It is not clear if it is connected with the masonry roomblock to the north, but it appears at this time that it is not. A row of rotting posts was also found in this area, indicating that jacal rooms may have been present at the site as well. A tree-ring date

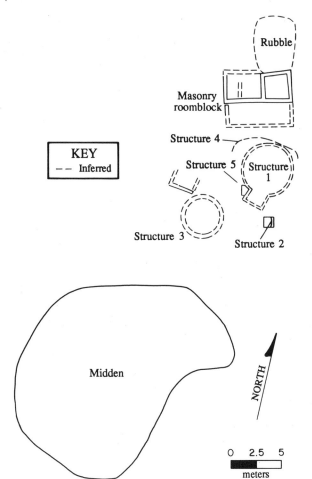

Figure 5.5. Main cultural features at Shorlene's site.

of 1145 + vv comes from the fill of a pit feature stratigraphically beneath both the masonry wall segment and the row of posts. This tree-ring date is also the latest one from Shorlene's site.

Dating the Pueblo III occupation is difficult, as none of the Pueblo III structures burned. The single tree-ring date referenced above indicates only that the late occupation was after A.D. 1145 and hence falls in the Pueblo III period. Mesa Verde Black-on-white pottery found on the site indicates a post–A.D. 1180 (and probably post–A.D. 1200) date for the occupation (Wilson 1991). The stratigraphy and character of the kiva fill are interpreted as evidence that the kiva roof was dismantled and the beams salvaged when the structure was abandoned, and that the kiva was intentionally partially filled. This, coupled with the paucity of floor artifacts, suggests that the occupants of Shorlene's site moved to another location in the area. Hence, the site was probably abandoned before the regional abandonment at approximately A.D. 1280–1290.

The stratified random sample also located architectural features that relate to earlier occupations of Shorlene's site. These include three pit structures. Two of these, Structures

4 and 5, were stratigraphically earlier than the Pueblo III kiva, Structure 1. Based on its depth and earth-wall construction, Structure 2 appears to be earlier as well, but the stratigraphic relationship of Structure 2 to the other pit structures was not observed.

Structure 4 burned; dated tree-ring samples and the architectural style of this pit structure indicate that it dates between A.D. 650 and 700 and, hence, that there was a residential occupation at the site in the late Basketmaker III period. Structure 2 also appears to date to this period and could conceivably represent either an antechamber associated with Structure 4 or a separate pit structure. Little is known about Structure 5, and its dating is ambiguous. Further excavation would be required to understand its form and chronology.

In addition to Pueblo III and Basketmaker III pottery, Pueblo I and Pueblo II style pottery have also been identified in small numbers in the site assemblage. This indicates that occupations from these periods may be present as well. The Pueblo II pottery is the more numerous, but the lack of architectural features assignable to this period may indicate that occupation at this time was nonhabitational. The Pueblo I sherds are so rare that any use of the site during this period must have been minimal.

Troy's Tower (5MT3951)

Troy's Tower (Figure 5.6) is a small site located at approximately 2120 m elevation on the mesa top overlooking the upper part of Sand Canyon. A collapsed masonry tower, Structure 1, is located in the center of the site. No other masonry structures were evident on the surface, but surface remains of burned adobe suggested that nonmasonry rooms might have been present. Structure 2, a masonry-lined kiva, was found when a shallow surface depression was tested. Test excavations also revealed a portion of what is believed to be a tunnel connecting the tower and kiva. A small midden is present south of the tower and kiva. Two large, bell-shaped pits—Structures 3 and 4—were found during testing and were partially excavated. Several lines of evidence indicate that the site was occupied in the middle to late A.D. 1200s and was probably contemporaneous with the occupation of nearby Sand Canyon Pueblo.

Test excavations in the tower, Structure 1, did not reveal clear evidence of how it was used or abandoned. Ash found in and around a shallow hearth depression in the floor contained botanical remains consistent with use of the hearth in food preparation.

The masonry-lined kiva, Structure 2, was not burned at the time of abandonment, but small pieces of unburned wood occurred in the fill. We inferred that the principal roof timbers had been salvaged at abandonment, with the remainder of the roofing material being left on the floor. Portions of the Structure 2 floor and bench were exposed; the relative paucity of artifacts indicates that the artifact

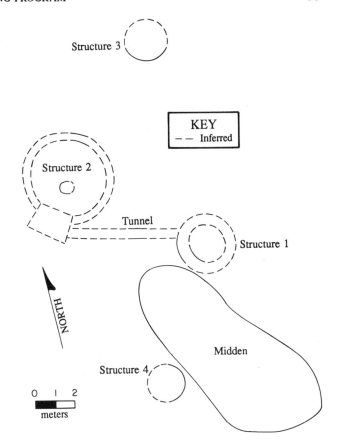

Figure 5.6. Main cultural features at Troy's Tower.

assemblage probably had been scavenged or drawn down at or near the time of abandonment. Most of the botanical remains from the Structure 2 hearth are best interpreted as fuel, so it is not clear that this feature was being used for food processing just before abandonment. An archaeomagnetic sample from the hearth of Structure 2 indicated its last intensive use was between A.D. 1225 and 1325.

Structure 3 is a large, burned pit found north of Structures 1 and 2. Strata above the floor include a layer of charcoal and ash covered by a layer of slabs that was covered by another layer of charcoal and ash. Botanical remains include charcoal interpreted as fuel and several economic plants that may have been used for food. The last use of Structure 3 appears to have been as a roasting pit, although it may have had other functions (e.g., storage) earlier. Tree-ring dates from charcoal in the fill of Structure 3 indicate that its last use was sometime after A.D. 1271.

Structure 4 is another large, bell-shaped pit found on the edge of the midden. Pueblo III pottery was found in its fill, so it is likely that it dates to the same period as the other architectural units recorded at Troy's Tower. What is not clear is this structure's function or its precise chronological placement within the Pueblo III use history of the site. A burial was placed in Structure 4 after it had been abandoned and had partially filled. Stones believed to be from the tower were placed around the burial, indicating that the tower had also been abandoned by this time. This is one of several examples of activity at Troy's Tower after the major architectural units were abandoned.

The question of site function can be addressed in more detail when analysis of artifacts and ecofacts is completed. The presence of the pit structure, food-preparation features, and a small trash area may indicate that the site is a habitation. On the other hand, the absence of a masonry roomblock, the relatively small midden, and the presence of pit storage features rather than above-ground masonry storage rooms may indicate that Troy's Tower site was used only as a short-term, seasonal, or intermittent habitation. The late use of Structure 3 as a roasting pit may document conversion of the site to a limited-use locus after its original function had ceased.

Alternatively, Troy's Tower may not have been a habitation site at all. It appears to have been occupied, or a least used, at the same time as Sand Canyon Pueblo, less than a kilometer away. So far, it is the only small mesa-top site found to date this late. Its position on the crest of the McElmo dome gives it a commanding view of the region; the locations of several large, late Pueblo III sites are clearly visible from Troy's Tower. The site may have had a specialized function, as a ritual, defensive, economic, or communications feature closely associated with Sand Canyon Pueblo.

Catherine's Site (5MT3967)

Catherine's site (Figure 5.7) is a small habitation located on a bench within upper Sand Canyon, at an elevation of 2060 m and approximately 1.4 km down-canyon from Sand Canyon Pueblo. The primary occupation of Catherine's site was in the A.D. 1200s. Structures present include two kivas and a masonry roomblock having at least four rooms. Nonmasonry rooms may also be present. Associated with these architectural features is a substantial midden.

In Structure 1—a masonry-lined kiva—testing encountered portions of the bench and main chamber floor, as well as the ventilator shaft. The structure has a prepared adobe floor.

Testing in Structure 2—a probable kiva—did not expose the walls, so the construction methods are unknown. Three, and possibly four, superimposed floors were documented in test pits. A hearth that had been remodeled several times was partially exposed. Archaeomagnetic dating indicates it was last used sometime between A.D. 1200 and 1325. The amount of remodeling observed in Structure 2 indicates it may have been the first kiva constructed during the Pueblo III occupation at Catherine's site, with Structure 1 being added later. The unusual location of Structure 1—west of the roomblock—may indicate that it was not part of the

original site plan. Room for expansion at this site is somewhat limited by steep slopes and closely spaced runoff channels.

Stratigraphic evidence indicates that roof timbers were salvaged from both kivas when they were abandoned. Neither burned nor rotted roof beams were found, although contexts in which either type of evidence is likely to have been preserved were sampled. Massive cultural deposits, possibly derived from dirt originally placed on the roof, cover both floors. Rubble that is probably derived from a partial dismantling of the roomblock was also thrown into the Structure 2 depression. Most of the masonry roomblock has walls that stand only one or two courses high. A room at one end of the block, however, has walls over 1 m high, with rubble completely filling its interior. This room may have been left more intact when the site was abandoned.

Masonry rubble was found on top of the large boulder at the north end of the roomblock, indicating that some type of structure once stood there. In the southeast portion of the site, downslope from the midden area (not shown in Figure 5.7), evidence of collapsed walls was found at the base of several large boulders that have slight overhangs on one side.

Several possible retaining walls occur in and near the midden south of the main habitation area. These evidently were built late in the site's occupation, because they are underlain by substantial midden deposits. Test pits in the midden revealed several areas of highly concentrated secondary refuse up to 90 cm thick.

A young cottonwood tree growing near the southeast edge of the site (not shown in Figure 5.7) indicates the location of moist sediments. A possible spring enclosure of unshaped sandstone surrounds the tree. Several stone alignments that may represent agricultural checkdams or terraces occur near the possible spring enclosure, not far east and south of the boundary of the artifact scatter that was used to define the site area for sampling purposes.

A few Mancos Black-on-white sherds were found at Catherine's site, generally outside structures and in the lower levels of the test pits. This suggests that Catherine's site may have had limited use—but almost certainly not as a habitation—in the Pueblo II period. Also, stratigraphy in three sampling units suggests that during the Pueblo III period there may have been a brief hiatus in trash disposal.

The predominance of Pueblo III style pottery at the site and the post–A.D. 1200 archaeomagnetic date from Structure 2 strongly indicate that the primary occupation of the site was in the Pueblo III period, and probably after A.D. 1200. Evidence that the roof timbers of both kivas had been removed at abandonment suggests that they were recycled to new construction at a nearby site and, hence, that the surrounding area was still populated when Catherine's site was abandoned.

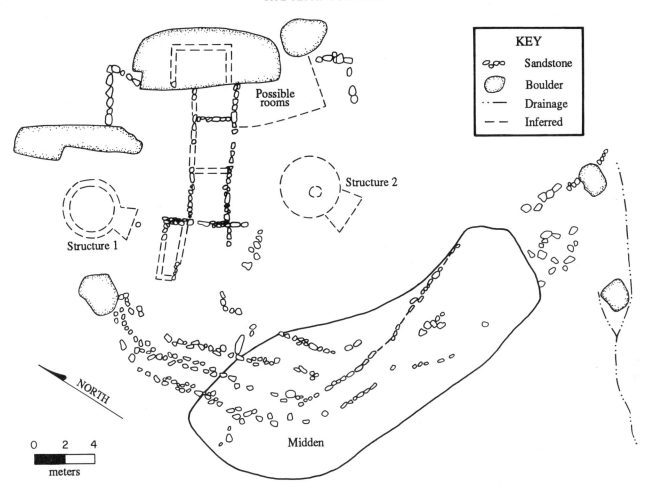

Figure 5.7. Main cultural features at Catherine's site.

Stanton's Site (5MT10508)

Stanton's site (Figure 5.8) is located approximately 100 m upslope from Catherine's site and approximately 1.4 km south of Sand Canyon Pueblo. Work at Stanton's site initiated the Testing Program's investigation of sites located at the junction of talus slope and cliff face, usually just below the canyon rim. Surveys in the Sand Canyon locality have documented many sites in this location, a large proportion of which have predominantly Pueblo III pottery on their surfaces. On these sites, the relative position of the structures usually does not conform very well to the standard unit-type pueblo layout, and heavy postabandonment deposition and erosion make the interpretation of surface remains difficult. One reason to test sites in this location is to determine the type and configuration of architectural features present and, hence, to improve functional and demographic interpretation of the survey data.

The principal cultural units at Stanton's site are a kiva, a boulder-top tower connected to the kiva by a tunnel, at least two small, masonry roomblock areas, and an extensive and deep midden.

The two roomblock areas abut the cliff and are located both northwest and southeast of the kiva. Extensive erosion and the difficulty of distinguishing fallen wall rubble from surrounding talus made definition of the surface rooms difficult, but we estimate there are at least two rooms in each of the two small roomblock areas.

The kiva—Structure 2—is at least partially lined with masonry. Multiple superimposed floors indicate more than a brief use of the structure. One of the test pits encountered a portion of the kiva's bench and the entrance to a tunnel extending south from the bench level. What is probably the other end of this tunnel was found in tests of the tower, Structure 1. The kiva roof had not been burned, and no evidence of unburned roof beams was found. The stratigraphy indicated that the sediments immediately above the floor were not naturally deposited; rather, they are probably the remains of adobe and earth that once covered the roof. The inference is that the roof was dismantled and the beams salvaged, presumably for use elsewhere, when the structure was abandoned.

The masonry tower—Structure 1—is built on and around a large boulder, about 6 m south-southeast of the kiva.

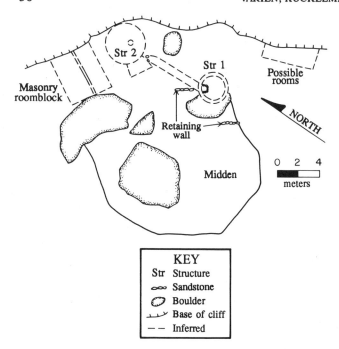

Figure 5.8. Main cultural features at Stanton's site.

Circular in plan and 2.25 m in interior diameter, this tower would have had a commanding view of Sand Canyon. From this structure, lower Sand Canyon is visible to the south as far as its confluence with McElmo Creek. To the north, one can see Troy's Tower, a mesa-top site near the west rim of Sand Canyon. Although the floor of the structure had been badly disturbed by rodent burrows, it was clear that a prepared surface had been present. No features except the tunnel opening were encountered in the one test pit excavated in the tower. Postabandonment fill was interpreted as roof fall and wall fall mixed with wind-deposited sediments.

Investigation of sites such as Stanton's can potentially help to date more precisely the apparent Pueblo III period move from predominantly mesa-top locations to canyon situations, including talus tops and cliff shelters. Unfortunately, no absolute dates were obtained in the test excavations at Stanton's site. The percentage of Mesa Verde Black-on-white pottery is higher than that in the mesa-top Prudden units. This suggests that Stanton's site was occupied in the middle or late 1200s. The fact that roof timbers were salvaged from Structure 2 at Stanton's site indicates it was abandoned before the locality was depopulated in the late 1200s. We estimate that Stanton's site was occupied between A.D. 1220 and 1270, though not necessarily for this whole interval.

The length and season of site occupation are other important questions addressed by the Testing Program. The Stanton's site midden has refuse deposits up to 1.25 m thick—greater than at any other tested site. This suggests that occupation lasted for more than a few years.

Stratigraphy in the midden shows no evidence of repeated occupations and abandonments. Therefore, our preliminary interpretation is that Stanton's site represents a year-round habitation site, occupied for perhaps a generation or longer in the middle to late A.D. 1200s.

Lester's Site (5MT10246)

Lester's site (Figure 5.9) is a small habitation located at an elevation of approximately 2060 m at the base of the cliff just below the north rim of Sand Canyon, only 30 m southwest of where the site-enclosing wall of Sand Canyon Pueblo meets the canyon rim. The decision to treat Lester's as a separate site was made during survey. Testing produced evidence that Lester's site was occupied at the same time as Sand Canyon Pueblo. It undoubtedly functioned as part of the larger settlement, even though it is "outside the wall."

The principal cultural features observed at this site include two kivas, two cliff-face alcove rooms, a minimum of three surface structures, one main site retaining wall, two kiva-associated retaining walls, and at least one rock alignment (a possible agricultural terrace wall) downslope. A substantial midden is present on the talus slope below the structures. Forty-three randomly selected 1-×-1-m test pits, four judgmentally selected pits, and two small trenches were dug, resulting in the sampling of both kivas, one alcove room, the site retaining wall, the two kiva-associated retaining walls, the midden, and the site periphery.

Structure 1 is a masonry-lined kiva. Test pits revealed segments of the upper lining wall, bench, pilaster, and remodeled hearth, as well as an exterior retaining wall. Only portions of the floor and bench were exposed; evidence from these areas suggests that most usable artifacts had been removed from the structure during abandonment. Numerous burned beam fragments in a roof fall stratum indicated that the roof had been burned. Naturally deposited sediments without trash lenses made up the kiva fill above roof fall, indicating that burning of the kiva probably coincided with abandonment of the site. Ninety tree-ring samples produced dates; the latest were 1270r and 1271vv, indicating that construction or repair occurred as late as the early A.D. 1270s. An archaeomagnetic date from the Structure 1 hearth indicated that it was last used between A.D. 1275 and 1650.

Structure 2 is a cliff-face alcove room with only the south wall constructed of masonry. The very limited data that were obtained indicate that the room was used for habitation rather than for storage.

Structure 3 is a very shallow, masonry-lined kiva. The shallowness of the structure was dictated by the shallow depth at which bedrock is encountered in that area of the site. Testing revealed portions of a retaining wall, upper lining wall, bench, pilaster, ventilator tunnel, deflector, hearth, and a very limited amount of incidental refuse on

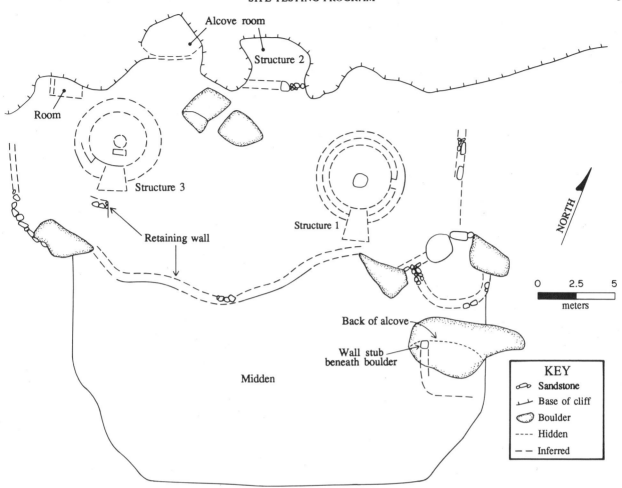

Figure 5.9. Main cultural features at Lester's site.

the floor. Stratigraphic evidence indicates that, unlike Structure 1, the roof of this structure had been dismantled when the structure was abandoned.

Each of the kivas (Structures 1 and 3) at Lester's site is partially surrounded by its own retaining wall. These walls are separate from the main site retaining wall and presumably served to further stabilize and level the areas used for kiva construction and to create level courtyard areas for daily activities.

Testing of the midden revealed accumulations of secondary refuse as much as 67 cm thick. This is an impressively thick deposit to have survived on a slope as steep as 34 degrees. However, the presence of artifacts as much as 35 m downslope from the south edge of the midden attests to downslope movement of artifacts as well. A rock alignment 15 m south of the midden may be a remnant of an agricultural terrace fashioned and used to form a field or garden by the inhabitants of this site.

The tree-ring and archaeomagnetic dates from Structure 1 indicate that Lester's site was abandoned after A.D. 1271. Pottery from the site is consistent with an occupation in the middle and late 1200s. These dates, plus the site's proxim-

ity to Sand Canyon Pueblo, indicate that Lester's site functioned as part of the larger settlement and was abandoned at approximately the same time. Another similarity between these two sites is the intentional burning of the kiva roofs, common at Sand Canyon Pueblo (Bradley, this volume) but rare in the small sites that have been tested.

Evidence from Sand Canyon Pueblo indicates that its enclosing wall was constructed relatively early in the site's history—perhaps in the 1250s (Bradley, this volume). However, aggregation of population, and hence building of facilities, continued in and around this site as late as the 1270s. Perhaps Lester's site was constructed by a small group that moved to Sand Canyon Pueblo late in the process of aggregation and settled just outside the site-enclosing wall.

Mad Dog Tower (5MT181)

Mad Dog Tower (Figure 5.10) is a single-component, Pueblo III site located in lower Sand Canyon at an elevation of approximately 1789 m. The most striking architectural feature at the site is a partially intact and stabilized masonry

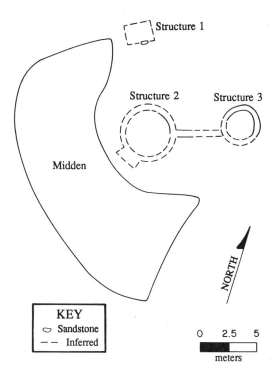

Figure 5.10. Main cultural features at Mad Dog Tower.

tower. It stands over 3 m high on the crest of a small hill on the first bench overlooking Sand Creek. Surface indications of a masonry roomblock and a trash midden are also present. Although evidence of a pit structure was not visible prior to excavation, the presence of such a structure was thought to be probable. Twenty-nine randomly located and three judgmentally selected 1-×-1-m test pits were excavated. Excavation revealed the presence of a single masonry room, a relatively shallow midden, a masonry tower, and an earth-walled kiva connected to the tower by a tunnel.

The surface room, Structure 1, has an estimated floor area of less than 2.7 m². The floor consists of unprepared, use-compacted ground surface, and wall stones are unshaped. No evidence of roofing materials was found. The tower, Structure 3, is circular in plan view and is constructed of pecked-block masonry. It appears to have originally been at least two stories in height. Its floor surface consists of unprepared, use-compacted natural ground surface. No artifacts or features were encountered in the portion of the floor that was exposed. Fill in both Structures 1 and 3 appears to consist primarily of naturally deposited sediments, plus the remains of wall collapse.

Structure 2, a kiva, is an unburned, earth-walled pit structure with masonry pilasters. Surface rubble to the south indicates that the southern recess may also have been constructed of masonry. Excavations exposed portions of the bench, a prepared floor, a hearth, and a possible sipapu. The entrance to a tunnel that heads in the direction of the

tower was also excavated. Few artifacts were recovered from the exposed portions of the floor and bench. The floor was covered with a thick, unburned roof fall stratum. The fill above this appeared to be naturally deposited sediments. An archaeomagnetic date from the Structure 2 hearth indicated the last intense firing was between A.D. 1010 and 1325. Two small pieces of charcoal from the Structure 2 fill yielded vv dates in the A.D. 900s and 1000s, respectively. These are not thought to date the construction or use of the structure.

Sampling revealed that the midden at Mad Dog Tower is small and shallow relative to the middens at most of the other small sites that have been tested. Together with the relatively low level of time investment in construction of the surface room and the kiva, this suggests that the builders of the site did not intend to use it for a long time, or that it was not primarily intended for habitation. The relatively high level of labor investment in the tower, which does not appear to have been a habitation structure, would support the latter interpretation.

Several other Pueblo III tower-kiva sites have been excavated in the northern San Juan region. The presence of a tunnel connecting the tower with the adjacent kiva appears to be common at these sites; many have surface roomblocks as well. In addition to Troy's Tower (discussed earlier in this chapter), isolated tower-kiva complexes include Cedar Tree Tower and Far View Tower at Mesa Verde National Park. Ferguson and Rohn (1986:42) believe that such tower-kiva complexes served dispersed communities, possibly as locations for religious rituals. They argue, for example, that Far View Tower served the whole early Pueblo III Far View community at Mesa Verde.

On the other hand, recent reevaluations of the "idea of the kiva" (Lekson 1988; Lipe 1989) conclude that most small Pueblo I through Pueblo III kivas were probably primarily domestic structures, and that the religious features they contain probably served only a small residential group—perhaps an extended family. Furthermore, it is not uncommon for the ratio of surface rooms to kivas to be very low in Pueblo III sites, including those—such as Lester's, Catherine's, and Stanton's sites—where there are heavy midden deposits, presumably indicating substantial domestic use of the location.

The paucity of tree-ring dates from Mad Dog Tower make its dating somewhat problematical. The pottery styles that are present indicate that the occupation was in the Pueblo III period, certainly after A.D. 1180, and probably after A.D. 1200. This is not inconsistent with the single archaeomagnetic date, although the dating range provided encompasses late Pueblo II through Pueblo III. The lack of either burned or unburned beams in the kiva roof fall stratum, where such evidence would be preserved had it been present, suggests that this structure's roof beams were salvaged when the site was abandoned and, hence, that occupation was continuing at other sites in the vicinity.

Saddlehorn Hamlet (5MT262)

Saddlehorn Hamlet (Figure 5.11) is a single-component, Pueblo III site located in and around a natural shelter within lower Sand Canyon, at an elevation of approximately 1770 m. The most prominent architectural features visible on approaching the site are two partially intact rooms located in an alcove at the base of a sandstone cliff and the remains of two dry-wall structures visible on a pinnacle approximately 30–40 m above the alcove. Surface evidence also indicates the presence of collapsed walls and a midden on the slope in front of the alcove.

To test this site, a stratified sample of 23 randomly located 1-×-1-m test pits was excavated. No excavations were conducted in the alcove because of the fragile nature of the structures and the thinness of the fill they contained. Cultural features documented by testing include a burned kiva, a relatively thick midden, and two or possibly three additional surface rooms located in the confined space between the kiva and the alcove rooms. Therefore, four or five surface rooms lie adjacent to the kiva, with two additional rooms resting on the cliff top above. The small amount of excavation conducted within the rooms was not sufficient to provide much information regarding their function. Some of these structures are large enough to have served as habitation rooms. It seems unlikely, however, that the rooms on the pinnacle above the alcove were habitation structures. Their position, which commands the view of a large area of lower Sand Canyon, suggests they may have functioned as lookouts or as part of some type of intersite communication system.

Testing in and around the kiva (Structure 1) exposed portions of the masonry-lined main chamber, floor, hearth, bench, southern recess, and ventilation system. Few artifacts were found on the floor or bench surfaces. The floor was covered with a 60-cm-thick roof fall stratum that included numerous large fragments of burned roof beams. From this context, 59 samples yielded dates. A strong date cluster at A.D. 1228–1232 included several cutting dates; this indicates that the kiva roof may have been constructed in the early A.D. 1230s. The roof fall stratum also yielded one date of A.D. 1256vv, indicating that construction or remodeling may have occurred in the 1250s. Like the tree-ring-dated structures at Sand Canyon Pueblo, the early cluster may represent reused beams. An archaeomagnetic date from the kiva hearth yielded a range of A.D. 1200 to 1375 for the last intensive use of this feature.

Midden deposits at the site were concentrated in an area south of the kiva and are up to 1.3 m thick. Two tree-ring samples from the midden area provided dates—1162vv and 1237r. The latter, which can be interpreted as a cutting date, is consistent with the hypothesis that the kiva was constructed in the early A.D. 1230s. Relatively high percentages of Mesa Verde Black-on-white pottery at the site are consistent with an occupation in the mid- to late 1200s.

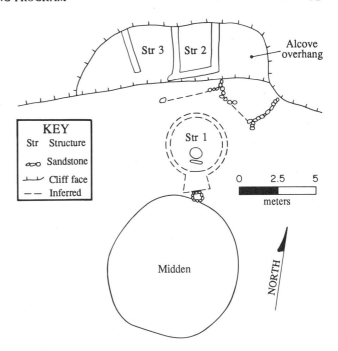

Figure 5.11. Main cultural features at Saddlehorn Hamlet.

The thick midden at the site, the number of surface rooms, and the relatively high level of labor investment in kiva construction indicate that Saddlehorn Hamlet was probably a year-round habitation. The burning of the kiva roof is a pattern that is common at Sand Canyon Pueblo, where it appears to have been part of final abandonment, not only of the site but of the region. If the Saddlehorn kiva was constructed in the A.D. 1230s, it seems unlikely that this structure would have remained in use until the late 1270s or 1280s, the presumed time of final regional abandonment. If burning of the kiva roof coincided with regional abandonment, the single A.D. 1250s date from the kiva may be closer to the actual construction date.

Preliminary Results

Analysis of the Site Testing Program data is in progress, but preliminary results are summarized below.

Chronology

Improved dating is critical to studies of community organization and interaction. Archaeologists studying Anasazi culture history in the Mesa Verde or northern San Juan region have suggested that there was a move from the mesa tops into the canyons in the A.D. 1200s and that the degree of aggregation increased through time (Eddy et al. 1984; Fetterman and Honeycutt 1987). However, they lacked the high-resolution chronologies necessary to test these hypotheses. By obtaining chronological data from sites in each of the physiographic zones listed above, we anticipate being able to address this question with considerable precision. We can also refine our community organization and interaction studies by being able to specify which sites were occupied contemporaneously. Finally, improved chronologies will enable us to better characterize the processes of aggregation and the role of big sites in community organization. Tree-ring, high-resolution ^{14}C, and archaeomagnetic dating have been or are being employed. In addition, Michelle Hegmon has initiated a study of late Pueblo II through Pueblo III period pottery in an attempt to refine pottery indicators of chronology. By dating sites with these methods, we expect to improve the chronological resolution of our work.

Tree-ring samples are abundant at Sand Canyon Pueblo, and Bradley (this volume) places its construction, occupation, and abandonment at approximately A.D. 1250 to 1280. Tree-ring and archaeomagnetic dates for the tested sites and Green Lizard are listed in Table 5.2.

In addition to these dating results, two ^{14}C samples from the Green Lizard site (5MT3901) were analyzed. These dates are A.D. 1258 ± 40 and 1259 ± 40 (as calibrated to calendar years). They are consistent with other chronological evidence from the site that indicates occupation in the early, or more probably the middle, 1200s. It seems likely that the Green Lizard occupation overlapped to some extent with the occupation of Sand Canyon Pueblo, fairly securely dated to between A.D. 1250 and 1280.

The dating results obtained from the Testing Program so far—plus work at Green Lizard and Sand Canyon Pueblo—indicate that the mesa-top unit pueblos were occupied in the first third of the A.D. 1200s, but that Troy's Tower, a mesa-top tower-kiva site, dates to the later part of the 1200s. The tested Pueblo III sites located off the mesa top in Sand Canyon appear to have been established after A.D. 1200, and at least some were occupied in the middle or late 1200s. Abandonment of the mesa-top unit pueblos may predate the construction of Sand Canyon Pueblo, whereas at least some of the sites inside Sand Canyon are probably partially contemporaneous with the large canyon-head aggregate. Recent tree-ring dating results from Castle Rock Pueblo, in McElmo Canyon, indicate that building was going on there in several locations in the mid-1250s and 1260s, and possibly in the 1270s, indicating that this smaller aggregate was also contemporaneous with Sand Canyon Pueblo. These results suggest that there was a move from mesa-top to canyon locations between A.D. 1200 and 1250, and that the formation of large aggregates—at least in the Sand Canyon drainage—did not occur until the mid-1200s. Further testing of these hypotheses will require testing additional sites or developing more refined pottery chronologies that can be applied to surveyed sites.

Basic pottery analysis has been completed for the sites tested in 1988 through 1990. Table 5.3 summarizes the frequencies of major types and categories of white wares

Table 5.2. Dating Summary, Tested Sites

Site Type/ Site Name	Latest Tree-Ring Cutting Date	Latest Tree-Ring Noncutting Date	Archaeo-magnetic Date
Mesa Top			
Shorlene's Site	—	1145+ +vv	—
Roy's Ruin	1213r	1223vv	—
Lillian's Site	1211rB	1214vv	1175–1250
Troy's Tower	1271rB	1271+vv	1175–1400 1225–1325
Cliff-Talus			
Saddlehorn Hamlet	1237r	1256vv	1200–1375
Lester's Site	1270r	1271vv	1275–1650
Lookout House*	—	1004vv	—
Stanton's Site	—	—	—
Canyon Bench			
Mad Dog Tower	—	1047+vv	1010–1325
Green Lizard Site	—	1233vv	1125–1300
Catherine's Site	—	1111vv	1225–1325
McElmo Canyon			
Castle Rock Pueblo*	1261r	1274vv	—

* Excavations incomplete at time of writing, but some dates available from the first season's work.

B = bark is present.

r = less than a full section is present, but the outermost ring is continuous around available circumference.

vv = there is no way of estimating how far the last ring is from the true outside. Many rings may be lost.

+ = one or a few rings may be missing near the outside whose presence or absence cannot be determined because the series does not extend far enough to provide adequate crossdating.

++ = a ring count is necessary beyond a certain point in the series because crossdating ceases.

from these sites. In an attempt to make pottery analyses reproducible by different analysts, and hence comparable, the Crow Canyon Center uses very strict criteria for the assignment of sherds to traditional types. Consequently, these types occur in low frequencies in Table 5.3. The majority of sherds are assigned to categories that have less rigorous criteria but provide some chronological placement, at least in comparisons across broad time periods. Thus, many decorated sherds are assigned to either Late Pueblo Black-on-white or Early Pueblo Black-on-white, depending on design elements, type of paint, rim form, etc. Whether paint is carbon or mineral is also recorded for sherds in these broad categories. Because the great majority of untyped sherds from the tested and excavated sites were assigned to Late Pueblo Black-on-white, we tabulated instead the relative frequencies of carbon- and mineral-painted sherds in the untyped categories as a possible chronological indicator.

Comparison of the white ware frequencies shown in Table 5.3 gives general support to the dating interpretations based on absolute dates (Table 5.2). The lowest percentages of Mesa Verde Black-on-white come from the mesa-top unit

Table 5.3. Painted White Ware Summary, Tested Sites

Site Type/ Site Name	Number of Sherds	Pottery Type				
		Mesa Verde Black-on-white %	McElmo Black-on-white %	Mancos Black-on-white %	Indeterminate Carbon Paint %	Indeterminate Mineral Paint %
Mesa Top						
Shorlene's Site	1,061	3.2	0.8	0.8	86.5	8.6
Roy's Ruin	973	6.2	1.5	1.2	85.8	5.2
Lillian's Site	912	4.6	1.3	2.0	78.3	13.8
Troy's Tower	336	7.7	3.3	2.4	85.4	2.4
Cliff-Talus						
Saddlehorn Hamlet	370	12.2	0.5	0	85.7	1.6
Lester's Site	920	9.6	0.8	0.7	87.6	1.4
Lookout House*	635	9.1	1.4	0.3	88.3	0.8
Stanton's Site	1,609	7.2	0.3	0.1	91.2	1.1
Canyon Bench						
Mad Dog Tower	106	9.4	0.9	0.9	85.8	2.8
Green Lizard Site	3,065	11.2	1.2	2.4	78.4	6.9
Catherine's Site	1,404	7.4	2.9	1.0	85.8	5.6
McElmo Canyon						
Castle Rock Pueblo*	398	7.5	0.3	0	92.2	0
Canyon-head Aggregate						
Sand Canyon Pueblo*	15,102	13.3	0.9	0.2	83.9	1.8

*Testing or excavation not completed; partial analysis results are reported here.

pueblos, which appear to date to the early A.D. 1200s. Troy's Tower, which is on the mesa top but is not a unit pueblo, has a higher percentage of Mesa Verde Black-on-white than the three upland unit pueblos. Canyon-bench and cliff-talus sites, which have absolute dates ranging from the middle to late 1200s, also have higher percentages of Mesa Verde Black-on-white and generally lower percentages of McElmo Black-on-white than do the mesa-top unit pueblos. Sand Canyon Pueblo, which appears well dated to the last half of the thirteenth century, has the highest frequency of Mesa Verde Black-on-white. Castle Rock Pueblo, however, which has tree-ring evidence of construction in the 1250s and 1260s, has intermediate levels of Mesa Verde Black-on-white. At the time this chapter was written, only a portion of the 1990 Castle Rock pottery assemblage had been analyzed, however.

The presence of small amounts of Mancos Black-on-white and of Early Pueblo white wares suggests the presence of a pre–Pueblo III component at a number of the sites. In some cases, archaeological contexts that could be assigned to an earlier component were identified. At Lillian's site, and quite probably at G and G and Kenzie Dawn hamlets, there is architectural evidence for structures dating to the Pueblo II period. The evidence at present is insufficient to determine whether these structures were used as habitations or as seasonal or limited-activity loci. The relatively low frequencies of pottery assignable to a Pueblo II date suggest the latter. At Shorlene's site, there is evidence for a pre–Pueblo III habitation dating to the Basketmaker III period.

In some cases, the frequencies of Pueblo II and earlier sherds in tested site assemblages are so low that they may represent heirlooms or merely be the product of imprecision in assigning small sherds to types and categories.

In general, it seems clear that the present scheme of types and categories is too blunt an instrument to provide the level of chronological resolution that is desired, particularly when relatively small samples of decorated pottery are all that is available. The next step in the use of pottery to refine chronologies is to develop an attribute-based seriation, or calibration, of pottery assemblages. The absolute dating results and the patterns revealed in initial comparisons using types and categories suggest that there is good potential for an attribute-based approach to refining pottery chronology. The sherds that did not meet the criteria for assignment to a traditional type nonetheless display attributes that may well have chronological significance. A project to refine the pottery chronology using attribute-level data has recently been completed by Michelle Hegmon (1991), but the results were not yet available at the time this chapter was written.

Continuity and Longevity of Occupation

Estimating the length and seasonality of occupation is critical to improving survey-based population estimates. Use of stratified random sampling at the tested sites allows us to estimate the total number of artifacts discarded on the site. Varien (1990a) has reported on a method based on discard theory and accumulation-rate studies that will use these estimates of total artifact populations to calculate the length of occupation at sites (see Kohler and Blinman 1987 and Pauketat 1989 for similar approaches). Results from the sites excavated in 1988 indicate that there is a large range in site use life based on the variation in the amount of pottery discarded on sites. Estimates of the total amount of sherds from four of the tested sites are presented in Figure 5.12.

Rim-arc/vessel-volume analyses will convert the estimates of the total number of sherds discarded on the site to estimates of the total number of vessels discarded. Cross-cultural and ethnoarchaeological studies have collected data on the number of vessels that households use and how often those vessels break. These studies will provide estimates of discard rates. These discard rates, together with architectural data on the number of households present at the site and the estimates of the number of vessels discarded, will permit estimation of the length of occupation at the tested sites.

This method holds promise and is being explored by researchers in several regions. Another Crow Canyon Center researcher, Ricky Lightfoot, has recently applied discard theory and accumulation-rate studies to evaluate abandonment assemblages at the Duckfoot site (Lightfoot 1990, 1992). Early in 1991, The Crow Canyon Archaeological Center hosted a small working session at which several archaeologists actively researching this problem met and presented their findings. As a result of this conference, several participants are working on the prob-

lem of cooking-pot use life and breakage rates. They plan to compare estimates of rates derived from the ethnoarchaeological literature and experimental studies with those obtained independently from archaeological evidence at the Duckfoot site and Sand Canyon Pueblo. At these sites, length of occupation, number of households, and standing inventories of cooking pots are known well enough to allow calculation of the breakage rates necessary to generate the observed discard assemblage. Data from the Testing Program will then be added to demonstrate how a sampling approach can use these rate-of-accumulation estimates to address the question of the length of site occupation.

Site Abandonment

Postabandonment fill sequences in kivas at each of the tested sites provide data on site abandonment. Of the 18 kivas tested between 1988 and 1990, all but three were unburned. The abandonment stratigraphy at tested sites and Green Lizard is summarized in Table 5.4. At Sand Canyon Pueblo, on the other hand, six of eight excavated kivas had been burned, although several appear to have been partially dismantled before burning.

In the unburned kivas at the tested sites and at the Green Lizard site, stratigraphic evidence suggests that roof timbers were salvaged at the time the kivas were abandoned. Two geomorphologists—Fred Nials of the Desert Research Institute and Eric Force of the U.S. Geological Survey—

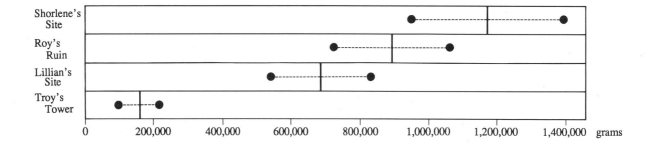

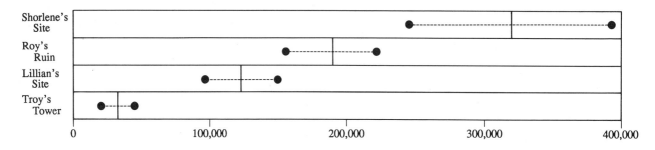

Figure 5.12. Population estimates of sherd weights (*above*) and counts (*below*), selected tested sites.

Table 5.4. Summary of Kiva or Pit Structure Roof Fall Strata, Tested Sites

Site	Roof Fall
Mesa Top	
Shorlene's Site	Unburned roof fall directly above floor; roof timbers salvaged
Roy's Ruin	Unburned roof fall directly above floor; roof timbers salvaged
Lillian's Site	Unburned roof fall directly above floor; roof timbers salvaged
Troy's Tower	Unburned roof fall directly above floor; roof timbers salvaged
Cliff-Talus	
Saddlehorn Hamlet	Burned roof fall directly above floor; roof burned at abandonment
Lester's Site	Burned roof fall directly above floor of one kiva; roof burned at abandonment; unburned roof fall directly above floor of second kiva; roof timbers salvaged
Lookout House	Unburned roof fall directly above floor of two kivas; roof timbers salvaged
Stanton's Site	Unburned roof fall directly above floor; roof timbers salvaged
Canyon Bench	
Mad Dog Tower	Unburned roof fall directly above floor; roof timbers salvaged
Green Lizard Site	Unburned roof fall directly above floor; roof timbers salvaged
Catherine's Site	Unburned roof fall directly above floor of two kivas; roof timbers salvaged
McElmo Canyon	
Castle Rock Pueblo	Burned and unburned roof fall present; a variety of abandonment processes present in the seven kivas sampled

have consulted on the recording and interpretation of the kiva stratigraphic profiles at several of the tested sites. They concur that the profiles they examined indicated that the major roof timbers had been removed, and that cultural rather than natural deposits cover the kiva floors. In other words, roofs appear to have been dismantled and a stratum of culturally derived sediment deposited on the kiva floors when they were abandoned.

The burned structures encountered by the Testing Program were at Lester's, Saddlehorn, and Castle Rock sites. It should be kept in mind that Lester's site is clearly an extension of Sand Canyon Pueblo and that the kiva that burned there was built late in the occupation of this site and of the region. Castle Rock Pueblo has yielded tree-ring dates indicating that occupation extended past A.D. 1270, placing it contemporary with Sand Canyon Pueblo and Lester's site. Consequently, it is possible that the burned kivas at these sites are related to final abandonment of the locality. Arguments were made above, however, that the burned kiva at Saddlehorn Hamlet may have been built as early as the A.D. 1230s. A tree-ring date in the 1250s and a "late" pottery profile suggest, however, that we cannot exclude the possibility that this kiva was also burned at the time of locality abandonment.

Test pits also permit us to evaluate whether complete tools (including pottery vessels) were abandoned on structure floors. The structures investigated on the small tested sites appear to have few, if any, usable tools associated with their floors.

Lightfoot (1990, 1992), following Stevenson (1982), has recently developed a model to explain the different ways sites are abandoned; we can apply this model to the Sand Canyon locality to evaluate the data from small sites summarized above and from Sand Canyon Pueblo. The tested sites' abandonment pattern of unburned structures, salvaged roof timbers, and salvaged tool assemblages is in sharp contrast to the abandonment documented at several excavated architectural complexes within Sand Canyon Pueblo (Bradley, this volume). Based on excavations to date, it appears that Sand Canyon kivas were often burned and rooms, kivas, and courtyards were sometimes abandoned with large assemblages of usable tools on their surfaces. Following Lightfoot's model (1990), the salvaging of roof timbers and usable tools from small sites indicates a gradual abandonment to a new site a short distance away. This implies that the tested sites where roof timbers had been salvaged were probably abandoned before their local communities came to an end, and hence before the abandonment of the Mesa Verde region. The former occupants of these sites probably moved to new sites within the Sand Canyon locality.

The abandonment of Sand Canyon Pueblo, with its intentionally destroyed structures and remaining usable tool assemblages, represents a more rapid abandonment in which there was no intent to return and where the distance to the new site was great. Sand Canyon Pueblo abandonment appears to have been terminal abandonment that coincided with the abandonment of the Sand Canyon locality and, very likely, of the Mesa Verde region. Tested sites with burned roofs may also represent sites abandoned simultaneously with the abandonment of the Mesa Verde region or moves undertaken when the distance to the next occupied site was great.

It is interesting that so many of the tested sites have abandonment stratigraphy that indicates they were abandoned before the abandonment of the region as a whole.

This is true not only for the mesa-top sites that appear to have been occupied in the early A.D. 1200s, but also for the other sites that appear to date to the middle and late A.D. 1200s. This information, combined with the late construction dates for Sand Canyon Pueblo (Bradley, this volume), suggests that aggregation continued through the 1200s, with the occupants of dispersed small sites increasingly moving into the large pueblo. This is supported by the construction dates in the A.D. 1270s from Lester's site, located just outside the site-enclosing wall at Sand Canyon Pueblo. Inside the wall, Sand Canyon Pueblo may have been full by the A.D. 1270s, and yet households were continuing to aggregate around it.

Community Organization

Studies of community organization are generally comparative in their approaches, and several such studies are currently in progress. The sampling methods employed by the Site Testing Program are largely designed to facilitate intersite comparisons of material culture.

The question of variability in site function can be addressed in a preliminary way by comparing the gross architectural remains and midden sizes among the tested sites. These data, for the Pueblo III components of these sites, are summarized in Table 5.5. The sites selected for testing are not, of course, a representative sample of all Pueblo III sites in the surveyed area or in the locality. The tested sites were selected on the basis of architectural, physiographic, locational, and chronological variability. The use of architectural characteristics as a criterion excluded from the program most, if not all, limited-activity sites and probably most seasonally used sites. Furthermore, reliance on surface pottery to assess the sites' chronological positions ensured that sites having relatively abundant surface pottery would be selected. Consequently, all the sites that were tested have a substantial occupation, based on the presence of multiple structures and a midden.

Variation in the maximum depth and surface extent of the midden may be useful as a preliminary measure of the length of occupation. Variation in the kind and number of structures may reflect some degree of functional variation among sites. Both types of variability are most apparent when we compare the two tower-kiva sites—Troy's and Mad Dog—with the rest of the tested sites. No masonry surface rooms are present at Troy's, and only one room is present at Mad Dog Tower. One function commonly associated with masonry surface rooms in pueblo sites is secure, long-term storage. There are typically several such storage rooms at Pueblo III unit pueblos. The absence of secure, long-term storage facilities at these sites suggests that occupation was seasonal or episodic. Masonry surface rooms at Pueblo III unit pueblos were also often the location of specialized activities, such as mealing. The absence of

Table 5.5. Summary of Structure and Midden Depths, Tested Sites

Site Type/ Site Name	Kiva	Room Estimate	Tower	Midden Depth[a]
Mesa Top				
Shorlene's Site	1	5–7	1	50
Roy's Ruin	1	5–7	1	42
Lillian's Site	1	7–10	1	57
Troy's Tower	1	0	1	30
Cliff-Talus				
Saddlehorn Hamlet	1	3–5	1?	90
Lester's Site	2	3–5	0?	60
Lookout House*	3	5–7	1?	40
Stanton's Site	1	3–5	1	125
Canyon Bench				
Mad Dog Tower	1	1	1	25
Green Lizard Site	2	15–20	0	120
Catherine's Site	2	5–7	0	95
McElmo Canyon				
Castle Rock Pueblo*	12–15	50–75	1	120

* Excavation not completed at time of writing.
[a] Maximum depth in centimeters.

these types of structures at the tower-kiva sites may also indicate they had a function different from that of the unit pueblos. Both tower-kiva sites also had middens that are not only relatively shallow but relatively small in area, as compared with the other tested sites. For example, the midden at Lillian's site is only slightly thicker than the one at Troy's Tower but is at least four times as large in area. Population estimates for the total number of sherds at the two sites (most of which come from their middens) indicate that Lillian's also has approximately four times the number of sherds as Troy's (Figure 5.12). The other mesa-top unit pueblos have even larger populations of sherds.

The next step in exploring possible functional differences among the tested and excavated Pueblo III sites in the Sand Canyon locality is to compare the artifact and ecofact assemblages from each. Comparisons between the Green Lizard site and Sand Canyon Pueblo are being carried out by Edgar Huber and Bruce Bradley. Comparative studies of the tested sites and between the tested and intensively excavated sites will be done after Testing Program fieldwork is concluded in 1991.

Site-Formation Processes

The stratigraphic information described in the previous section on site abandonment (Table 5.4) also provides expectations regarding patterns of de facto refuse associated with occupation surfaces. Although relatively small areas of occupation surface were uncovered by the Testing Program, the assemblage evidence that was obtained was generally consistent with evidence from roof fall stratigraphy. That is, when unburned roof fall strata lay directly on the floor, the floor assemblage had few or no usable tools. This depletion of floor assemblages is consistent with planned movement to a nearby location. Stratigraphic information, plus the spatial coverage provided by the test pit sample, will also enable us to evaluate the degree to which erosion has moved artifacts downslope and has concentrated artifacts in the upper portions of middens.

We are also attempting to evaluate the extent to which historic land use has altered site assemblages. An important study in this regard is the Goodman Point Oral History Project recently completed by Marjorie Connolly (this volume; Connolly 1990). In addition to recording the process of homesteading of the Goodman Point area, this project has documented early farming practices and their impact on sites, including sites that have been removed by landowners to clear farmland. It has also documented the types of artifacts that have entered private collections.

The sites sampled by the Testing Program have been affected by a variety of historic land-use practices. This variability may allow us to make some estimates of the effects of these practices on assemblages of artifacts, structures, and features. The tested sites are in areas that are currently being farmed, areas that have been chained and grazed, areas that are grazed but have not been chained, and areas that have had little direct alteration of the land or vegetation during the historic period. In addition, the tested sites show varying damage by artifact collectors, ranging from no prior excavation, to repeated digging in middens and occasional pitting of rooms. By studying aspects of assemblage composition in relation to types of historic alteration, (e.g., the ratio of painted sherds to corrugated sherds, and the ratio of sherds to flakes on surfaces and in middens) we hope to be able to better understand how historic practices have altered the archaeological assemblages.

Perhaps most importantly, the sampling methods employed in the Site Testing Program enable us to estimate the total number of features and artifacts on sites and to calculate statistical confidence intervals with which to evaluate these estimates of populations of artifacts and features. This information will provide a better understanding of survey data, and will provide agencies which manage archaeological resources in this area with a better means to measure site significance and future impacts to sites.

6

Excavations at the Green Lizard Site

Edgar K. Huber and William D. Lipe

Introduction

The Green Lizard site (5MT3901) is a small, Pueblo III habitation site located in the middle reaches of Sand Canyon, approximately 1 km down canyon from Sand Canyon Pueblo (Figure 1.3). In the summers of 1987 and 1988, intensive excavation was carried out in the western half of the site. A kiva, an adjacent masonry roomblock, and the floors of several jacal structures were excavated; the midden lying to the south of these features was sampled with test pits (Figure 6.1).

The Green Lizard site was first recorded by Crow Canyon Center researchers in 1984 (Adams 1985a). The layout of the site is essentially two adjacent Prudden units (Prudden 1903, 1914, 1918). It consists of two kivas, approximately 20 more or less contiguous, masonry-walled surface rooms, and an extensive and relatively deep midden deposit located to the south of the structures (Figure 6.1). Portions of several retaining walls are located in the midden area, and several checkdams or similar erosion control features occur a few meters to the west, east, and possibly north of the architectural portion of the site.

Surface pottery and masonry styles at the Green Lizard site indicated to the survey crew that it was occupied during the Pueblo III period, probably in the A.D. 1200s. It was selected for excavation to obtain data on Pueblo III community organization in the Sand Canyon locality. Questions guiding the work included: (1) When and how long was the Green Lizard site occupied? Was it earlier than Sand Canyon Pueblo, partially contemporaneous, or fully contemporaneous? (2) If it was contemporaneous, at least in part, with Sand Canyon Pueblo, were activities at this small site similar to activities at the nearby large site, or did the two settlements play different roles in the upper Sand Canyon community? (3) If the Green Lizard site was earlier than Sand Canyon Pueblo, or was abandoned before the end of occupation at the larger site, does comparison of artifacts and ecofacts from the two sites provide evidence that may help us understand the shift from a dispersed to an aggregated settlement pattern and/or the eventual abandonment of the Sand Canyon locality?

In planning for the Green Lizard excavations, we decided to excavate a full *kiva suite* (kiva and associated surface rooms) to obtain a data set fully comparable to those being produced by the intensive excavations of kiva suites at Sand Canyon Pueblo (Bradley, this volume; see also Adams 1985a; Bradley 1986, 1987, 1988a, 1990; Kleidon and Bradley 1989).

Environmental Setting

The Green Lizard site is located within Sand Canyon on a small, south-facing erosional bench at an elevation of 2025 m (6645 ft). A large spring, which flowed throughout the relatively dry summer of 1987, is located on the floor of Sand Canyon approximately 30 m below the site. The site is in the mixed pinyon-juniper woodland that blankets the upper reaches of Sand Canyon. A small riparian vegetation community is present below the site but is restricted to the vicinity of the spring and the narrow main drainage channel of Sand Canyon.

The site commands an excellent view down the canyon to its confluence with McElmo Creek and of the northern flank of Sleeping Ute Mountain. Within the canyon, potentially arable soil can be found on broad colluvial terraces less than 1 km south of the site. Numerous small colluvial benches near the site may also contain sediments suitable for agriculture. The wind-deposited, arable silts on the mesa top are accessible within 1 km. The bench on which the site is located is formed of colluvium and talus resulting

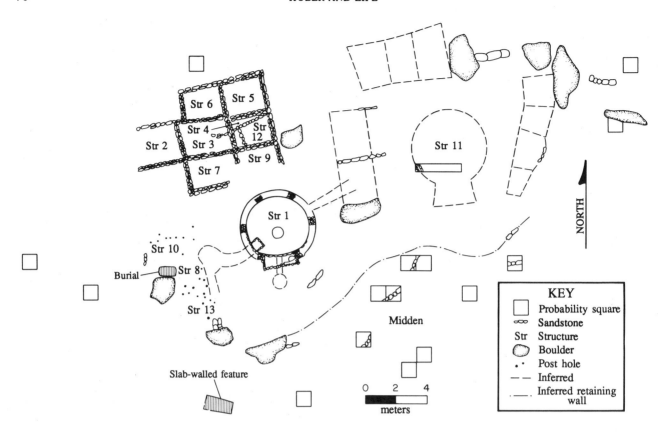

Figure 6.1. Excavations and main cultural features at the Green Lizard site.

from the erosion of the Brushy Basin Shale Member of the Upper Jurassic Morrison Formation, which also underlies the bench. The Brushy Basin Member consists of banded and variegated gray, green, brown, and red shales accompanied by thin bands of limestone, sandstone, conglomerate, mudstone, claystone, and bentonite. It is conformably overlain by the Cretaceous Burro Canyon Formation, which consists of variegated conglomerates, sandstones, limestones, shales, and cherts. Lying unconformably on the Burro Canyon Formation is the Cretaceous Dakota Sandstone Formation, which consists of variegated sandstones interbedded with variegated clays, gray shale, and lignite, as well as massive silicified and cemented quartz sandstone (Northrop 1973). The Dakota Formation forms the canyon rim and upland surface and is the uppermost rock formation in the Sand Canyon drainage. In the uplands, unconsolidated eolian silts of varying thicknesses commonly lie on the Dakota Sandstone.

Sampling Design

The site was sampled by a combination of intensive excavation and a stratified random sample employing 1-×-1-m test pits. Intensive excavations focused on the architectural features in the west half of the site; the entire midden area was sampled with randomly located test pits. In addition,

randomly located test pits were excavated in peripheral areas of the site. No clear kiva depression was evident in the eastern half of the site, so a test trench was excavated to determine if a kiva was present; evidence of a kiva was encountered (Figure 6.1). The site sampling strategy employed six sampling strata.

Sampling Stratum 1 consists of the peripheral zone north, east, and west of the architectural and midden features of the site. The external boundaries of this sampling stratum (and hence the site boundary) are defined by the falling off of artifact densities to near zero, except on the south, where the boundary coincides with an abrupt steepening of the slope below the site. Due to erosion of the midden, some surface artifacts do occur south of this boundary. To sample Stratum 1, four randomly selected 1-×-1-m sampling units were excavated to sterile deposits. This is the minimum number of sampling units from which quantitative data can be subjected to statistical manipulation with viable results (Blalock 1979).

Sampling Stratum 2 consists of the architectural component of the site, including all rooms, kivas, and associated courtyard areas. This sampling stratum was investigated by intensive excavation of the western kiva and associated western roomblock, or approximately 50 percent of the architectural features in Stratum 2. The only sections of the western kiva suite left unexcavated are the two kiva tunnels and the ventilation system, which could not be completely excavated in the time available. The only excavation in the eastern half of Stratum 2 was a test trench through a portion of the eastern kiva to determine its placement and depth. Although the intensive excavation of only half of Stratum 2 produced a sample that is not strictly comparable to that yielded by the random test-pit design in the other strata, this approach did yield data comparable to similar intensive excavations of kiva suites at Sand Canyon Pueblo. It was thought that the Stratum 2 sample would be large enough to be reasonably representative of the stratum, and that it could be adjusted to permit comparison with data from the randomly sampled strata.

Sampling Strata 3 through 6 are located in the midden area of the site. To create these samples, the midden was initially divided into an upper, or "formal," midden and a lower, or downslope, portion. Based on surface evidence, it was inferred that the upper portion represented relatively intact deposits, whereas the sediments in the lower portion were much more likely to have been redeposited or reworked by erosion and slopewash. This upper/lower dichotomy was then bisected by a division into eastern and western halves, so that samples of midden materials likely to have originated from the eastern and western Prudden units could be compared. As a result of this scheme, the western upper portion of the midden was designated as Stratum 3, the eastern upper portion as Stratum 4, and the western and eastern lower portions as Strata 5 and 6, respectively.

Five 1-×-1-m grid units were randomly selected from each stratum (a total of 20 units). Alternative sampling units were drawn in case any of the units was subject to one or more of the following rejection criteria: (1) excavating the unit would require removing a tree; (2) the unit was in a looter's pit; or (3) the unit coincided with the single test pit that had been excavated during the 1986 Sand Canyon Survey and Testing Program (Van West et al. 1987). Units were not rejected if they landed on a large boulder or similar "stable" natural feature that had been part of the midden area prehistorically.

The midden sampling was conducted in two stages. First, the 20 sampling units were surface-collected to obtain a representative surface sample from the midden. The second stage consisted of excavating five randomly selected 1-×-1-m test pits in both Strata 3 and 4—the upper portion of the midden. Strata 5 and 6, located in the "slope-washed," or lower, portion of the midden, were not tested because of lack of time. The surface collections from the randomly selected squares in these strata do provide some assemblage data from this part of the site, however. Two units that were excavated close to the southern boundary of the formal midden had shallower deposits than those upslope, supporting the original inference that the lower slope deposits were more likely to be thin and eroded.

Excavations in Structure 1 (Kiva)

Excavations in the kiva were carried out in both the 1987 and 1988 field seasons. The most notable structural characteristic of this kiva is its almost complete lack of masonry in the lower and upper lining walls. Most of the lower lining wall consists simply of plastered sterile sediments rather than masonry. Masonry is largely confined to the pilasters and to the southern recess, where several large boulders intrude through the wall. It appears that the builders decided that a masonry wall around the boulders was necessary to stabilize the southern recess. East of the southern recess, a section of boulder intrudes onto the floor of the kiva below the pilaster; this boulder has been carefully pecked away to conform to the arc of the kiva floor. The edge of the bench surface above the southwestern tunnel was faced with a single row of stones. It is probable that this stone facing was added to reinforce the edge of the earthen bench surface that had been undercut by the tunnel opening.

Fill Stratigraphy

The postabandonment depositional record of the kiva-fill sediments is relatively straightforward. Although a number of individual strata were recorded, these can be grouped into three major depositional units, labeled 1 to 3 from top to bottom. Units 1 and 2 represent postabandonment/post-occupational filling, primarily by slopewash. Because the site is on a relatively pronounced slope, this postabandonment deposition was probably rapid. These units contain a considerable amount of masonry rubble that probably washed into the kiva depression as the roomblock walls deteriorated and fell. Unit 1 has darker sediments and less structural rubble and rocky colluvium than does Unit 2, which lies below it. These differences probably indicate that Unit 2 was deposited quite rapidly, relatively early in the site's postabandonment history. Unit 1 was deposited later, when the kiva depression was shallower. The darker sediments probably record more growth of plants in the depression during intervals between deposition episodes.

Unit 3, which overlies the benches and floors, consists of two discontinuous deposits. First to be deposited (Strata 7 and 9, considered together) was a thin layer, or mat, of decayed vegetal matter that lies directly on portions of the benches and around the periphery of the floor. Several thin lenses of ash are associated with this organic layer on the benches. On the floor, the organic mat ranges up to 10 cm thick in places near the kiva wall and is partially overlain by, or intermixed with, Stratum 8, a deposit that contains chunks of beam-impressed daub and that probably represents the remains of roofing material, without the beams. This stratum is absent over some portions of the floor but exists as thick lenses in the center and northeastern quadrant of the kiva.

Some questions remain regarding the interpretation of Unit 3. In the field, the organic deposit was initially interpreted as the remains of burned and decayed closing material from the roof. Closer examination of samples in the laboratory showed that it is composed primarily of decayed but unburned juniper needles and small twigs. It closely resembles woodland-floor duff that occurs under juniper trees in the vicinity today. It is possible that this layer of organic material washed into the kiva not long after abandonment, at a time when portions of the roof had been breached by decomposition or by partial dismantling. Alternatively, the mat of juniper needles and twigs may have been deposited as part of activities associated with abandonment of the structure or with its reuse not long after abandonment. The deposit does not have the characteristics of packrat middens.

Stratum 8, which contains chunks of beam-impressed daub, clearly appears to have been deposited on the floor and, in some places, over the organic layer as a result of salvaging the kiva roof beams. Conditions of preservation are good enough in the kiva that wood or wood fragments would have been preserved if the beams had been left in the fill.

Features

Thirty-nine features were recorded. Included in this total are six benches and pilasters, the ventilation system, two tunnels, 17 floor features, and seven features found in the lower lining wall.

The bench features were all constructed of unexcavated native sediments and plastered with a fine red-brown silt. Except for the edge of the southwestern bench, no masonry was used in bench construction. There are six masonry pilasters in the kiva; they are relatively uniform in height, ranging from 48 to 54 cm. All of these heights appear to be original; only the upper, inward-facing courses of Pilaster 6 had collapsed. Pilasters 1 and 6, which bound the southern recess, are tied into the masonry upper lining wall of the recess.

Wall Features

Six of the seven wall features that occur in the kiva's lower lining wall are small niches assumed to have had a ritual function (Rohn 1971; Cattanach 1980). The seventh wall feature is a large, rounded cist-like structure (Feature 29) located below the northwestern bench. A similar wall cist was found in the kiva at Sun Point Pueblo at Mesa Verde National Park (Lancaster and Van Cleave 1954).

Feature 29 opens partially onto the floor of the kiva. The primary function of this feature is interpreted to have been storage. Evidence of decayed organic material was abundant in the fill in this feature, and a single corn cob fragment was identified from a sample of the feature fill. Numerous

squash seeds (*Cucurbita* sp.), as well as cactus seeds and needles (*Opuntia* sp.) and cheno-am seeds, were recovered from floor fill adjacent to this feature. Plant macrofossil and flotation samples collected from fill in the vicinity of this feature also yielded numerous squash seed fragments (*Cucurbita moschata*), as well as seeds and macrofossils of several other economically useful plants (K. Adams 1989b). Whether the seeds and other plant remains recovered from the contexts near the mouth of this cist feature had originally been stored in the cist or whether they were brought in by rodents is not clear, but the first interpretation is preferred.

The niches in the lower lining wall are all located in the northern and eastern quadrants of the kiva. All of these features are simple plaster-lined openings in the lower lining wall. They are of various sizes, have round or rounded openings, and all appear to have been available for use at abandonment.

Floor Features

Two plastered floors were present. The upper, Floor 1, had a hearth, an ash pit, a bell-shaped storage pit, and two small cylindrical pits that evidently had been open and available for use when the structure was abandoned. Another small cylindrical pit was visible in Floor 1 but had been sealed over. No sipapu was visible in Floor 1. Any or all of these features might also have been used with Floor 2; certainly the hearth, and probably the ash pit, would have been associated with Floor 2. Set in the base of the ash pit was a small segment of a sandstone slab that was interpreted as the base of a deflector. The Floor 2 features that had been covered when Floor 1 was constructed included a number of cylindrical pits, several possible storage pits, and two small overlapping pits interpreted as sipapus. The rim of a white ware jar had been set into the floor to form the opening of the later of these two sipapus.

Only a portion of the ventilator tunnel was excavated. The tunnel opening is in the masonry lower lining wall below the southern recess but is itself not masonry lined. The ventilator shaft was not investigated. The deflector was not encountered in place, but a large, thin sandstone slab was found leaning against the lower lining wall near the ventilator tunnel opening. It appears likely that this was the deflector. The presence of a probable deflector base set into the floor of the ash pit, covered by apparently undisturbed ash, indicates that the deflector slab may have been removed before the last use of the hearth and ash pit.

Two tunnels leading from the kiva were found. Because of time constraints and safety considerations, neither was fully excavated. Tunnel 1 was entered through an opening in the southwestern part of the kiva floor and extended west to a small, irregular, subterranean chamber. From there the tunnel exited to the south. It may have extended to the area of Structures 8 and 13, but its southern end was not found during excavations in this area. The floor entrance to Tunnel 1 appears to have been filled with trash while Structure 1 was still in use or shortly after it was abandoned.

Tunnel 2 exited from the kiva at bench level in the northeastern part of the structure. It led in the direction of a small, north-south trending block of surface rooms located between the eastern and western portions of the site. The entrance to Tunnel 2 appears to have been open at the time of kiva abandonment.

Floor and Bench Artifacts

A diverse set of artifacts was found on and in the fill just above the bench and floor surfaces. Although some of these may have been associated with the roof fall stratum (Stratum 8), most are probably items left in the kiva when it was abandoned. There is also a possibility that a few artifacts were introduced during a brief reuse of the structure, after its initial abandonment. Some amount of secondary refuse may also have been dumped into the kiva depression relatively early in the postabandonment period. Since the stratum produced by dismantling the roof did not fully cover the floor and benches, trash deposited after abandonment might have become mixed with the de facto refuse produced by artifacts left on floors, benches, and roof when the structure was abandoned.

In addition to sherds, flakes, and several ground-stone fragments, the bench and floor assemblage includes a number of complete bone awls, a small metate or lapstone, a one-hand mano, a large biface, several polishing stones, a ground and faceted lump of hematite, a modified sherd, and a bowl fragment that may have been used as a shallow container. These items are likely to have been used or stored in the kiva; together they indicate a diverse range of activities. The lack of complete pottery vessels and of many usable stone tools suggests that these artifacts represent a depleted assemblage—that many usable items had been removed prior to abandonment. The occurrence of numerous bone awls in this context is somewhat anomalous, but it is likely that these tools required relatively little manufacturing investment and could have been replaced fairly rapidly.

Excavations in Surface Rooms

Two types of construction, masonry and jacal, are present in the surface structures excavated at the Green Lizard site. The masonry structures are located to the north and west of the kiva (Structure 1). Of these, only the northern structures (Structures 2–7, 9) have been excavated. The remains of earlier masonry-walled rooms (Structure 12) were found below the floors of Structures 3 and 4. It is not known whether the unexcavated surface rooms located directly northeast of Structure 1 (the western kiva) were

related to it or to Structure 11 (the eastern kiva). The former interpretation is supported by the probable link between Tunnel 2 in Structure 1 and one of these surface rooms. The jacal structures (Structures 8, 10, and 13) found to the west of Structure 1 were encountered in the course of excavating what was originally thought to have been a small masonry structure (Structure 8) in a courtyard area.

Masonry Roomblock

Excavation in the northern roomblock revealed the remains of Structure 12 beneath the floor of Structure 4. Structure 12 was a surface room with walls of unshaped stone masonry a single stone wide. The presence of small quantities of Mancos Black-on-white in association with Structure 12 and in the midden indicates that this structure may have been constructed during the late Pueblo II period. The floor of Structure 12 was the use-compacted surface of the underlying sterile sediments. A shallow, basin-shaped firepit was associated with the Structure 12 floor.

The Pueblo III period rooms (Structures 2–7, 9) north of Structure 1 have masonry walls that are generally two stones wide; many of the stones were shaped by flaking, but not by pecking. On the basis of evidence of wall bonding, Structures 4 and 5 were built first; then Structures 3 and 6 were added to the west. Finally, Structure 2 was added to the west wall of Structure 3, and Structures 7 and 9 were added to the south of Structures 3 and 4, respectively.

The floors in all of these Pueblo III structures are unprepared and unplastered use surfaces, generally on top of use-compacted constructional fill, but in some cases overlying sterile sediments. No features clearly associated with these floors were defined.

The fill sequences of the Pueblo III structures were not complex. Wall rubble lay on the floors, and was overlain by compacted colluvial sediments. Little evidence for a definable roof fall zone was noted in any of the structures; if roof fall material was present, it was mixed with the wall fall stratum. There was no indication that any of these rooms had been used as trash dumps. There were few artifacts in their fills or on their floors, although the remains of two partial gray ware vessels were found. It is probable that most usable artifacts were removed from the rooms before abandonment.

The occurrence of a masonry-plugged doorway in the south wall of Structure 3 indicates a possible change in the function of this structure, perhaps related to the construction of Structure 7 to the south. No other door features were found in the roomblock.

Jacal Rooms

Patterns of postholes in the area immediately to the west of the kiva indicate that at least three jacal structures

(Structures 8, 10, and 13) were present. The floor of Structure 13 appears to have been excavated through the floor of Structure 8, indicating that remodeling or additions occurred during the use lives of these structures.

It is possible (but not likely, in our opinion) that some or all of these jacal-walled structures were constructed during the proposed late Pueblo II occupation of the site noted above. The pottery types from this complex of structures are predominantly Pueblo III types, but most or all appear to have been introduced as secondary refuse after abandonment of all or most of the jacal structures. Assemblages that represent de facto refuse associated with use and abandonment of the structures' initial functions could not be distinguished.

A concentrated deposit of Pueblo III refuse rested on the floor of Structure 10 and was also present in Structures 8 and 13. In Structure 8, however, this trash deposit overlay a stratum composed in part of melted daub that also contained Pueblo III artifacts. This stratum lay on the floor of Structure 8 but extended into Structure 13, where it was separated from the floor by a trash deposit containing Pueblo III artifacts. Sherd refitting data indicate that despite their differing sedimentological characteristics, the strata that filled Structures 8, 10, and 13 may represent a single depositional event or a series of closely related ones.

A pit feature interpreted as a hearth was associated with the floor of Structure 13. Functions of other pit features associated with the floors of Structures 13 and 8 are unclear. An adult burial was found in a prepared pit just south of Structure 10. The stratigraphic relationship of the burial to the jacal rooms is unclear. Several Mesa Verde Black-on-white vessels were found in association with the burial, however, indicating that it dates to the Pueblo III occupation of the site.

Midden Excavations

All 10 randomly selected midden excavation units were excavated in arbitrary 20-cm levels; these levels paralleled the natural contours of the modern ground surface. All units were excavated until culturally sterile sediments were encountered, and all sediments removed from the pits were screened through ¼-in mesh.

Midden stratigraphy in the six deepest midden units, located in the formal midden area near the kiva retaining walls, shows that depositional processes across the main midden area were similar. Within each of these units, three strata can be distinguished on the basis of color. The lowest stratum overlies sterile, noncultural deposits and is grayish brown. The middle, and by far the thickest, stratum is reddish brown, similar to the sterile sediments underlying the midden. This middle stratigraphic unit also contains the largest number of artifacts. The uppermost stratum is a

dark gray-brown in color, but unlike the lowest stratum, it is not compacted.

Granulometric analysis of sediments from the upper two depositional units of test pit 124S 117E indicates that all of the strata are sandy loam despite differences in sediment color. However, sediments from the middle depositional unit tend to contain slightly more sand and less silt and clay than those from the upper depositional unit. These changes are probably related to decreasing velocity of water runoff onto and over the midden and hence to decreasing capability of water to transport sediment as the midden built up (Bloomer 1988).

Retaining walls constructed of large, unshaped pieces of sandstone rock were encountered in several excavation units in the formal midden. All these wall sections are "floating," in that they are built on, and covered by, midden deposit. It appears that these walls were built either to prevent erosion of the midden, to create more level surfaces in the southern part of the occupation area, or both.

The midden assemblage contains a great diversity of artifact and ecofact types, ranging from sherds and flaked and ground stone to bone and charred plant remains. The midden is relatively thick—over 1 m of deposits in Sampling Strata 3 and 4—and has a high content of ash. There is also a high density of artifacts. For example, over 40 percent of the approximately 12,500 sherds from the excavations came from the 10 test units excavated in the midden. All these characteristics combine to indicate that the midden represents secondary refuse deposited primarily, and probably entirely, during use of the site as a habitation. The midden appears to have accumulated largely, if not entirely, during the Pueblo III period. The presence of small numbers of Mancos Black-on-white and of unidentified mineral-painted white ware sherds, however, suggests that there may have been a light occupation of the site and some deposition of artifacts in the midden area in the late Pueblo II period. The Mancos Black-on-white sherds from the midden tend to occur in the lower levels, but Mesa Verde Black-on-white—the dominant decorated type at the site—occurs in these levels as well.

Excavations in Sampling Stratum 1

Sampling Stratum 1 includes the areas west, east, and north of the portion of the site containing the midden and architectural features. Four 1-×-1-m randomly selected sampling units were excavated in this stratum. No features were encountered in any of the units. Two units were located to the west of, and downslope from, the jacal structures (Structures 8, 10, and 13). Artifacts were encountered in the upper 15 cm of each unit; they appear to derive from slopewash from the trash deposits in the area of the jacal structures. The other two units were located to the east of the eastern, unexcavated kiva suite. Very few artifacts were encountered in the sediments, which appeared to be colluvial in origin. Sterile sediments were encountered within 30 cm of the surface. One judgmentally located test unit was placed just north of Structure 6 to check for features or midden deposits north of the western masonry roomblock. Available time permitted the excavation of only one 20-cm level in this unit; culturally sterile sediments had not yet been encountered by the close of excavation. The deposits could not be characterized as a midden, however.

Feature 1 in Sampling Stratum 1 is located immediately south of the jacal structures and west of the midden area. Surface indications of this feature were three upright slabs forming a right angle. Upon excavation, this feature was found to be a completely slab-lined, rectangular box measuring 190 cm long, 95 cm wide, and 45 cm deep. The feature had been partially excavated into sterile sediments. The sandstone slabs exhibited a variable degree of fire-reddening. The lowest stratum of fill consisted of a 4-cm-thick layer of charcoal with very little ash, indicating that the last fire in the feature was extinguished—either by the people who were using the feature or by natural phenomena such as rain—before much of the wood had burned to ash.

The function of this feature is unclear. Its size and the charcoal layer at the base of the fill are characteristic of Pueblo III features from southwestern Colorado that have been interpreted as kilns (Fuller 1984; Larry Hammack, personal communication). Remains of common fuel woods were identified from the hearth. This would be consistent with use of the feature as a kiln. However, the definitive evidence—sherd clinkers or wasters (Fuller 1984)—is absent. An alternative possibility is that the feature is a large roasting pit. However, no potential food remains were identified in the analysis of charred plant materials from the feature (K. Adams 1989b).

Site Chronology and Function

The presence of Mancos Black-on-white sherds in midden contexts and below the floors of the Pueblo III roomblock indicates there was a Pueblo II occupation of the site. The absence of earlier types indicates that this occupation was probably in the late A.D. 1000s or early 1100s. Structure 12 and the ill-defined architectural remains below the floor of Structure 3 may relate to this occupation, but the evidence for this is not conclusive. If these structures were part of the surface roomblock of a late Pueblo II Prudden unit, the associated kiva would have been approximately where Structure 1 is now located. It seems unlikely that Structure 1 was built as early as 1150; the bulk of evidence (see below) would place the site's Pueblo III structures in the A.D. 1200s. It is possible, however, that an earlier structure in this location was dismantled and Structure 1 built in its place.

Another possibility is that the late Pueblo II occupation at the Green Lizard site was seasonal and did not result in construction of a full complement of habitation structures. A number of the small Pueblo III sites in canyon and cliff-talus settings in Sand Canyon appear to have had light use in the late Pueblo II period (see Varien et al., this volume), at a time when Prudden-unit-type habitations appear to have been located predominantly on the mesa.

In the succeeding Pueblo III occupation, the Green Lizard site appears unquestionably to have been used as a year-round habitation for a number of years. Several lines of evidence support the inference that this occupation was primarily in the A.D. 1200s and that abandonment did not occur until after A.D. 1250.

First, the ratio of Mesa Verde Black-on-white to McElmo Black-on-white is high, as is the ratio of Mesa Verde Black-on-white to all decorated white ware. Of the Pueblo III sites tested and excavated by the Crow Canyon Center in the Sand Canyon locality, the Green Lizard site most closely resembles Sand Canyon Pueblo in these ratios. The occupation at Sand Canyon Pueblo appears well dated by tree-ring evidence to between about A.D. 1250 and 1280 (Bradley, this volume). The preliminary results of attribute-level analysis of design styles (Hegmon 1991) also appear to place the Green Lizard site closest to Sand Canyon Pueblo and to Lester's site, which has kiva construction dates in the A.D. 1270s. The set of site assemblages being compared includes several with fairly good evidence for occupation in the middle 1200s (see Varien et al., this volume), so Hegmon's analysis indicates that Green Lizard was as late or later than these sites.

Twenty-five tree-ring dates were obtained from the excavations, most of them from small pieces of wood collected from kiva fill or secondary refuse contexts. None are clearly from construction elements, although some may be. A number of the dated specimens probably represent fuel wood. Unfortunately, none of the specimens produced cutting dates. The latest dates were A.D. 1230vv and 1233vv, from small pieces of wood in a large, basin-shaped floor feature in Structure 8, one of the probable jacal structures. These samples were collected from what is probably a trash or rubble fill that was deposited at, or soon after, the abandonment of Structure 8. Consequently, they may relate to the use of this area for the disposal of refuse during the main occupation of the site. A tree-ring sample from just above the floor of Structure 13, another of the jacal units, dated to A.D. 1204vv. The majority of the remaining dated tree-ring samples yielded vv or +vv dates in the A.D. 1100s.

An archaeomagnetic dating sample from the rim of the hearth in Structure 1 yielded two possible dating ranges: A.D. 1015 to 1125, and A.D. 1125 to 1300. The latter range clearly seems the more probable for the latest intensive heating of the hearth. The archaeomagnetic dating is not precise enough to help refine the chronology of the Pueblo

III occupation, but it is not inconsistent with the other lines of evidence.

Two "high precision" [14]C determinations (Stuiver and Pearson 1986; Jope 1986) were made on samples from the Green Lizard site. This method requires use of large samples of plant materials thought to reflect a brief period of time (e.g., annuals or twigs instead of heartwood samples with many annual rings). The two samples submitted to the University of Washington Quaternary Isotope Laboratory were from the stratum of matted organic material (predominantly juniper twigs and needles) found on the floor and benches of Structure 1 and from a mass of charred plant remains located in the midden. Although the samples from these contexts were not as large as desirable, the results were fairly good: the kiva sample (QL 4391) yielded a radiocarbon age of 780 ± 40 (calibrated to a calendrical date of A.D. 1259 ± 40) and the midden sample (QL 4395) yielded a radiocarbon age of 785 ± 40 (calibrated to a calendrical date of A.D. 1258 ± 40). The calibration of radiocarbon years to the Christian calendar follows Stuiver and Reimer (1986). Both dates were also corrected for ^{13}C fractionation. Although not as precise as might be wished, they clearly appear to place the occupation and abandonment of the site in the A.D. 1200s—between approximately A.D. 1220 and 1300.

Overall, the various lines of chronological evidence are consistent in placing the main occupation of the Green Lizard site in the A.D. 1200s. A reasonably strong case can be made that this occupation was in the middle or late 1200s and that it overlapped, at least to some extent, with the occupation of Sand Canyon Pueblo.

Evidence for an increasing intensity of site use in the Pueblo III period is present in the growth of the masonry roomblock from two to seven rooms. The remodeling in Structure 3 (a blocked doorway) is consistent with accretional growth of the roomblock. There may actually have been as many as 12 rooms associated with Structure 1, if the jacal structures and the small roomblock located just east of the kiva are included. The exact chronological placement of these last two sets of rooms is not clear, however. They may or may not have been used contemporaneously with the masonry roomblock north of Structure 1. The chronological relationships of the eastern and western parts of the site also are unknown, but their layout indicates that their occupations probably were at least partially overlapping. Full contemporaneity is not ruled out.

Although we lack precise dating of the duration of the Pueblo III occupation of the Green Lizard site, subjective interpretation of the evidence indicates that it probably extended for at least a generation and perhaps more. In addition to evidence of accretional growth and remodeling in the surface roomblock, there is evidence that the kiva was fairly extensively remodeled. The thickness and high artifact density of the midden deposits also support this estimate.

It is clear that the jacal structures were abandoned before occupation ceased in other parts of the site. The refuse placed in these structures most likely came from occupation in the nearby kiva and masonry roomblock. The lack of trash fills in these latter structures suggests that they were used until the end of occupation at the site. The roof of the kiva evidently was dismantled at, or shortly after, abandonment, with the roof beams presumably recycled for use elsewhere. Also, the artifact assemblages in both the kiva and the surface masonry rooms appear to have been depleted prior to abandonment, with most of the usable artifacts being removed. From this evidence, it is inferred that the former occupants of the Green Lizard site moved to a relatively nearby location. Their most likely destination would have been Sand Canyon Pueblo, which apparently was still growing as late as the mid–A.D. 1270s. There are tree-ring-dated construction episodes at this time both inside the wall at Sand Canyon Pueblo (Bradley, this volume) and at Lester's site, located just outside the wall (Varien et al., this volume). Construction at the latter site has been interpreted as possible evidence that in the 1270s the population of Sand Canyon Pueblo was beginning to "overflow" the confines of the walled space that had been established earlier—probably in the 1250s (Bradley, this volume; Varien et al., this volume). The similarities between the Green Lizard and Sand Canyon Pueblo pottery assemblages indicate a substantial temporal overlap between the occupations of the two sites. Consequently, the inhabitants of the Green Lizard site may have moved to Sand Canyon Pueblo (or elsewhere) not very many years before the abandonment of the Sand Canyon locality, estimated at approximately A.D. 1280.

Throughout its Pueblo III occupation, the Green Lizard site appears to have been a year-round habitation. The archaeological evidence demonstrates that all the activities associated with daily living in one place occurred regularly at the site. Environmentally, the site's location is a favorable one—especially because of its proximity to the largest spring in Sand Canyon. Arable land occurs on colluvial benches near the site, as well as on the mesa above the site. From this location, the inhabitants could exploit various wild resources in the relatively diverse canyon environment and employ a risk-reducing farming strategy by farming both the mesa top and the canyon benches.

Evidence has been presented that the occupation of Green Lizard overlapped in time with that of Sand Canyon Pueblo. Certainly during this period, the smaller site would have been a part of the primary, or face-to-face, community centered at Sand Canyon Pueblo. Understanding the social and economic roles of both the small sites and the large one in this community is a principal theme of the Sand Canyon Research Project (Lipe, this volume: Introduction). A number of comparative studies of architecture, artifacts, and ecofacts are underway to pursue this topic. These include comparisons between the kiva suite excavated at the Green Lizard site and the several suites that have been investigated at Sand Canyon Pueblo (Huber 1991).

Preliminary architectural comparisons show that construction of kiva suites at Sand Canyon Pueblo required a somewhat higher investment of time than did those at Green Lizard. In general, the Sand Canyon structures have a more formal appearance, with greater use of pecked surfaces on masonry blocks, etc. Of course, Sand Canyon Pueblo also has elements of "public architecture," including a great kiva and a D-shaped building, that are not present at Green Lizard or other small sites. These results suggest at least a modest level of social differentiation between the two sites.

Initial comparisons of midden-context assemblages show that lithic materials and pottery originating outside the local area are quite rare at both sites, though Green Lizard had slightly higher frequencies of nonlocal lithic materials (Huber 1991). These results do not indicate significant differences between the two sites in their occupants' ability to obtain exotic materials.

It has been argued (e.g., Lightfoot 1984) that larger household sizes and use of feasting to validate leadership are associated with the formation of social hierarchies. If the sizes of pottery cooking and serving vessels are related to the size of commensal groups, the residences of "big persons" should have somewhat larger vessel sizes. Comparisons of jar and bowl sizes from refuse at both Sand Canyon Pueblo and the Green Lizard site indicate that under these assumptions, commensal group sizes may have been slightly larger at the Green Lizard Site (Huber 1991). Assemblage-formation variables, such as differences in vessel-breakage rate by size and in length of occupation at the two sites, may be affecting these results, however. If the Sand Canyon occupation was shorter than the occupation at Green Lizard (a distinct possibility), and if large vessels break at a lower rate than smaller ones, the larger

vessels might be underrepresented in the Sand Canyon assemblages (Huber 1991).

Comparison of functional categories of artifacts between midden assemblages from the two sites showed some differences. For example, the "general utility" tool group at Green Lizard is dominated by a large number of abraders, while fewer of these occurred at Sand Canyon. In the "grinding tools" category, Green Lizard had a higher percentage of discarded manos and metates than did Sand Canyon Pueblo. At Sand Canyon, modified and shaped sherds had a much higher frequency in the "pottery tools" category than they did at Green Lizard. Sand Canyon Pueblo also possesses substantially higher frequencies of modified flake and other chipped-stone artifacts within the "processing tools" category (Huber 1991). These results suggest some possible functional differences between activities at Sand Canyon Pueblo and at the Green Lizard site, although much more work needs to be done to understand the assemblage-formation processes operating in the contexts sampled at the two sites (Huber 1991).

Overall, initial comparisons are suggestive of some subtle social and functional differences between the two sites. Intrasite comparisons among kiva suites at Sand Canyon Pueblo will be needed to determine if the differences between Sand Canyon and Green Lizard are within or outside of the range of variability observed within Sand Canyon Pueblo itself. Some of the preliminary results may be a function of differences in assemblage-formation processes operating at the two sites, or at least among the contexts sampled. Much better understanding of these processes needs to be achieved. In general, the differences and similarities observed do not at this time appear to support the presence of a strongly hierarchical model of community organization, or a strong differentiation between the economic roles of the sites in the community settlement system.

7

Excavations at Sand Canyon Pueblo

Bruce A. Bradley

Introduction

Sand Canyon Pueblo includes an estimated 420 rooms, 90 kivas, 14 towers, an enclosed plaza, a D-shaped multiwalled structure, a great kiva, and various peripheral structures and features (Figure 7.1). The site is situated around a spring at the head of a small canyon that divides the site into east and west areas. This canyon drains into upper Sand Canyon. A large percentage of the architecture at Sand Canyon Pueblo is inside a masonry wall that encloses the site on the west, north, and south. Inside the wall, structures occur both on the canyon rim and on the slopes below the rim. Current interpretations of site chronology place the construction and use of the pueblo between approximately A.D. 1250 and A.D. 1285.

The chronological and functional interpretation of Sand Canyon Pueblo plays a key role in the overall research design for the Sand Canyon Archaeological Project (Lipe, this volume: Introduction; Adams 1984; Lipe and Bradley 1986, 1988). As in the Sand Canyon Project as a whole, the principal questions addressed in research at this site have to do with (1) community structure and (2) change and abandonment during the thirteenth century A.D. In the first domain, we wish to know whether there is evidence for social or functional differentiation within Sand Canyon Pueblo itself. On a larger scale, we wish to know whether this site functioned as a religious, economic, or political center for the smaller settlements that were contemporary with it in its immediate vicinity and in the Sand Canyon locality as a whole.

With respect to the second domain, we need to know when and how Sand Canyon Pueblo formed, what changes in activities and organization took place while it was occupied, and when and how it was abandoned. Its construction in the mid-thirteenth century exemplifies the intensive aggregation of settlement that was taking place in the Pueblo III period in the northern San Juan area. Was Sand Canyon preplanned and built as a unit, or did it develop more gradually, as individual residence units were added? Was this large site abandoned all at once, or did population decline gradually? Does the archaeological record at this late site display evidence of social or economic stresses that might be related to the abandonment of the site and of the region?

These questions are being addressed by ongoing analytical studies of architectural, feature, and assemblage data from the site, as well as by continuing excavations. This chapter is designed primarily to present a brief account of the excavations conducted in 1984 through 1989, to set forth the chronology of site construction and abandonment as it is currently understood, and to present some preliminary data and interpretations regarding possible spatial and functional differentiation at the site. Although the artifact and ecofact assemblages from the excavations have been analyzed, the use of these data for functional comparisons among contexts is still in process. Consequently, assemblage data are used very sparingly in this preliminary report. Architectural and chronological data provide the bulk of the evidence used to support interpretations.

History of Research

At the outset of the Sand Canyon Archaeological Project, it was decided to focus on the Pueblo III occupation of the McElmo drainage and, in doing so, to attempt to learn more about the very large settlements that characterized this time period in that area (Adams 1983, 1984). Sand Canyon Pueblo was selected as the centerpiece of this study because its architectural plan is relatively clear on the modern ground surface, and its surface pottery, site location, and

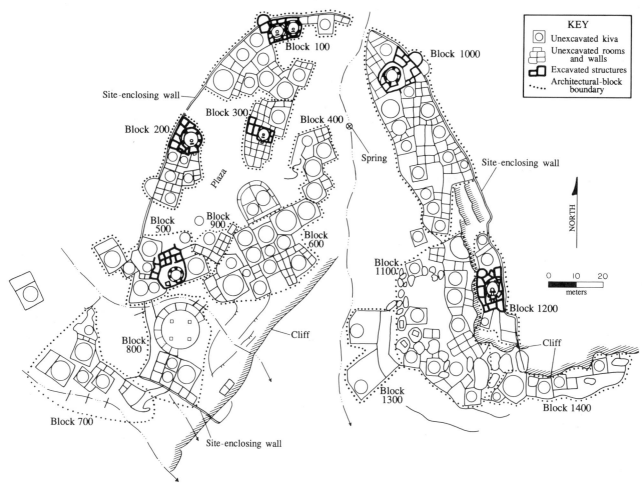

Figure 7.1. Plan map of Sand Canyon Pueblo.

architectural form indicated that it had been occupied in the middle to late thirteenth century. Unlike nearby Goodman Point Ruin, there was little evidence of an earlier occupation that might confuse architectural and chronological interpretations made from surface indications.

In 1983, a detailed surface map of the site was made with plane table and alidade by E. Charles Adams and the author. A contour map was produced by James Grady in 1985 by photogrammetric means, using aerial photographs (Grady 1986). Excavations were begun on a small scale in 1984 (Adams 1985a, 1986). Bradley took over direction of the work in 1985 and continued a program of excavation through 1989 (Bradley 1986, 1987, 1988a, 1990, 1991b; Kleidon and Bradley 1989). No excavations were conducted in 1990, while Bradley drafted a descriptive report of the 1984–1989 excavations for publication.

In planning the fieldwork at Sand Canyon Pueblo, Adams and Bradley (Adams 1984) concluded that the research questions they wished to answer could best be examined by fully excavating groups of structures selected to sample the architectural variability that was visible from surface evidence. The *kiva suite* and the *architectural block*

were defined as the primary elements for sampling. As a first step, the site was subdivided into 14 architectural blocks (Figure 7.1), each of which consists of a cluster of contiguous architecture, regardless of what types of structures it contains. Architectural block boundaries were defined by horizontal or vertical (e.g., cliff-edge) breaks in structural continuity. The 14 architectural blocks were numbered as 100, 200, etc., through 1400.

Literature on Pueblo III sites in the Mesa Verde area (such as the large cliff dwellings at Mesa Verde National Park) indicated that the typical ratio of rooms to kivas was approximately 10 or 12 to 1. Yet it was clear from inspection of the newly made map of Sand Canyon Pueblo that the ratio there was considerably lower than this, although there was also a great deal of variability among the various architectural blocks (Adams 1984, 1986). Consequently, the architectural blocks were assigned to one of three groups on the basis of the most obvious pattern of architectural variability at the site—differences in the ratios of rooms to kivas. Kiva-dominated blocks have surface evidence of fewer than four rooms per kiva, as averaged over the block; standard blocks have 5–16 rooms per kiva, and the single block where rooms appear strongly predominant has surface evidence of more than 20 rooms per kiva.

Within each of these classes of architectural block, kiva suites were judgmentally selected for full excavation. A kiva suite consists of a single kiva and all the structures (including open courtyard spaces and refuse areas) inferred to have been directly associated with it. Architectural and other associations were determined primarily by proximity and accessibility. In one case (the excavations in the 100 Block), the application of these principles led to excavation of three kivas (one unexpected from surface evidence) as part of a suite of closely associated structures. In most cases, however, the elements most closely associated with a given kiva are surface rooms and open courtyard spaces. Within a kiva suite, the *core unit* refers to the original architecture and open utilized spaces that were constructed or defined prior to, or concurrent with, the construction of the kiva. Excavated structures and areas were assigned numbers that identify the architectural block in which they occur (e.g., Architectural Block 200 includes excavated Structures 202, 203, 204, etc., and Nonstructures [unroofed areas such as courtyards and middens] 201, 209, and 210). Kiva suites are identified by the structure number of the kiva (e.g., the kiva suite that has been excavated in Architectural Block 1200 is called Kiva Suite 1206 after the kiva of that number).

Between 1984 and 1989, six groups of structures were excavated (Figure 7.2)—three in kiva-dominated blocks (100, 200, 500), two in standard blocks (1000 and 1200), and one in the room-dominated block (300). This work has resulted in the excavation of a total of 8 kivas and 38 rooms (not counting the small "corner rooms" associated with circular-plan kivas that are set into rectangular masonry enclosures). Because the set of structures excavated in the 100 block included three kivas, this group by definition included three kiva suites—Nos. 102, 107, and 108. The architectural areas selected for excavation do not necessarily conform to the same room-to-kiva ratios as the architectural block in which they are located. Specifically, Kiva Suite 501 is a unit-type pueblo in form, but in an architectural block that is kiva-dominated; consequently, Kiva Suite 501 is surrounded by kiva suites that have few rooms. Kiva Suite 501 was selected to allow comparisons between unit-type pueblo kiva suites occurring in different types of architectural blocks—specifically with Kiva Suites 1206 and 1004, which occur in standard architectural blocks on the eastern side of the site.

Data from the 1984–1989 excavations have confirmed the general accuracy of the original surface estimates of ratios of rooms to kivas and have permitted refinement of the estimates of numbers of kivas, rooms, and towers. In identifying various classes of structures from surface indications, the label *kiva* was assigned to circular depressions larger than three meters in diameter. Towers were inferred on the basis of high piles of masonry rubble that are either circular or D-shaped. Identification of individual surface rooms was more difficult; generally speaking, individual rooms are not always identifiable from surface indications, though groups of surface rooms can be recognized as accumulations of stone rubble that lack kiva depressions. In Figure 7.1, only surface room walls that were visible from surface indications are shown; consequently this map underrepresents the numbers of rooms actually present.

To obtain a more accurate estimate of numbers of surface rooms actually present, data were compiled from excavated rooms and from mapping of surface rubble areas in these same roomblocks. This exercise indicated that only 64 percent of a mapped room-rubble area is occupied by room floors, with the average floor area being 4.25 m². Using these data, room counts were estimated for the remainder of the site, using the following equation:

$$number\ of\ rooms\ =\ \frac{rubble\ area\ (m^2)\ \times\ .64}{4.25}$$
or
$$number\ of\ rooms\ =\ rubble\ area\ (m^2)\ \times\ .15059$$

The results of this study are presented in Table 7.1. The estimated total of 421 surface rooms is an increase of 170 over the minimal count of 251 (Adams 1986) obtained by mapping room walls evident from the surface.

In 1987, testing of the nonarchitectural areas of the site began, through excavation of a stratified random sample of 2-×-2-m test pits. The strata consisted of a peripheral area outside the site-enclosing wall, the nonarchitectural areas inside the wall and above the canyon rim, and the non-

Table 7.1. Structure-Type Estimates and Ratios for Architectural Blocks, Sand Canyon Pueblo

Architectural Block	Room Estimate	Kiva Estimate	Tower Estimate	Kiva-to-Room Ratio
100	24	11	1	1:2
200	20	6	1	1:3
300	30	1	0	1:30
400	7	3	1	1:2
500	19	9	0	1:2
600	27	12	1	1:2
700	16	5	0	1:3
800*	46	3	1	1:15
900	10	1	1	1:10
1000	89	13	3	1:7
1100	52	12	1	1:4
1200	21	2	2	1:11
1300*	31	2	0	1:16
1400	29	3	0	1:10
Other	0	7	2	—
TOTAL	421	90	14	1:5

*Architectural blocks that are heavily disturbed and may yield inaccurate estimates. Room counts may be high and kiva counts may be low. Excluding these blocks, the kiva-to-room ratio for the site is 1:4.

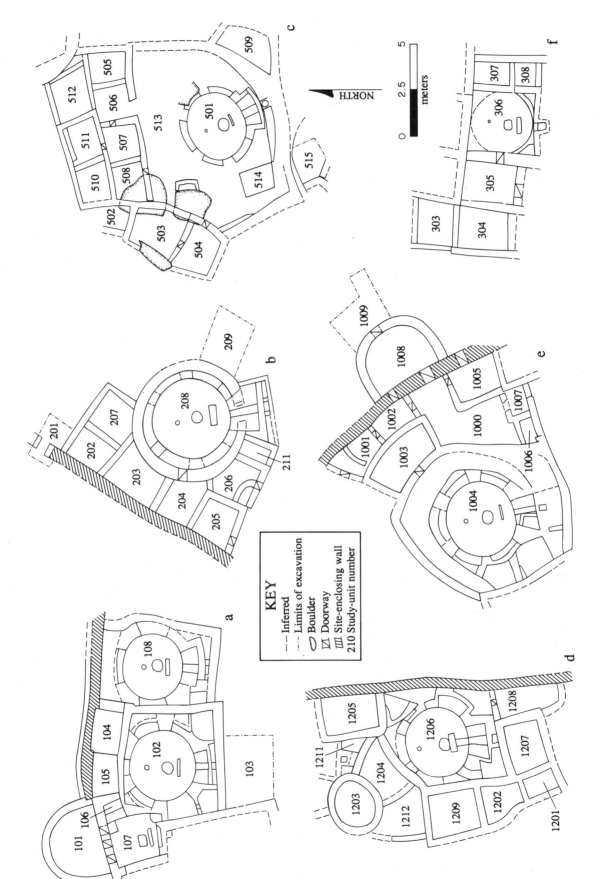

Figure 7.2. Plan maps of excavated structures in architectural blocks at Sand Canyon Pueblo: *a*, Architectural Block 100; *b*, Architectural Block 200; *c*, Architectural Block 500; *d*, Architectural Block 1200; *e*, Architectural Block 1000; and *f*, Architectural Block 300.

KEY

— — Inferred
—·· — Limits of excavation
◯ Boulder
▨ Doorway
▥ Site-enclosing wall
210 Study-unit number

NORTH

0   2.5   5

meters

architectural areas inside the wall and below the canyon rim. The test pit sample was completed in 1989.

In 1991, Bradley returned to the field to begin sampling two elements of "public architecture"—a great kiva and a large, biwalled D-shaped structure (Bradley and Lipe 1990). This work, which continued in the 1992 field season, is partially supported by Research Grant 4544-91 from the National Geographic Society. At least one more year of excavation is planned at Sand Canyon Pueblo after 1992. Currently, less than 10 percent of the architectural area of the site has been excavated. The Crow Canyon Center does not plan to excavate more than a small additional percentage of the site in the foreseeable future, leaving the majority of it intact for research in the future.

The 1984–1989 Excavations

Architectural Block 100

Structures excavated in Architectural Block 100 (Figure 7.2a) include two circular above-ground kivas (Structures 102 and 108), a subrectangular kiva (Structure 107), a D-shaped tower (Structure 101), and two rooms (Structures 104 and 105) (Adams 1985a, 1986; Bradley 1986, 1987, 1988a, 1989). Architectural Block 100 has an overall low ratio of rooms to kivas and hence is considered one of the kiva-dominated blocks.

The excavated area in the 100 Block is bordered by the site-enclosing wall to the north, internal open space to the south and east, and an unexcavated kiva to the west (Figure 7.1). From surface evidence, only two kiva depressions (Structures 102 and 108) were evident; Kiva 107 was evidently constructed by remodeling a room-size rectangular structure. Since a kiva suite has been defined as a kiva and associated nonkiva structures, this architectural group represents three separate kiva suites.

Of the excavated suites, the first to be built consists of a single kiva—Structure 102, which abuts the wall of an unexcavated kiva immediately to its southwest. Based on current interpretations of its date of construction and on evidence from other areas regarding the date of the site-enclosing wall, Structure 102 almost certainly was built after the site-enclosing wall was constructed. Next to be added to the complex was Kiva Suite 107, consisting of Structures 107 (a kiva) and 101 (a D-shaped tower). Subfloor excavations in this area indicate that other structures preceded these two. This may account for the extension of Kiva Suite 107 through the site-enclosing wall (Figure 7.2a), which other evidence indicates preceded the construction of this kiva suite. Kiva Suite 108, consisting of Structures 108, 104, and 105, was built last. The latter two structures, interpreted as storage rooms, are assigned to Kiva 108 rather than to 102 because of their position in the construction sequence of the complex and also because

of certain stratigraphic and assemblage evidence that indicates they were related to the use of Kiva 108 at the end of occupation in the complex.

The time intervals between these construction episodes is unknown, but tree-ring dates indicate that the roof of Structure 102—a kiva—was built in or after A.D. 1274. There are also several clusters of dates earlier in the 1200s from this kiva roof, so an alternative (but not preferred) interpretation would be that this kiva roof was built earlier but repaired and remodeled in or after A.D. 1274. The general principles used to infer construction dates at Sand Canyon Pueblo are discussed in the section entitled "Dating."

Kivas 102 and 108 were built inside rectangular, masonry enclosures, as was customary at Sand Canyon Pueblo when the architectural complex was built atop bedrock. In most cases, the spaces between the circular lining wall of the kiva and the corners of the enclosing rectangle were filled, but occasionally they were left open to serve as small corner rooms that probably were used for storage. (These spaces are not included in the counts of surface rooms presented in Table 7.1.) Two corner rooms were associated with Kiva 102. Both were accessible from the kiva bench through small "pass-through" apertures in the lining wall of the kiva banquettes. Both corner rooms had been intentionally filled before abandonment of the complex.

A number of complete or near-complete artifacts evidently had been left on the roof, benches, and floor of Kiva 102 when its primary use ceased. Subsequently, there was an accumulation of debris on the floor, resulting at least in part from decomposition of the structure after maintenance had ceased and from the deposition of small amounts of trash, presumably by people still using other parts of the site. It is possible, however, that at least some of these cultural materials resulted from temporary use of the structure at this time. After this probably brief "peri-abandonment" period, the kiva roof was burned.

A partially vandalized midden deposit located just south of the Structure 102 enclosing wall was sampled (Nonstructure 103). This deposit contained lenses of ash and high concentrations of sherds, lithic items, and animal bone. The closest, most probable, source for the refuse is Kiva 102.

Kiva 108 had a single, small, corner room, accessed through a pass-through extending from the lining wall of its southern recess. The floor of this kiva was a thin layer of adobe over bedrock. Subfloor excavations revealed a large petroglyph—apparently of the Puebloan mythical figure Kokopelli—pecked into the bedrock below the floor (Bradley 1989). Because the figure was pecked into a bedrock surface that was modified as part of the construction of Structure 108, it could be inferred that the petroglyph was also made as part of the construction of this kiva.

Numerous artifacts were encountered on the floor of Structure 108 and in the fill immediately above the floor, including a number of complete (i.e., restorable) pottery vessels and other items. After the initial abandonment, sediments accumulated on the floor as the structure began to decompose. A fire was built atop this thin layer of sediments, and it appears that some cultural materials were deposited during this episode, indicating a temporary reuse of the structure. The partial, disturbed remains of an individual were found in the lower fill and on the floor of Structure 108; the body of this person may originally have lain on the floor of the structure. The disturbance of these remains and the sediments in which they lay took place during a period of unknown duration between the placement of the body on the floor and the collapse of the structure's roof. The roof of Structure 108 did not burn but evidently was allowed to decompose in place.

Structure 107 was built in a space that had been occupied by one or more earlier structures, which probably were razed when this subrectangular kiva was built. Preexisting walls on the south and southeast were incorporated into Structure 107, but new walls were constructed on the west, north, and northeast. The southern wall was modified so as to create a small southern recess with a ventilator tunnel running through it, and a deflector was built between the ventilator opening and the firepit. In the northeast corner of the room is a small raised platform that is similar in form to shrine areas in some historic pueblos (Adams 1986). The structure also has four niches built into the walls, features that are common in kivas. There also is a petroglyph on one of the wall stones (Bradley 1989). In the southeast corner of the room was a subfloor pit into which was set a corrugated jar with a stone slab cover.

A human skeleton was found on the floor of Structure 107. Evidently it was placed there at approximately the time of abandonment of this structure. The moderate number of artifacts found on the floor appear to be de facto refuse not associated with the human remains. The roof of Structure 107 was not burned.

Connected with Structure 107 by a doorway is Structure 101, a D-shaped tower that extends outside of the site-enclosing wall. Two other passages between Structures 107 and 101 had been blocked prior to abandonment. On the floor of Structure 101 was a probable small firepit. In the fill of the structure was a piece of sandstone shaped into a zoomorphic head. It probably had protruded, gargoyle-like, from the interior of the masonry wall of the structure. One of the stones in the curved wall had a petroglyph composed of three concentric circles (Bradley 1989).

Structures 104 and 105 appear to have been storage rooms entered through their roofs. Structure 104 did, however, have evidence of an informal fire area on its floor surface. On the floor and extending over the fire feature was an assemblage of artifacts that appeared to have been stored in the structure and left at its abandonment. This included several pottery vessels and a number of ground-stone tools. In Structure 105, a burial with several associated artifacts was found on the floor. Few other artifacts were found on the floor of this structure.

Architectural Block 200

The excavated area in Architectural Block 200 (Figure 7.1) is located at the north end of this kiva-dominated block. It is bordered on the north and east by the central plaza, on the west by the site-enclosing wall, and on the south by two unexcavated kivas. One kiva (Structure 208) and seven surface rooms (Structures 202–207 and 211) were excavated (Figure 7.2b) (Bradley 1986, 1987, 1988a, 1989). During excavation it was found that Structures 205 and 206 have doorways opening into unexcavated kiva suites to the south, so they are not considered part of Kiva Suite 208. The relationship of Structure 211 to Kiva Suite 208 is not clear; it is contiguous to Structure 208 but also to Structure 206 and the unexcavated structures to its south.

Construction in Kiva Suite 208 began with the building of Structure 208 as a free-standing, circular, tower-like structure, 6 m in diameter. The chronological relationship of Structure 208 to the site-enclosing wall is unclear. However, the enclosing wall was clearly in place when Structures 203, 204, 202, and 207 were built in the space between it and Structure 208. At some time during the construction of this kiva suite, Structure 208 was remodeled into an above-ground kiva. It seems likely that the associated rooms were built at the same time that this remodeling took place.

The construction of Suite 208 as a whole remains poorly dated. The remodeling of Structure 208 from a tower-like building into a kiva must postdate A.D. 1244 because a tree-ring specimen with this cutting date was recovered from below the floor of the southern recess. One of the rooms (Structure 204) also yielded a noncutting date of A.D. 1267. On the basis of these dates, a relatively weak argument can be made that the kiva and associated rooms date from the A.D. 1260s and the original circular structure from the 1240s or 1250s.

Despite its unusual history, the remodeled Structure 208 conforms to Pueblo III northern San Juan kiva "standards," with a central firepit, deflector, and vent system, a sipapu, wall niches, six pilasters, a bench, and a southern recess. Subfloor excavation revealed groups of small, pecked depressions in the underlying bedrock; these may have been made during the construction of the building or during its remodeling into a kiva (Bradley 1989).

The artifact assemblage recovered from the floor of Structure 208 was large and varied. It includes several corrugated jars and several white ware vessels, as well as a canteen, a kiva jar, a mug, a ladle, and at least one large water jar. In addition, numerous bone tools, polishing stones, a mortar and pestle, projectile points, and ground-stone axes were found.

Artifacts were also recovered from the roof fall stratum, which lay directly on the floor; these materials appear to represent items that had been on the roof of the structure or that had been placed or suspended among the beams inside the kiva. The roof of Kiva 208 was not burned and appears to have been allowed to decompose in place. In the roof fall stratum, enough evidence of decomposed and partially decomposed beams was found to suggest that wood had not been salvaged from the roof after abandonment of the structure. None of the unburned pieces of wood encountered in this stratum was well enough preserved to permit tree-ring dating.

The surface rooms associated with Kiva 208 (Structures 202, 203, 204, 207, and 211) exhibit certain similarities. Apparently all were entered through their roofs. Several have wall niches. Heights of preserved walls, rubble accumulations, and the presence of only a single roof fall stratum in their fills indicate that the four associated rooms on the northwest (Structures 207, 202, 203, and 204) were as tall as two-story buildings, although they each contained only a single story. Most of the surface rooms had floors that consisted entirely, or in part, of irregular bedrock, none had formal floor features, and the roofs of most or all had apparently been allowed to decompose in place. Large, partially decomposed beams were found in the roof fall stratum in several of these rooms, suggesting that wood had not been scavenged from the roofs after abandonment of the structures.

An ashy midden deposit just outside the southeast wall of Structure 208 was sampled as Nonstructure 209. This deposit displayed a high density of ash, sherds, lithic items, and animal bones. It appears clearly to be associated with the use of Kiva Suite 208, and probably specifically with Structure 208 itself. Because of the lack of formal firepits or hearths in the associated surface rooms, the most likely source for the highly concentrated ash in Nonstructure 209 is the hearth in Structure 208.

Architectural Block 500

Kiva Suite 501 is located in the center of kiva-dominated Architectural Block 500. It is bordered on the north by the central plaza, on the west and east by unexcavated kivas, and on the south by an eroded architectural area and the great kiva (Figure 7.1). Excavations in this suite (Bradley 1988a; Kleidon and Bradley 1989) included a kiva (Structure 501); nine definitely associated surface rooms (Structures 503–508 and 510–512); one possibly associated surface room that was not fully excavated (Structure 502); a subterranean room (Structure 514); and a courtyard surrounded on three sides by a retaining wall (Nonstructure 513). In addition, several nonstructural areas outside the retaining wall were also excavated (Nonstructure 509 and Other 515) (Figure 7.2c).

Tree-ring dates from the burned roof fall of Kiva 501 indicate that Kiva Suite 501 was probably constructed in or after A.D. 1252. The first construction in the suite was probably a large room that was partitioned into two rooms (Structures 503 and 504). Next to be added were two rooms

(Structures 510 and 511), a southern retaining wall, a subterranean room (Structure 514), and a kiva (Structure 501). At this stage there were four rooms and a kiva, with a prepared courtyard (Nonstructure 513) in front of the rooms and extending on top of the kiva roof. This architecture is considered the core unit of Kiva Suite 501.

Although wall abutments suggest that this core unit was constructed by accretion, there is no direct evidence to indicate that any of the structures were in use while the others were being built. From this I conclude that the core unit was constructed rapidly to a plan that was completed in three stages.

Secondary refuse accumulated southeast and east of the northern surface rooms (Structures 510 and 511) while they were in use, after which four rooms (Structures 505–508) were added onto them, utilizing the existing courtyard surface and a thin secondary refuse deposit as floors. Finally, another room (Structure 512) was added to the northeast corner of this roomblock, after additional refuse had built up in this space. Structure 502 appears to have been added sometime after the original four surface rooms were built, but it was not fully excavated, and its chronological position (or whether it was even roofed) has not been determined.

Kiva 501, unlike Kivas 102, 107, 108, 306, and 1206, was not built above ground surface and within a rectilinear, masonry enclosing wall. Instead, the northern portion was excavated into the natural slope, while the southern part was built into constructional fill deposited behind the massive retaining wall that also defines the courtyard area. This courtyard separates the kiva from the surface rooms to its north and northwest.

An exceptionally large and varied assemblage of artifacts, representing de facto refuse left at abandonment, was found on the floors of structures, in and on their roof fall deposits, and on the occupation surface of the courtyard. The assemblage pattern suggests either some type of ritual abandonment or a relatively rapid, unplanned departure. The lack of evidence of postoccupational use or scavenging suggests that the abandonment occurred at or very close in time to the final abandonment of the site, or else that a very rigid prescription against disturbing this area was in place after its use ceased.

Especially notable in this regard is the assemblage evidence from Kiva 501. The kiva roof evidently was burned at abandonment, with the roof fall stratum lying directly on the floor and benches and covering a number of artifacts left on these surfaces. These included a number of reconstructible, complete, corrugated and white ware vessels, bone tools, and lithic artifacts. A number of other easily portable, and presumably high-value, items were present in the assemblage. For example, two small black-on-white pottery boxes were found in one of the kiva's wall niches. The articulated, but partially burned, remains of a single individual were found in the roof fall stratum. It appears that this individual had been placed on the roof of the kiva not long before it was burned.

Structure 514 is a small, largely subterranean room located in the courtyard just southeast of Kiva 501. Luebben and Nickens (1982) excavated a similar, but completely subterranean, room at the Grinnell Site, a small Pueblo III site near Yucca House National Monument south of Cortez. This room was connected by tunnels to two kivas. At Kiva Suite 501, however, there was no evidence of a tunnel entrance to Structure 514; it must have been entered through a roof hatchway. Functionally, Structure 514 may be equivalent to the corner rooms found in fully enclosed kivas elsewhere at Sand Canyon Pueblo.

Seven of the nine surface rooms in Kiva Suite 501 appear likely to have been used entirely or primarily for storage. This inference is based on the absence of formal floor features and on the presence of small, raised wall entries, or on the absence of any wall entries, implying access through the roof. These structures varied considerably in the size and composition of the artifact assemblages found on their floors and in their roof fall strata. Nearly all had at least one reconstructible complete vessel on the floor, however. Structure 505 had a small, informal fire hearth in its northeast corner, suggesting that it may have had some use as a sleeping or food-processing space in addition to being used for storage.

Structure 506, which is adjacent to Structure 505, has a floor-level doorway that opens onto the courtyard north of the kiva. It had a large and varied assemblage of floor artifacts, but no hearth or other formal floor features. A high, raised-sill doorway connects this structure to adjacent Structure 507, which had a storage bin and a corrugated jar which was set into the floor. Structure 506 is tentatively interpreted as a multiple-function space, probably a habitation room.

Structure 503, the largest surface room, has much of its floor space taken up by four mealing bins. One had been converted to use as a fireplace prior to abandonment. This structure has a floor-level doorway that opens onto the courtyard and a raised-sill aperture—now sealed—that once had connected it to adjacent Structure 504. The floor assemblage from Structure 503 consists primarily of stone artifacts probably related to mealing activities, but a greater diversity of items, including several reconstructible pottery vessels, were found in roof fall and presumably represent items left on the structure's roof at abandonment.

As noted, this kiva suite includes storage rooms, a living room, a primary food-processing room, an adjacent courtyard space, a kiva, and a small subterranean room. Functionally and architecturally, this kiva suite is a classic unit-type pueblo (Prudden 1903:11–16). It probably served as a habitation for a single household, whose size and membership are likely to have varied through time.

Architectural Block 1200

Kiva Suite 1206 (Figure 7.2d) is located in the eastern portion of the site, in the center of Architectural Block 1200—a standard one in terms of room-to-kiva ratios. The excavated area is bordered on the east by the site-enclosing wall, on the north by an unexcavated kiva suite, on the west by a cliff that drops off to additional, unexcavated architecture, and on the south by a small open space that contains an unexcavated tower (Figure 7.1). Structures excavated in this kiva suite include a kiva (Structure 1206), a tower (Structure 1203), and eight surface rooms (Structures 1201, 1202, 1204, 1205, 1207, 1208, 1209, and 1212) (Bradley 1986, 1987, 1988a).

Kiva Suite 1206 exhibits a construction history similar to Kiva Suite 501, but in a different configuration. Tree-ring dates were recovered from both the kiva (Structure 1206) and one of the rooms (Structure 1205), allowing detailed reconstruction of the core unit by year. The first structures in this area were a round tower (Structure 1203) and the massive site-enclosing wall. Their chronological relationship could not be determined. Tree-ring dates from the roof beams of Structure 1205 indicate that this two-story structure (with one room on each story) was added to the inside of the site-enclosing wall in or shortly after A.D 1260. An L-shaped line of rooms (Structures 1201, 1202, 1207, and 1209) was then built, largely enclosing an open space between the cliff drop-off and the site-enclosing wall. A wall, bonded to and extending from the northeast corner of Structure 1209, abuts the southwest corner of Structure 1205. This L-shaped group of rooms has not been directly dated. On the basis of tree-ring dates from burned beams in the roof fall, it was inferred that the kiva (Structure 1206) was built into the enclosed space in A.D. 1262 (Figure 7.2d). Together, these structures formed the core unit of Kiva Suite 1206.

This well-dated sequence is clear evidence that this core unit was built as a staged construction plan over a three-year period. The tree-ring date clusters indicate that no appreciable number of beams were stockpiled, but that many of them had probably been recycled from the dismantled roof of a kiva constructed in A.D. 1242. Using estimates of the original wall volumes and a formula for person-hours required to construct the estimated volumes, the effort required to build the core unit in three yearly episodes could have been accomplished by three adults working for three months each year (see Bradley 1988a:36–43). Therefore, construction could have been accomplished by a household-size social group. Next, two rooms (Structures 1208 and 1204) were added to the core unit, one between the line of rooms and the tower (Structure 1203) and one on the southeast side of the kiva. Since the north wall of Structure 1208 also forms a portion of the south wall of the kiva enclosure, and a opening in this wall connects Structure 1208 to the southeast corner room of the kiva, Structure

1208 may well have been built at about the same time or shortly after the kiva was constructed.

Structure 1204 was used for a while and then subdivided into two rooms, one of which became a mealing room (Structure 1212) and the other a trash dump (Structure 1204). Eventually the mealing room was abandoned and partially dismantled and the entire space used as a midden. Several strata of accumulated organic and inorganic trash were visible, and there was evidence of episodic in-place burning of the midden.

Structure 1211 was built sometime after Structure 1204 and appears to have been intentionally filled before the abandonment of the site. Probably it was associated with the use of the unexcavated kiva to the north, and it may in fact be a small corner room of this kiva. Consequently, it is not considered part of Kiva Suite 1206.

The kiva, Structure 1206, was constructed above ground on a ledgy and irregular bedrock surface in a space formed by the site-enclosing wall and the exterior walls of the surrounding rooms. Three small corner rooms were constructed in the angles between the kiva wall and the surrounding walls. Two were accessed by tunnels leading from different portions of the kiva bench; there is evidence that both also had roof hatch openings, enabling them to be entered from the courtyard surface formed by the kiva roof. The third corner room, in the southeast angle of the kiva enclosure, was joined to the kiva by a small pass-through opening suitable for transferring small objects. A larger aperture joined this corner room to Structure 1208, as previously noted.

Few artifacts were found on the floor or bench surfaces of Structure 1206. A thin stratum of wind- and/or water-deposited silt and clay occurred over the hearth and floor in the kiva main chamber. The top of this stratum was compacted, forming what has been interpreted as a use surface. Several artifacts were recovered from this surface. The roof fall stratum included burned beams in some areas and decomposed unburned wood in others. The jumbled condition of the roof fall stratum, plus the lack of evidence for very many roof beams, indicated that the roof had been at least partially dismantled and that a number of beams had probably been salvaged. This pattern of abandonment indicates that Structure 1206 went out of use at some time prior to the abandonment of the site as a whole.

Structure 1203, the tower, was built on sloping bedrock at the edge of the cliff. It was positioned so as to incorporate a wide portion of a crack in the bedrock; this may have allowed entry to the tower from below. The amount of fallen wall rubble associated with the structure was sufficient to suggest an original height of 4 or 5 m. A mixed stratum of wall fall, roof fall, and nonstructural sediments rested on the unprepared bedrock floor of the structure. This deposit included several decomposed beams, indicating that the upper floors or roof of the structure had been at least partially intact at abandonment. Few artifacts were found

in this stratum, but it did include materials tentatively identified as avian (turkey?) gastroliths and decomposed corn cobs.

Structure 1205 was a two-story building that would have "towered" above the site-enclosing wall, which it adjoins. The lower floor was entered through a hatchway in the second-story floor. Access to the second story may have been through a doorway in the west wall; evidence is inconclusive, however. The roof and the second-story floor did not burn but collapsed in place; preservation was good enough to infer the method of roofing. There was no evidence of a hearth or other features on either floor.

Moderate numbers of "hard" artifacts such as bone and lithic tools were associated with the ground floor and with the remains of the collapsed upper floor. Large quantities of organic materials, ranging from well preserved to largely decomposed, were also present in these two contexts. The majority of these materials were food remains or materials related to food processing, but fragments of basketry and several other organic artifacts were also found.

The assemblages associated with the last use and abandonment of this structure and the lack of hearths or other formal floor features are consistent with a storage function for Structure 1205. It is possible that the last use of Structure 1205 was related to occupation of the kiva suite to the north of it, which may have continued to be occupied longer than all or part of Kiva Suite 1206.

Structure 1204 had a well-prepared floor, but no floor features. Adjacent to it is Structure 1212, which has three metate bins. Adjacent to the east end of the southernmost bin was an accumulation of ash produced by in-place burning of fuel. This was not a formal, constructed hearth, but appears to have been an area where small temporary fires were built.

There is some evidence that Structure 1204 began to be used as a trash dump while Structure 1212 was still in use. Eventually, the metates and some of the mealing bin slabs were removed from Structure 1212, which also began to be used as a dump. This continued after the east wall collapsed into the fill and the roof had been removed. The trash appears to have been dumped primarily in the north portion of the structure and may have originated in the kiva suite to the north of Suite 1206. The trash consisted primarily of organic materials, plus ashes from hearth cleanouts. It appears that the organic material periodically caught fire and partially burned in place. Late in the buildup of the deposit, the remains of a single individual were placed on or in it. Overlying and surrounding organic materials then burned, largely cremating the body.

Structures 1201, 1202, 1207, and 1209 yielded few artifacts in floor-contact situations. Structure 1209 had a corner hearth with a low rim of stones and mortar. It did not appear to have been used intensively. All of these structures except Structure 1207 had a roof fall stratum resting on the floor, with wall fall above this; 1207 had wall fall all the way to the floor, indicating that its roof had probably been removed prior to abandonment. It is probable that all these structures were entered from their roofs, which would have been accessible from the courtyard that was formed on the kiva roof. A possible exception might have been Structure 1207. The amount of wall fall in its fill was large enough to indicate that this room may have been as tall as a two-story building, though without an intermediate floor level.

Structure 1208 had a small fire area in a natural depression in the northwest corner of its floor. It did not appear to have been intensively used. The floor was covered with a deposit of sandstone spall rubble that appears to have been added before the abandonment of the site. Above this was a stratum that contained a few pieces of roofing material, possibly the remains of the dismantling of the roof.

Except for Structure 1205, then, the assemblage and stratigraphic data indicate that Kiva Suite 1206 fell into disuse before the abandonment of nearby living areas. Prior to abandonment, Kiva Suite 1206 included spaces that appear to have been used for living, food processing, and storage, indicating that the unit as a whole probably served as a residence for a household, perhaps one built around an extended family. The size of the unit and the type of functional differentiation displayed by the structures conform to the Prudden-unit model (Prudden 1903; Lipe 1989). The spatial configuration does not conform to the classic Prudden unit, however, in which the surface rooms are largely to the north or northwest of the kiva and the tower, if present, lies to the south, southeast, or southwest.

Architectural Block 1000

Kiva Suite 1004 (Figure 7.2e) is located at the north end of Architectural Block 1000 on the east side of the site. It is bounded on the north and south by kivas, on the west by rooms, and on the east by the site-enclosing wall (Figure 7.1). A D-shaped tower, interpreted as part of the kiva suite, is appended to the outside of the site-enclosing wall. The kiva (Structure 1004) is associated with a surrounding courtyard and retaining wall and two small corner rooms. The tower (Structure 1008) and six surface rooms were excavated (Structures 1001–1003 and 1005–1007), as were an enclosed but unroofed space (Other 1000) and a midden area adjacent to Structure 1008 (Nonstructure 1009) (Kleidon and Bradley 1989; Bradley 1990).

Kiva Suite 1004 has a construction history somewhat different from the other kiva suites. The site-enclosing wall and two structures existed in the area before the beginning of this kiva suite. These two structures were not excavated and are associated with architectural complexes located south and west of Kiva Suite 1004.

The first stage in the development of the kiva suite was construction of a massive kiva-enclosing wall and a large room (Structure 1003). These were built on a stepped, bedrock slope between the site-enclosing wall and the existing structures to the southeast and southwest. Presumably, the kiva (Structure 1004) and its associated corner rooms were also constructed at this time. This was followed by the addition of two smaller rooms (Structures 1001 and 1002) between Structure 1003 and the site-enclosing wall. This group of three rooms and a kiva are considered the core unit of Kiva Suite 1206. Because of the curving walls of Structure 1003, this core unit resembles a small segment of a triwalled structure (see Vivian 1959).

Other 1000, the unroofed space south of Structures 1003 and 1002, was probably used as a courtyard; in addition, trash was dumped into its southwestern portion, near the kiva-enclosing wall and the preexisting unexcavated structure. This refuse area was then intentionally filled and leveled with sterile deposits. The resulting surface was probably used as part of the courtyard. After the resurfacing, three rooms were added in this area (Structures 1005, 1006, and 1007).

At some point in the construction history of the kiva suite, a multistory, D-shaped tower (Structure 1008) was added to the exterior of the site-enclosing wall and connected to the courtyard by the addition of a rough doorway through the site-enclosing wall. While this access was still in use, the south end of the courtyard and the two small rooms (1006 and 1007) were filled with midden deposit while the northern end of the courtyard remained unobstructed, allowing continued access into the tower and the adjacent rooms and onto the kiva roof.

The rubble from the site-enclosing wall included two clusters of sill stones and the finished stones used in the sides of doorways. This suggests that two raised-sill doorways had been constructed in the wall, at approximately the locations of the southwest corner of Structure 1002 and the center of Structure 1005. Whether these doorways were blocked or remained open after the construction of these rooms is not known. Several small apertures extended through the standing portion of the site-enclosing wall. These are in the area where Structure 1008, the D-shaped tower, was built. One evidently was still open at abandonment.

Tree-ring dates from the burned roof of the kiva indicate it was constructed in or after A.D. 1265, and a noncutting date of A.D. 1266 from a roof member of the D-shaped tower may indicate a slightly later construction date for it. The dates from the kiva roof beams include a strong date cluster in A.D. 1249–1251. It is possible that the kiva was originally constructed at this earlier time and that the roof was rebuilt when some of the later rooms and tower were added to the kiva suite. Since no other evidence of major structural remodeling was encountered in the kiva, this earlier date probably represents reused beams.

Structure 1004, the kiva, showed evidence of minor remodeling and perhaps of a change in function, with the construction of a mealing bin against the east wall and a small masonry bin in the southern recess. Also, two small firepits were cut consecutively into the compacted ash fill of the central hearth.

Few artifacts were found on the floor of the kiva, suggesting that items customarily used or stored there had been removed. The last use of the kiva and its two corner rooms was evidently as a burial place for the dead. The remains of nine individuals were encountered on the floor of the kiva and in the corner rooms. All but one individual appeared to have been placed in the normal, semiflexed position, and several of the interments had probable associated grave offerings. Stratigraphic evidence indicated several episodes of interment in the structure and that several of the individuals lay on, or were covered with, secondary refuse or what appeared to be constructional fill. This indicates that occupation was continuing elsewhere in the site while the kiva and corner rooms were still basically intact but were being used as a burial area.

The fill sequences in the kiva indicate that, after its use as a burial place ceased, the roof collapsed (or was partially dismantled) and plaster sloughed off the walls before the burning of the remainder of the roof. It is not clear whether the burning was intentional or accidental.

Structure 1003, the C-shaped room attached to the kiva-enclosing wall, appears to have been open and in use from its construction as part of the core unit to the end of occupation at this kiva suite. It had no floor features other than evidence that numerous small fires had been built on the floor at various times; the resulting ashes had been removed from all but one of these episodes. Few artifacts were found on the floor, and it is not clear whether the ones found were associated with the activities that normally took place there. The room was not used for deposition of secondary refuse, however.

Structure 1001 had two stories. After abandonment, either the upper floor collapsed into the lower story or the upper floor and roof were intentionally dismantled. The remains of two incomplete human skeletons were associated with the fallen floor, suggesting that they had originally been placed in the upper story. Few artifacts were associated with either the upper or lower floor, and there was no evidence of floor features.

Structure 1002, which appears to have stood only one story tall, had two shallow, basin-shaped firepits and a subfloor pit associated with its floor surface. An intact, semiflexed human skeleton was found lying atop the ash fill of the firepit in the southwest corner of the room. No artifacts were associated with the human remains. The skeleton and the remainder of the floor were covered with what seems to have been roof fall, though no wood was recovered.

Floor features in Structure 1005 consisted of a slab-lined bin and two fire features, one consisting of a firepit in the northwest corner of the room. The fill of the structure consisted primarily of wall fall from the east and south walls. There was no roof fall stratum, and the amounts and distribution of wall fall indicated that much of the north and west walls might have been dismantled before the walls began to collapse. The skeletons of three humans were encountered in the lower area of wall fall in the southeast quadrant of the room. All three were lying mostly on their backs, with arms and legs extended in various positions. One skeleton lay directly over the other two and had been substantially disturbed, probably by carnivore activity. No artifacts were associated with these remains. It is clear that Structure 1005 was already collapsing (or being dismantled) when these individuals were introduced into the room, probably all at the same time. Their positions suggest they may have been dropped rather than placed into the structure, perhaps from the roof of the tower (Structure 1008) or from the unexcavated room adjoining Structure 1005 on the south.

Structure 1008, the D-shaped tower, stood at least two stories high, perhaps higher. The position of the ground-story roof (second-story floor) was indicated by a series of beam sockets; it was only 1.3 to 1.5 m above the ground-story floor. This floor had a prepared surface, with a firepit adjacent to the south wall segment and another near the northwest corner of the floor. Both had been plastered over before the abandonment of the structure. Several shaped, sandstone slabs, a metate, and several manos were found on the floor surface near the aperture that extended from Structure 1008 to the courtyard area (Other 1000). In immediate contact with the floor surface was a thin layer of powdery, yellow-ochre-colored deposit, perhaps the remains of decomposed organic materials. This stratum contained a number of small artifacts (mostly sherds and flakes) and a relatively large concentration of avian gastroliths (gizzard stones).

The upper-story floors/ceilings of Structure 1008 were represented by a thick stratum of daub and mixed silt/clay sediments containing a multitude of decomposed and partly decomposed beams and shakes, indicating that the roof and upper floor(s) had probably deteriorated in place. A concentration of ash and oxidized and sooted daub near the center of the roof fall stratum indicated that a hearth or burn spot had probably existed on the second-story floor of the structure. A substantial collection of animal bone fragments was also recovered from the upper floor/roof stratum. A cluster of shaped, wall edge stones in the wall fall stratum both inside and outside the structure indicated that a doorway had probably existed in the northeast portion of the tower wall at second-story level.

Structures 1006 and 1007, at the south end of the courtyard (Other 1000), apparently did not have roofs or full-height walls at the time of abandonment, and it is possible that neither was ever roofed. The fill in Structure 1006 may have been constructional fill, suggesting that the structure may never have been used. Structure 1007's fill was mostly a concentrated ash deposit resulting from extensive dumping of secondary refuse; this was capped by a small amount of wall fall.

In its final use-context configuration, Kiva Suite 1004 included living, storage, and food-processing areas, indicating that it served as a habitation and was functionally equivalent to a Prudden unit, even though its layout departs somewhat from the standard unit-pueblo form. It seems clear that after its habitation function ceased, the unit continued to be used for an unknown but probably relatively brief time as a burial place and as a locus for trash deposition, indicating that occupation was continuing elsewhere in the site.

Architectural Block 300

Five rooms (Structures 303, 304, 305, 307, and 308) and a kiva (Structure 306) were excavated (Figure 7.2f) in the central portion of Architectural Block 300 (Adams 1985a, 1986; Bradley 1986, 1987), which is located at the northeast edge of the central plaza (Figure 7.1). The surface estimates of structures (30 rooms and one kiva) for this block clearly indicate that it is room-dominated. The excavations revealed a second kiva (Structure 306), which evidently had been built in a space originally occupied by one or, more probably, two rooms. The discovery of this intramural kiva that was not identified from the surface does not change the overall characterization of the architectural block. If, however, there are more unrecognized kivas, this block will have to be reclassified.

The excavated architecture in the 300 Block does not include a complete kiva suite, since some rooms that are spatially associated with Kiva 306 were not excavated, while some that are not closely associated (e.g., Structures 303 and 304) were excavated. The kiva-suite model may not be appropriate for this architectural block, because for many of the presumed large number of rooms there would not be a close spatial relationship to a kiva. In the case of "Suite" 306, it is evident that there was not a kiva in this part of the block when it was originally constructed.

The relative construction sequence of the excavated structures is incompletely known, but there is evidence that they were built in stages. The unexcavated rooms to the north of Structures 305, 306, and 307 appear to have been present when the rooms that now have been excavated began to be added. Patterns of wall abutment indicate that Structure 305 and an unexcavated room south of it were the first to be added. Next were Structure 307 and another room in the space now occupied by the north part of Structure 306. Structure 304 and 303 may have been added at this time as well. Structure 306 was also built after 307 and probably required the demolition of one or more rooms to provide space for its construction. Structure 308 appears to have been built after Structure 306 was in place.

Because no datable tree-ring specimens were encountered, the structures excavated in Architectural Block 300 are the most poorly dated of the six groups of structures studied in 1984–1989. Pottery and masonry styles associated with this group of structures indicate, however, that they are similar in age to other excavated structures at the site—certainly Pueblo III period, and most probably middle to late Pueblo III.

Structure 306 lacks benches and pilasters and hence does not fully conform to the norm for Pueblo III kivas in the northern San Juan area. On the other hand, it is nearly circular in plan and has a hearth, deflector, ventilator system, and sipapu. Also, three of the four angles between the curved kiva wall and the corners of the rectangular enclosure were left open and used as small corner rooms accessed from inside the kiva. A door extending through the wall separating Structure 306 from Structure 305 had been plugged, perhaps at the time the kiva was constructed. A floor-level pass-through also extended through this wall, but it may have been blocked by the construction of the southwest kiva lining wall.

A moderate number of complete pottery containers and bone and stone tools were found on the floors of the main chamber and corner rooms, in addition to a relatively low density of sherds, flakes, and unworked animal bones. These materials appear interpretable as de facto refuse—an assemblage perhaps somewhat depleted during the abandonment process. A roof fall stratum lay on the floor. It contained numerous pieces of decomposed wood—the probable remains of roof timbers. Whether the roof had been left complete or was partially dismantled at the time of abandonment was not determined.

Structures 303, 304, 305, 307, and 308 lacked evidence of lateral entries, except for the plugged floor-level doorway in the east wall of Structure 305 and a raised-sill doorway in its south wall. However, the walls of Structures 303 and 304 had been reduced to a meter or less in height, so raised doorways could have been present. Floor features are not common in these structures. Room 303 had a subfloor pit that contained a metate, three manos, and three stone axes. A burned spot, 40 to 50 cm in diameter, was also found near the southwest corner of the room. Structure 305 had a rectangular, slab-lined bin in its northeast corner.

As in Structure 306, several of the surface rooms (e.g., Structures 303, 305, and 307) had moderate amounts of de facto refuse in their floor and roof fall contexts, including several complete (reconstructible) pottery vessels. Most of these structures also had evidence of unburned roof fall resting on the floor.

The location of Architectural Block 300 adjacent to the site's plaza and near the D-shaped structure, plus the relatively small size of the rooms and the low ratio of rooms to kivas, suggests that this complex may have primarily served a storage function associated with a suprahousehold level of use. The addition of Kiva 306, the presence of a rather varied de facto assemblage in this structure and in some of the excavated rooms, and the presence of an informal fire feature on the floor of Structure 303 suggest that the excavated portion of the block may have been converted to some type of residential use before abandonment. The lack of food-processing features such as mealing bins may be a result of the small sample of structures excavated, or it may indicate that domestic use was not intensive here. Abandonment of the excavated structures does not appear to have been ritualized or catastrophically rapid, but the relatively large number of usable items left behind does not indicate a planned, short-distance relocation to another area of the site or locality.

Interpretations

Dating

Several excavated structures contained large numbers of burned or unburned structural beams that produced tree-ring dates. Analysis of the patterning of tree-ring dates has allowed probable construction dates to be inferred for these structures. If a tree-ring sample retains evidence of the outside (or bark) ring, it is concluded that the date of the sample represents the year of the tree's death and is considered a cutting date (coded as "B" by the Laboratory of Tree Ring Research at the University of Arizona). For samples without bark dates, the year of the tree's demise may in some cases be estimated on the basis of other characteristics of the sample. Such cases are indicated by a variety of codings (e.g., "G" and "v"). For other samples, an unknown number of rings is missing, and the year the tree died cannot be estimated (these are "vv" dates, in the coding used by the Laboratory of Tree Ring Re-

search). In this analysis, both actual and estimated cutting dates are grouped together.

Tree-ring dates from Sand Canyon Pueblo are presented in stem-and-leaf diagrams (Figures 7.3 and 7.4). In these, the two- or three-digit numbers in the left column represent centuries and decades A.D. The numbers to the right represent individual years, with each number derived from an individual sample. Thus, **124 2 2 2** represents three samples dated to A.D. 1242. If all of the dates from a particular context or grouping of contexts are illustrated, the result can be a very long diagram with many decades not represented by samples. To reduce the length of the diagram in Figure 7.4, the dates have been put into two groups: unclustered noncutting dates, and clustered dates (including cutting and noncutting). The unclustered dates are grouped by decade and only the decades with dates are illustrated. Clustered dates are grouped by half decades and illustrated as a continuous series. The phrase *End Values* identifies the break between the two forms of presentation. Cutting dates are underlined to distinguish them from "vv" dates. One hundred and seventy-nine cutting dates and 171 noncutting dates are used in this analysis.

A stem-and-leaf diagram of all cutting dates from the architectural units used in this study is presented in Figure 7.3. Although the results suggest that Sand Canyon Pueblo was constructed throughout the thirteenth century, analysis and detailed interpretation of the individual structures indicate otherwise.

Ranges of cutting dates occurred in each structure with tree-ring-dated structural elements (Figure 7.4), not including dates from hearth or midden charcoal. Construction dates are inferred using the tree-ring interpretation methods presented by Ahlstrom (1985). These include consideration of the temporal distributions of date clusters and their relationships to archaeological contexts. Strong

```
119  5 6
120  0 0 1 2 3 3 3 3 3 3 3 3 3 3 3 3 3 3 3 3 3 3 3 3 3 3 3 3 3
120
121  2
121  5 5
122  0 0 1 1 1 1 2 2 3 4 4 4 4 4 4 4
122  5 8 9
123  0 1 2 3 3 4
123  5 5 5 5 5 5 5 5 5 5 5 5 5 6 8 8 9
124  1 2 2 2 2 2 2 2 2 2 2 2 2 2 2 2 2 2 2 2 2 2 3 4 4
124  5 6 8 9 9 9 9 9 9 9 9 9 9
125  0 0 0 0 0 0 0 0 0 0 0 0 0 0 0 0 0 1 1 1 1 1 1 2 2 2     Construction of Structure 501
125
126  0 0 0 1 2 2 2 2 2 2 2 2 2 2 2 2 2 4 4 4 4 4 4 4     Construction of Structures 1205 and 1206
126  5 5 5 6 6 7     Construction of Structures 1004 and 1008
127  0 1 1 1 1 4 4     Construction of Structure 102
```

Figure 7.3. Stem-and-leaf diagram of all tree-ring cutting dates from architectural units at Sand Canyon Pueblo.

Structure 1206

```
 93  4
103  1 6
104  9
105  8
113  8
End Values
117  1 1
117  6
118  1
118
119  3
119
120  2
120
121
121
122  4
122
123
123
124  1 2 2 2 2 2 2 2 2 2 2 2 2 2 2 2 2 2 2 2 2 2 2 2 2
124  5
125
125  9
126  1 2 2 2 2 2 2 2 2 2 2   Construction
126  5
```

Structure 1205

```
102  6
103  1
106  1
118  1
120  8
End Values
122  9
123  1
123  6
124
124  9
125  1 2
125
126  0 0
```

Structure 1004

```
 91  1
 92  2 2
 99  4
105  2 4
106  0
112  3
114  4
115  5 6
117  0
118  1 1 3 4 9
119  0 5
End Values
120  0 1
120  5 9
121  0
121  5
122  3 3
122
123  2
123  8 8 9
124  0 1 2 2 3 4 4
124  6 7 7 8 9 9 9 9 9
125  0 0 0 0 0 3
125
126  0 0 2 3 4 4 4 4 4 4
126  5 5 6   Construction
```

Structure 501

```
 90  4
 92  5 8
 97  7
 98  3 7
 99  4 4 8
100  7
101  9
103  8
106  1 3
108  4 8
112  5
114  1 5 6 9
115  2
117  0
End Values
118  8 9
119  0 4
119  5 6 6
120  0 0 1 1 2 3 3 3 3 3 3 3 3 3 3 3 3 3 3 3 3 3 3 3 3 3 3 3 3 3 3 3 4
120
121
121  5 5
122  0 0 0 1 1 1 1 1 2 2 3 3 3 4 4 4 4 4 4 4 4
122  5
123
123  8 8
124
124  6 9
125  0 0 0 0 0 0 1 2 2 2   Construction
```

Structure 102

```
 92  7
 93  3
 95  8
 98  8
100  5
103  9
107  5 6
111  2 5
112  4
113  0 0 7
114  6
116  0 5 7
117  2 5
118  0 1
119  0 5 8
120  0 0
End Values
121  3 3 4
121  7
122  0 0 3
122  6 6 8 8 9
123  0 2 2 3 3 4 4
123  5 5 5 5 5 5 5 5 5 5 5 5 5 5 5 5 6
124  2 2 2
124  7 8 9 9 9
125  0 0 0 0 0 0 0 0 1 1 1 1
125  7
126  1 4 4
126  7
127  0 1 1 4 4   Construction
```

Figure 7.4. Stem-and-leaf diagrams of all tree-ring dates from selected structures at Sand Canyon Pueblo.

Table 7.2. Construction Labor Estimates for Architectural Blocks, Sand Canyon Pueblo

Architectural Block	Room Estimate	Room Labor Estimate (Person-hours)	Kiva Estimate	Kiva Labor Estimate (Person-hours)	Tower Estimate	Tower Labor Estimate (Person-hours)	Total Labor Estimate (Person-hours)
100	24	9,276	11	18,103	1	2,323	29,702
200	20	7,730	6	9,874	1	2,323	19,927
300	30	11,595	1	1,646	0	0	13,241
400	7	2,706	3	4,937	1	2,323	9,966
500	19	7,344	9	14,811	0	0	22,155
600	27	10,436	12	19,748	1	2,323	32,507
700	16	6,184	5	8,229	0	0	14,413
800*	46	17,779	3	4,937	1	2,323	25,039
900	10	3,865	1	1,646	1	2,323	7,834
1000	89	34,399	13	21,394	3	6,969	62,762
1100	52	20,098	12	19,748	1	2,323	42,169
1200	21	8,117	2	3,291	2	4,646	16,054
1300*	31	11,982	2	3,291	0	0	15,273
1400	29	11,209	3	4,937	0	0	16,146
TOTAL	421	162,720	83	136,592	12	27,876	327,188

* Architectural blocks that are heavily disturbed and may yield inaccurate estimates.

cutting-date clusters (five or more cutting dates in a five-year period) are considered to be cutting events that probably represent building episodes. A problem arises when a single roof contains more than one strong date cluster. There are several possible interpretations. For example, the roof of Structure 102 has strong cutting-date clusters in A.D. 1230–1236, 1248–1251, and 1270–1274. It is possible that the roof was built in the early A.D. 1230s and remodeled in the early A.D. 1250s and 1270s. Another possibility is that it was built in the early A.D. 1250s, reusing some wood from an earlier structure, and remodeled in the A.D. 1270s. It also may have been built in the A.D. 1270s, reusing wood from one or more earlier structures. Finally, it may have been built after A.D. 1274 with only reused wood.

If the first or second option is correct, one might expect to find the beams that were added during remodeling to cluster together in the roof, and there would probably be other structural evidence of remodeling. Neither was the case. A total lack of any new beams in a roof is also unlikely; therefore, I have concluded that construction occurred in the early 1270s and that it included the reuse of beams from several structures. In each structure at Sand Canyon Pueblo that had multiple cutting-date clusters (Figure 7.4), the final cluster is inferred to represent construction, based on several lines of evidence. The earlier date clusters resulted from beam reuse, a common practice in late Pueblo III sites in the Mesa Verde region (William Robinson, personal communication 1988).

Five structures have construction dates inferred from tree-ring and excavation data. These include A.D. 1252 for Structure 501, A.D. 1260 and 1262 for Structures 1205 and 1206 respectively, A.D. 1265 for Structure 1004, and A.D. 1274 for Structure 102. Wall abutments, midden accumulations, and remodeling have been used along with these dates to infer the construction and use history of each excavated architectural area. Use histories and fuller information on tree-ring dating of the individual excavation areas have been presented above. More detailed discussions of these topics are also presented in the annual fieldwork reports cited above and in the monographic report on the 1984–1989 excavations that is being prepared for publication.

Construction Labor Estimates

The amount and intensity of construction labor that is expended on the building of an architectural unit may be an indication of the size of the labor force (if the period of construction is assumed) or of the length of time needed for construction (if the size of the labor force is assumed). This information may be used to help interpret the organization of labor, which may reflect social organization and may have implications relating to architectural evidence for social or functional differentiation among the various areas of the site. As compared with structures constructed less intensively, architecture with a higher labor investment per unit of space covered may represent a longer anticipated use life, elaboration intended to show social distinctions, etc. Cross-culturally, there is a tendency to invest relatively more labor in structures and buildings that are considered symbolically special or important.

Construction labor estimates made for the excavated architectural areas have been extrapolated to the architectural blocks and the site as a whole (Table 7.2). These estimates are based on formulas derived from observations and experimental replication data from Sand Canyon Pueblo (Bradley 1988a:41) and from work reported by Lekson (1984:277–286). The results indicate that the ob-

Table 7.3. Construction Labor Indices for Excavated
Architectural Areas, Sand Canyon Pueblo

Architectural Unit	Surface Area (m²)	Estimated Person-hours	Estimated Person-hours per m²
100*	104	5,349	51.4
200*	81	4,623	57.1
300	56	1,122	20.0
500	120	3,337	27.8
1000	140	6,385	45.6
1200	106	4,321	40.8

*Kiva-dominated architectural units.

served rooms, kivas, and towers at Sand Canyon Pueblo could have been built by approximately 157 people working 40-hour weeks for a year. Such estimates are, of course, only indicative and are not intended as a reconstruction of "what actually happened."

The estimates are taken a step further for the purposes of this study by deriving a labor estimate index which determines labor investment per unit area of architecture (Table 7.3). If relatively high labor investment is assumed to represent specialized function because of a greater symbolic value, then Kiva Suites 102, 107, 108, and 208 may have been special-function buildings.

Spatial Analysis

A method of analyzing the spatial interrelationships of buildings and components of buildings that goes beyond visual examination of plan maps has been presented by Hillier and Hanson (1984). They assume that spatial relationships in architecture that cannot be explained by randomness theory reflect cultural choices related to the function of the structure(s). Rooms and other spaces in general-use buildings such as habitations tend to be spatially well integrated with one another as well as with an adjacent open space. They also tend to be highly permeable; i.e., most rooms are readily accessible from a common open space. Although restricted access spaces may be included, these are relatively few in number and unrestricted space is the rule. Special-function structures and buildings may also be readily accessible from adjacent open spaces, but they are frequently poorly integrated internally. This is especially true of buildings whose functions include activities by groups with restricted membership.

This approach to spatial analysis necessitates knowledge of all the access points between spaces in a building. Fortunately, the preservation of doorways and other access points into structures is excellent at Sand Canyon Pueblo. Even when doorways collapsed with walls, it has often been possible to interpret their presence and original locations on the basis of clusters of wall corner-stones, sill stones, and lintels found in wall rubble. It has also been possible

in many cases to infer the presence of roof hatchways, either from fallen roofing materials or the lack of any access points through walls that retained enough height to have included part of even the highest raised-sill doorways, had they been present.

Each space in an architectural unit can be assigned a number that classifies its relative ease of access from a given location. An important part of this analysis is how and where spaces are connected by access points (doorways and hatchways) and an assessment of how easy or difficult access would have been. For example, a high, wide doorway that opens through a wall at floor level would have been easier to pass through than a small, raised-sill doorway. In the same way, a hatchway into a subterranean structure from the ground level would have been easier to get through than a roof hatchway in a room where access to the roof was by ladder. One can classify access in terms of the distance one has to travel and the difficulty one has to overcome to get from one space to another. Each step of distance and difficulty can be considered another depth from the point of origin. For example, if a door leads directly from the front of a building into a room, the access depth of this room would be assigned the value of 1. If another room opens from the back of the first, the second room would have an access depth of 1 from the first room but an access depth of 2 from the front of the building.

This basic technique has been applied to the excavated kiva suites at Sand Canyon Pueblo. There are two types of doorways (floor-level and raised-sill), and roof hatchways occur in ground-level as well as raised roofs. Each access point was classified, and then its relative depth from outside and in front (to the south or east) of the kiva unit was determined. Four depth values have been identified, with 1 being the most direct and 4 being the least. Each depth has also been assigned a qualifying term relating to how controlled the access might have been. An access depth of 1 is considered unrestricted, 2 is considered controlled, 3 is limited, and 4 is restricted.

Access analysis has been done for each of the kiva suites, except for 102, 107, and 108, which were combined and treated as a single unit. These data have been used to evaluate the degree to which the kiva-suite structures are integrated with the adjacent outside space. A measure of integration can be derived by the formula:

$$RA = \frac{2(MD - 1)}{K - 2}$$

where RA = the measure of integration,
MD = the mean depth, and K = the number of spaces (see Hillier and Hanson 1984:108–102).

This calculation results in a number of less than 1, with low values indicating well-integrated spaces and high values indicating poorly integrated spaces.

Three of the kiva suites (501, 1004, and 1206) are relatively well integrated with the adjacent open space, whereas two architectural units—the cluster 102–107–108, and Kiva Suite 208—are poorly integrated with the adjacent open space. I believe these results may denote that Kiva Suites 501, 1004, and 1206 served a variety of functions indicative of habitation and that the other two units were the locations of specialized functions. These conclusions correspond with interpretations of the suites based on room-to-kiva ratios, range of room functions present, and differences in labor intensity.

It is interesting to note that the two units that are being considered special function are in architectural blocks that are adjacent to the plaza, which may be interpreted as public space. Kiva Suites 102 and 208 are also directly adjacent to a smaller open space (Figure 7.1). In terms of the site as a whole, these units are easily accessed from public spaces, whereas the domiciles are more difficult to access. This observation may be heavily biased by the sampling design, but I believe that there may be some significance in the accessibility of special-function kiva suites from public spaces.

Summary and Conclusions

Synopsis

The excavated architectural areas in Sand Canyon Pueblo have shown that original estimates of structure types and numbers based on surface indications are reasonably accurate. Of the six areas excavated, one included three kiva suites (102, 107, and 108) interpreted as special function, and one contained a single special-function kiva suite (208). All of these kiva suites are located on the west side of the site and are in kiva-dominated architectural blocks. Three kiva suites interpreted as having primarily habitation functions have also been excavated—two (1206 and 1004) on the east side of the site and one (501) on the west side. The two suites on the east side are located in standard architectural blocks, while Kiva Suite 501 is in a kiva-dominated block. Excavations in room-dominated Architectural Block 300 were inconclusive in terms of function, although storage at a community or suprahousehold level has been suggested for the initial use of these structures, with a possible shift to temporary or permanent residential use later.

Even though unit-type pueblo architecture does occur in the kiva-dominated architectural blocks (e.g., Kiva Suite 501), these units are surrounded by kivas with few associated rooms. Although these unit-type kiva suites were probably habitations, they may have served a special function within the architectural blocks. Could they have been the residences of people who served as caretakers for surrounding, more specialized kivas when these structures

were not in use? Standard architectural blocks appear to consist primarily of habitations, with the exact layout partially determined by the form of the space available for construction.

Site Construction and Use History

Excavations to date, when combined with surface evidence of structures, allow a tentative interpretation of the growth of the site as a whole. The manner of growth of the individual architectural blocks is unclear because of the noncontiguity of the sampling areas. However, wall abutments have allowed the relative placement of some excavated areas relative to other construction in the blocks. Kiva suites 102, 107, and 108 were built late in the history of Architectural Block 100; growth seems to have been from the west. Kiva Suite 208 was also built late in the history of its architectural block; growth was from the south. Kiva Suite 501 is in the center of the architectural block and may have been one of the first units constructed. Kiva Suite 1206 was built before the unexcavated architecture to the north but may have been built after that to the south. This would put its construction either early or intermediate in the architectural block. Kiva Suite 1004 was constructed after the unexcavated units to the south and west had been built, but before those to the north. Growth seems to have been from the south in Architectural Block 1000, with Kiva Suite 1004 being added near the end of the construction sequence. There is no evidence that would indicate that any of the architectural blocks were built as single construction episodes. They seem to have formed by the addition of kiva suites onto the exterior of existing architecture, including the site-enclosing wall. On the other hand, this process may have taken place within a relatively few years.

In all four architectural areas where the site-enclosing wall has been exposed, wall abutments indicate that it preceded the adjacent structures. The masonry in the site-enclosing wall is massive and exhibits minimal stone sorting or shaping, possibly indicating that it was constructed hastily, or at least without the formalized style seen in many other external structure walls. The presence of yellowish green clay in the mortar of the site-enclosing wall in every exposure around the site may indicate that the wall was built as a single construction event, utilizing materials close at hand. This interpretation is strengthened by the complete absence of the yellowish green clay in any other walls, even though this material was extensively used as constructional fill. The date of the construction of the site-enclosing wall is unknown, but kiva suites that incorporate it into their construction have been dated at A.D. 1262, 1265, and 1274. Labor estimates indicate the site-enclosing wall could have been built as a community project in about two months, assuming that 5 percent of the estimated population of 725 people (Adler 1990) had been available. In contrast, for a single-household social unit that could have made available three people for this work, it would have taken nearly three years of continuous labor to construct the wall. The only other structures of a size that may indicate labor at a social scale greater than the household or multiple-household group are a large, D-shaped, multiwalled structure and a possible great kiva. These structures are only now undergoing testing, and specific labor estimates cannot be made until more is known about them.

Two of the three core units of the habitation kiva suites (501 and 1206) were built in planned stages. Each included three stages, each in consecutive years, with two room-construction stages followed by the construction of the kiva. Additional rooms were added during the use of the kiva suites. Construction of these core units clearly was planned, and completion took three years. The third habitation kiva suite (1004) may have been originally built as a special-function structure, resembling a segment of a triwalled structure, and then later converted into a habitation.

Special-function kiva suites (102, 107, 108, and 208, and the core unit of 1004) were constructed either without associated rooms or with rooms that were built at the same time as, or after, the kiva.

Although growth by accretion is indicated within individual kiva suites, and probably within architectural blocks, there is evidence that the overall layout of the site was preplanned. The construction of the site-enclosing wall in relation to cliffs and ledges preconditioned the spatial organization of the individual architectural blocks to some extent. Furthermore, the spacing of the architectural blocks in relation to each other, as well as to the central plaza, the D-shaped multiwalled structure, and the great kiva, may indicate that there were preplanned zones of construction, and that they may have been dedicated to specific uses and functions. If this is an accurate assessment, the east side of the site functioned primarily as a habitation area, while the west side was more specialized in function. This is seen in the proximity of kiva-dominated blocks to public architecture and in the apparent lack of these relationships between most of the standard architectural blocks and public spaces. This is evidence of overall preplanning at the site level, in which the location of architectural blocks was anticipated and the allocation of habitation, specialized function, and public areas predetermined. Rather than total site planning at the architectural-unit level, this pattern most closely resembles functional zoning. Is this form of aggregated site organization typical of the northern San Juan Anasazi? Do eleventh- and twelfth-century aggregated sites show similar patterns of planning and growth, and is there a continuity from these forms into the late thirteenth century?

A Regional Context for Sand Canyon Pueblo

Large, aggregated sites were present in the northern Southwest as early as the late ninth century (Lipe et al. 1988;

Windes and Ford 1990). Specialized architectural forms such as great kivas go back even further (Roberts 1929; Vivian and Reiter 1965:99–102). In the tenth and eleventh centuries, another kind of specialized architectural form known as a great house was developed (Lekson 1984). Some investigators have interpreted these structures as habitations consisting of a number of household units (Vivian and Mathews 1965; Vivian 1970, 1990). This interpretation has held sway until the last two decades, during which the great-house architectural form has been reassessed and reinterpreted by some researchers as a centralized religious and/or administrative center (Judge et al. 1981). The best known examples are the great houses in Chaco Canyon and around Aztec and Bloomfield, New Mexico. Smaller versions of this type of structure have also been identified throughout the San Juan Basin, southwestern Colorado, southeastern Utah, and in the Cibola region around and to the west of Zuni, New Mexico (Bradley 1988b; Marshall et al. 1979; Powers et al. 1983). Along with other traits, this distribution of great houses surrounded by a community of clustered small settlements has been used to define a regional sociopolitical system: the Chaco Phenomenon (Irwin-Williams 1972). Most researchers see the collapse and disappearance of this regional system by A.D. 1150.

Recent pioneering work by Fowler et al. (1987) and Fowler and Stein (1990) in the Cibola region and Stein and McKenna (1988) in the Aztec area has questioned this conclusion. Rather than viewing the Chaco communities simply as a combination of specialized and generalized structures, they see them as highly integrated communities with specifically designed and planned cultural landscapes (associated habitations and specialized structures and features, and their spatial and functional relationships), including a complex group of features that make up a ritual landscape such as great houses, roads, etc. (see Fowler et al. 1987). By detailing the features and traits they view as integral to the Chacoan cultural landscape, these researchers have been able to look at later aggregated settlements and recognize a survival of aspects of this symbolic form through the end of the thirteenth century, at least in the Cibola region. One of the key traits is evidence of settlement planning and construction within the central sites.

A relevant question is whether or not this apparent functional and symbolic survival of the Chaco system occurs in other areas. Recent work in the vicinity of Aztec National Monument has identified a series of structures exhibiting many of the traits that are used to describe the Chaco cultural landscape (Stein and McKenna 1988). Many of these structures and features clearly date to the late eleventh and early twelfth centuries, but others seem to date to the following period and have previously been assigned to the late twelfth and thirteenth centuries.

The distribution of aggregated communities in southwestern Colorado has also been examined, identifying some very massive aggregated structures that clearly postdate A.D. 1150 (Ferguson and Rohn 1986; Varien et al. 1990, 1991; Lipe and Lekson 1990). These sites are only now being examined in detail and their cultural and ritual landscapes described. This process is hampered by the long use histories of most of these sites and the difficulty of assigning specific architecture and features to any but the broadest of time periods.

Fortunately, enough information is available from Sand Canyon Pueblo to make an initial attempt at functional analysis. Detailed mapping of the main area, along with the results of sample excavations, has identified several traits that may define a ritual landscape at the site. These include site-scale preplanning, massive architectural forms sited and constructed so as to emphasize size and verticality, internal public spaces (central plaza), public architectural features (the D-shaped, multiwalled structure and the great kiva), intrasite functional differentiation (kiva-dominated architectural blocks as compared to standard architectural blocks), and community-scale public works (the site-enclosing wall and the D-shaped, multiwalled structure). There is also evidence of extramural features, including boulder alignments, possible shrines, and isolated kivas. It is also clear that there is a substantial amount of habitation in the site. Surveys and test excavations surrounding Sand Canyon Pueblo (Adler, this volume; Adler 1990; Varien et al., this volume) have indicated that there was probably only a small settlement cluster of small sites that were contemporary with it. It seems that the majority of the population was living in Sand Canyon Pueblo. This contrasts with the earlier pattern of aggregation, which exhibited centralized, probably special-function, structures surrounded by a dispersed cluster of habitation sites.

Conclusions

Sand Canyon Pueblo is a large, aggregated site that was constructed, used, and abandoned in the last half of the thirteenth century. It was built to a general plan initiated by the communal construction of a massive site-enclosing wall. Internal site zoning defined the locations of architectural blocks and open spaces with specialized functions, as well as habitation areas. The site formed very quickly in the A.D. 1250–1270s, with individual kiva suites constructed as planned core units consisting of a kiva, several rooms, and occasionally a tower, or as individual kivas. Habitations grew by accretion during their use.

Detailed analyses of kiva suites have indicated that Sand Canyon Pueblo includes a combination of domestic habitations and functionally more specialized architecture. The majority of the domestic architecture is located on the east side of the site, whereas most of the special function architecture appears to be located on the west side. That the site is more than a simple aggregation of individual household units as expressed in unit-type pueblos is clear. Whether Sand Canyon Pueblo represents a continuation or a revival of the architectural symbolism attributable to the Chaco system or is an expression of a generalized Anasazi symbolism related to population aggregation awaits further research in the Sand Canyon locality, the Mesa Verde region, and the entire Anasazi province.

Acknowledgments. Portions of this chapter represent a substantial revision of a paper presented at the 1990 Society for American Archaeology meetings in Las Vegas. Research was sponsored by the Crow Canyon Archaeological Center in Cortez, Colorado, under permits 84–CO–046, C–39466a, and C–39466c, through the Bureau of Land Management, San Juan Area Office, Durango, Colorado. Partial funding was also supplied by the National Geographic Society (Grant 2892–84) and by the National Science Foundation (Grant BNS–8706532). As with all large archaeological projects, many individuals have contributed greatly to this project and much of its success has depended on their support and encouragement. Foremost is the Board of Directors of the Crow Canyon Archaeological Center. Their commitment to the support of long-term archaeological research has allowed the implementation of a community-scale study rather than a site-focused investigation. The excavations and many of the laboratory analyses relied on work done by members of the lay public through Crow Canyon's public involvement programs. Although the list of individuals is too long to include, their help and support has been critical to the completion of this study.

The data used in this study were obtained through fieldwork directed by Dr. E. Charles Adams in 1983 and 1984 and by myself in 1985 through 1989. Able assistance was provided by Crow Canyon research staff members James Kleidon, Val Whitley, Ricky Lightfoot, Carla Van West, Carrie Lipe, and Steve Shelley. In addition, Crow Canyon educators Luther Allen, Cindy Bradley, Margie Connolly, Megg Heath, Lew Matis, Roger Walkenhorst, and Beth Wheeler and research interns Matthew Bandy, Alan Denoyer, Julie Endicott, Allison Hoff, Maripat Metcalf, Sarah Oliver, and Geoff Thompson greatly assisted in field operations. Special thanks are also due to volunteer research assistants Betty Havers, George Havers, and Cindy Paul, whose enthusiasm and commitment to the project have been inspiring.

Volunteers from the Amaterra organization, working under the direction of Dr. Roger Irwin, provided many weeks of invaluable research and logistical support in each field season, starting in 1984. Amaterra volunteers also constructed and maintained shelters, trails, and other facilities at Sand Canyon Pueblo that made the research there easier and more productive in many ways.

Laboratory work was under the direction of Angela Schwab, assisted by Mary Etzkorn and Louise Schmidlap and by research interns Kari Chalker, Molly Davies, Michael Gomez, Steve Lakatos, Nikki Lamberg, Rachael Myron, Julie Sidel, Nick Scoales, and Gary Wood. Draft versions of this chapter were read and critically evaluated by Mark Varien, William Lipe, Ricky Lightfoot, David Breternitz, Kristin Kuckelman, and Frank Hole. Their comments have been very helpful and are much appreciated. William Lipe helped substantially in condensing material from earlier reports into the descriptions of the excavations presented above.

8

The Environmental Archaeology Program

Karen R. Adams

Introduction

The Environmental Archaeology program was established at the Crow Canyon Center in January of 1990 to coordinate and integrate all ongoing environmental studies and to initiate new ones. The broad scope of environmental archaeology includes studies aimed at

- Reconstructing various aspects of the regional and local paleoenvironment
- Modeling agricultural productivity through time and comparing this to archaeological estimates of population
- Analyzing faunal and floral materials recovered from archaeological sites
- Providing both physical anthropological and chemical-constituent analysis of human skeletal material for insight into demography, pathology, and diet
- Devising modern studies to provide data on the potential supply and the resource properties of a series of key native plants
- Implementing projects designed to help understand the processes involved in the formation of assemblages of plant and animal remains in archaeological sites

Each of these major areas will be briefly reviewed to establish their current status and to suggest where future efforts will be directed.

Paleoenvironmental Reconstructions

Regional Views

Tree Rings. The excellent, multicentury tree-ring record for the Four Corners area not only offers the potential for dating archaeological construction events but also serves as a source of information on annual regional precipitation and, to a lesser extent, temperature. Van West (1990; Van West and Lipe, this volume) has incorporated these paleoclimatic-reconstruction data into a model of agricultural productivity (discussed below) for the period A.D. 900–1300 in an approximately 1800 km^2 area that includes the Sand Canyon locality. We are also interested in pursuing any studies that may enable us to infer temperature more directly. New evidence from tree-ring studies of limber pine (*Pinus flexilis*) in northern New Mexico suggests that this species may respond significantly to temperature as well as to precipitation (Henri Grisson-Mayer, personal communication 1991; K. Adams 1991a). This is a long-lived species with records extending back into the prehistoric period we are most interested in. Consequently, we may be able to develop a long-term temperature reconstruction from tree-ring records in limber pine stands in or near the Four Corners area. This would be most helpful in modeling absolute (instead of relative) values for both growing season temperature and growing season length during Anasazi times.

Pollen Records from Wetlands. Pollen grains that accumulate in riparian locations close to vegetation lifezone boundaries often provide a view of the changing nature of plant communities through time. Shifts in pollen influx are often interpreted as movements of plant taxa to higher or lower elevations in response to changing patterns of precipitation or temperature in an area. These data provide a record of variation in environmental parameters through time that is complementary to the tree-ring record, though less chronologically precise. In some cases, pollen records may provide better data on broad, regional climatic shifts than do tree-ring records. Pollen data may also provide information on changing proportions of summer-versus-winter rainfall (Petersen 1988).

Petersen's (1988) palynological work, based on cores from the La Plata Mountains and the Dolores River valley, provides a useful reconstruction of vegetation and climate for southwestern Colorado during the period of Anasazi occupation, and hence it is relevant to our work in the Sand Canyon locality. Obtaining wetland pollen records in or near the Sand Canyon locality may permit refinement or modification of Petersen's reconstruction, with more direct application to the Sand Canyon locality. The Sand Canyon locality and nearby areas have been surveyed for suitable locations for a wetland pollen core, and few are available. The best candidate is a small lake on Ute Mountain, but permission to core there would need to be granted by the Ute Mountain Ute Tribal Council. At this point, no proposal or permit request has been submitted.

Fluvial Records. Various events in the histories of drainages are often recorded in exposed alluvial stratigraphy. The timing and scale of lowland aggradation or degradation may well have important implications for Anasazi farming strategies and success (Dean et al. 1985; Karlstrom 1988; Plog et al. 1988). Efforts to understand the fluvial history of an approximately two-mile stretch of the McElmo drainage are well underway (Force 1990). The presence of a low bedrock sill across the McElmo valley in Anasazi times created a low-gradient segment of the drainage that may have appealed to prehistoric farmers interested in farming on upslope, side-canyon fans. Anasazi pottery, checkdams, and deposits of cultural organic debris are providing a means to classify fluvial events into pre-Anasazi, Anasazi, and post-Anasazi periods. Whether particular bodies of sediments originated in side canyons or were deposited by the main stream of the McElmo can be determined in some cases by differing characteristics of the sediment, as well as by elevation, position, and bedding plane strike and dip. Preliminary indications are that a braided, aggrading stream dropped up to 3 m of accumulated sediment in Pueblo II times, and that fans continued to be built at the mouths of side canyons during the Pueblo III period. Aggradation of the main flood plain may have ceased during the Pueblo III period. This excellent beginning in understanding fluvial history needs to be expanded along the McElmo drainage and into other nearby drainages, as local factors can figure heavily in stream gradient dynamics.

Local Views

Packrat Middens. The generalized collecting habits of packrats (*Neotoma*) have permitted paleoecologists to reconstruct local vegetation assemblages and, from hundreds of these reconstructions, to infer vegetation histories through time and across space in the arid southwestern

United States (Betancourt et al. 1990). Packrat middens are abundant in the Sand Canyon locality, and some may represent periods before, during, and after Anasazi occupation. Organic remains in the middens can be dated by the ^{14}C method. Middens in areas devoid of archaeological sites could provide a record of regional vegetation and possibly of human impact (field clearing, specific resource depletion). Middens in or adjacent to archaeological sites might reveal the nature of disturbed vegetation around an occupied settlement and track the recovery of vegetation after abandonment. At present no formal packrat study is underway, although there are active efforts to recruit an interested student or researcher.

Faunal Records from Sites. While faunal materials recovered from archaeological sites primarily provide a view of Anasazi utilization of specific animals and animal parts (see discussion below), faunal assemblages from sites offer indirect evidence on the characteristics of the local fauna available to the Anasazi and how it may have changed through time. Analysis of archaeological assemblages from the Sand Canyon locality to date indicates that the animals found in Pueblo III sites are also present in the Sand Canyon locality today (Walker 1989, 1990a, 1990b; Brand 1991), leading to the preliminary conclusion that if environmental change occurred in the twelfth and thirteenth centuries, it was not expressed in the species composition of the local fauna. This does not necessarily imply similarities in abundance of available individual taxa between the two periods.

Floral Records from Sites. Larger plant parts recognized by archaeologists (macrofossils) and smaller ones, such as seeds and pollen grains secured in soil samples (microfossils), have the potential to reveal the composition of local floral communities in the past. As in the faunal record, the heavy influence of human preferences and habits, and of site-formation processes, can affect the ability of an ancient plant record to reveal the details of local prehistoric plant communities. Currently, the accumulated macrofossil (Scott and Aasen 1985; K. Adams 1989a, 1989b, 1989c, 1989d) and pollen records (Scott and Aasen 1985; Gish 1988, 1991) do not suggest major differences between present and past plant communities in terms of taxa present. The close correspondence between prehistoric and modern local taxa does not suggest that people traveled long distances for floral items or engaged in trade for items unavailable locally.

Modeling Agricultural Productivity through Time

Van West (1990; Van West and Lipe, this volume) utilized tree-ring data and soils information from the region to model paleoclimate (A.D. 900–1970) and agricultural productivity for the A.D. 900–1300 period—Pueblo II and III in the Anasazi sequence. She reconstructed Palmer Drought Severity Indices (PDSI) for June for local soils within five elevational bands. The mapping unit was a 4-ha cell; each was assigned to the soil class that was predominant in the area of the cell. In combination with data on the potential productivity of each soil class, the reconstructed annual PDSI values were used to estimate potential yields of maize and beans under a dry-land farming regime.

Van West (1990) integrated, quantified, and visually displayed these productivity values with Geographic Information System (GIS) technology. This permitted her to display, both graphically and numerically, the changing and variable nature of potential annual maize production for the study area in the period A.D. 900–1300. Using assumptions about per capita human caloric needs, percent of needs supplied by maize, and level of production required to accommodate various levels of maize storage, she was also able to estimate potential carrying capacity of the study area for human populations.

On the basis of this modeling of precipitation, soil moisture, maize production, and potential human population, Van West concluded that potential maize yield in the study area had always been great enough to support a population density of 21 persons/km^2 in the study area, even in the driest periods in the middle 1100s and late 1200s, and that climatic fluctuations, as they affected crop production, cannot be considered the sole and sufficient cause for the total abandonment of the region in the late 1200s. Van West (1990) points out that these estimates assume mobility and per capita or per household access to productive land were not restricted, so populations were able to adjust their population density in keeping with both spatial and temporal variations in potential productivity.

The strengths of Van West's model are the high temporal resolution of climatic variation—on an annual scale—and the high spatial resolution of soil productivity—by 4-ha plots. The use of a GIS system represents an efficient means to integrate and quantify thousands of pieces of data and to provide visually meaningful displays. Van West (1990) suggests that this research can be enhanced to (1) test the overall robustness of the model by changing the values assigned to key variables (e.g., production of a soil type under extreme drought conditions); (2) reconstruct August PDSI values; (3) factor in soil nutrient depletion and erosion over time; (4) consider roles for insects, molds, and other pathenogens that could affect crop yield and successful storage; and (5) consider ways to integrate temperature reconstructions, especially in relation to length of past growing seasons. This last factor may be a critical one; Petersen (1988) concludes that decreased growing seasons, in combination with drought, made dry-farming in areas of southwestern Colorado perilous for farmers in the thirteenth century A.D.

Faunal and Floral Material from Archaeological Sites

Faunal Material. The Sand Canyon locality faunal record that is accumulating (Walker 1989, 1990a, 1990b; Brand 1991) is similar to that of other prehistoric Southwestern sites, revealing heavy Anasazi reliance on lagomorphs (primarily cottontail rabbits and jackrabbits), large birds (turkeys), rodents (primarily prairie dog), artiodactyls (deer, with some pronghorn antelope and bighorn sheep), and to a lesser extent other birds and carnivores. Calculation of relative frequencies of species shows little variation between contemporaneous sites and little change through time. The relative homogeneity of faunal assemblages suggests comparable rates of access to edible species at all sites during the twelfth and thirteenth centuries, and there is currently only slight evidence (Hoffman 1985) to suggest that protein was a limiting factor in this area. Evidence of possibly increased reliance on large mammals in Sand Canyon Pueblo agrees with Speth and Scott's (1985, 1989) prediction that aggregated communities would deplete local small game and have to search further for larger game.

Future analysis efforts will evaluate what portion of the faunal assemblage may be intrusive, assess the distribution of faunal-element frequencies, examine the nature of bone-processing intensity, characterize assemblages across space and through time in relative terms, evaluate evidence of reliance on domesticated turkeys through time and at different site types, and look for any signs of feasting or ritual activity involving animals. These studies must take into account differences in sample size, site-formation processes, and the nature of the deposits examined (primary activity, midden debris, abandonment context, etc.).

Although preliminary analysis has suggested a substantial degree of homogeneity in the faunal record from Pueblo III sites in the Sand Canyon locality, the work has been confined primarily to identification and descriptive characterization of the assemblages. Systematic comparative studies among various temporal, spatial, site type, and intrasite contexts have barely begun. There may well be subtle patterns of differentiation and change that have not been evident upon initial inspection of the data, or that can be revealed by types of analysis not yet attempted. The numerous contexts now available for study, the comparability of the sampling methods employed in the field, and the interpretations of site-abandonment mode and assemblage-formation processes that are now emerging make forthcoming comparative studies of faunal assemblages an exciting prospect.

Floral Material. A number of analyses of plant materials from Sand Canyon locality sites have been accomplished. These include pollen reports (Scott and Aasen 1985; Gish 1988, 1991; Huber 1990) and reports on seeds and larger macrofossils, including wood charcoal (Scott and Aasen 1985; K. Adams 1989a, 1989b, 1989c, 1989d).

In general, the archaeobotanical studies reveal a consistent reliance through time, for both large and small sites, on domesticated corn (*Zea mays*), on some disturbed-ground wild plants likely promoted by ancient farming activities (*Chenopodium/Amaranthus, Physalis*), and on some local members of the cactus family (*Opuntia*). A grass that produces ripe grains in late spring (*Oryzopsis hymenoides*) also provided a common resource. Three additional domesticates—beans (*Phaseolus*), squash (*Cucurbita*), and gourd (*Lagenaria*)—along with at least 17 additional wild plant taxa, were also recovered, many in archaeological contexts suggestive of food use. Foods common in Sand Canyon locality sites in the Pueblo III period are also common in the Pueblo III coprolite record from the area (Minnis 1989) and in the few Dolores Archaeological Project sites examined from that time period (Matthews 1986).

In addition to dietary data, the archaeobotanical record has provided information on other topics. Modern observations on the timing of plant availability tentatively suggest some differences in the seasonality of occupation of Pueblo III sites in the Sand Canyon locality. Wood of pine (*Pinus*), juniper (*Juniperus*), and leftover corn (*Zea*) cobs consistently provided hearth fuel through time for all sites, and branches and twigs of up to 17 additional local trees and shrubs were burned on occasion by the Pueblo III Anasazi. Some insight is also available on materials gathered for basketry, utensils, ritual smoking, and wooden artifacts. Functional differentiation of roomblocks has been suggested for Sand Canyon Pueblo (Bradley, this volume; Bradley 1991b) through a variety of architectural analyses; the plant assemblages from these roomblocks tentatively support some of the architectural interpretations and contrast with others. A series of rigorous standards for evaluating the ethnobotanical significance of plant remains has been established, with future experimental projects planned to help strengthen interpretations of archaeobotanical materials. The current database of analyzed plant materials from Sand Canyon locality sites is imbalanced in terms of spatial and temporal representation, a problem that can be remedied by significant investment of time and effort in analysis of additional samples. As with the faunal assemblages from the locality, systematic comparative studies are just beginning on samples from contexts chosen to provide data on questions of functional and social differentiation and on social and economic change.

Physical Anthropological and Chemical Analyses of Human Skeletal Material

More than two dozen human skeletons representing the Puebloan period in the Sand Canyon locality have been examined by physical anthropologists (Hoffman 1985, 1987, 1990b; Kice 1990, 1991). This assemblage has provided information on the pathology (trauma, growth disturbances, nutritionally related disorders) and demography of the Anasazi in the locality. Studies of stable carbon isotopes extracted from bone collagen are currently planned as a way of estimating aspects of the diet of these individuals.

Pathological data are informative but cannot provide information on many acute stressors such as gastrointestinal disease, etc. A preliminary paleodemographic reconstruction of the (admittedly small) population of individuals recovered at Sand Canyon Pueblo reveals a high incidence of infant mortality and an unusually high incidence of death among older children and adolescents (ages 5–20). Individuals in the Pueblo III sites generally reveal no remarkable cases of pathology, although there was some evidence of health disruption during growth (Kice 1991; Hoffman 1990b). Their oral health appears better than that of individuals from the Pueblo I period Duckfoot site (Hoffman 1990a), but whether this is due to the relatively young age of the individuals in the Sand Canyon population and/or to dietary causes is unknown. Hints of protein deficiency in both Duckfoot and later populations is suggested by tooth crowding, implying inadequate jaw growth (Hoffman 1985). Perimortem trauma has been recognized on the skulls of some Pueblo III individuals (Annie Katzenberg, personal communication 1991); the significance of this finding is currently unknown.

Reconstructions of prehistoric diet can be accomplished by analysis of stable carbon and nitrogen isotopes in bone collagen (Van der Merwe 1982; DeNiro 1987). A broadly based approach being undertaken in the Sand Canyon project includes analysis of (1) carbon isotopes from human skeletal material as an indicator of human consumption of maize and native C_4 plants and of consumption of animals eating C_4 plants; (2) nitrogen isotopes in human bone collagen, as an indicator of meat consumption; and (3) isotopes of plants and animals these individuals presumably depended upon, to provide baseline evidence for interpreting the human isotopic data. Another potential application of stable isotopic data is the identification of relatively recent immigrants into an area through their anomalous isotopic signatures. Limited trace-element (strontium) analysis as an indicator of reliance on agricultural products is also scheduled for human remains.

Such a multifaceted approach provides locality-specific estimates of isotopic and trace element signatures. Without this precision, dietary differences expressing social distinctions or other causes might be difficult to perceive. Elsewhere in the region, carbon isotopic analyses in the Mesa Verde region revealed a consistent (up to 70–80 percent) reliance on maize from Basketmaker III/Pueblo I through Pueblo II/Pueblo III times (Decker and Tieszen 1989). Most regional studies to date, however, have focused primarily on the human skeletal material, with little or no attention to the characteristics of the associated faunal and floral materials.

Modern Studies: Availability and Qualities of Key Plant Resources

Since the organic remains in the archaeological record are susceptible to differential degradation over time, and because the record itself may be biased by the diverse nature of human/plant interactions, we assume that ancient plant parts recovered from sites only imperfectly reveal the nature of Anasazi use or reliance on specific taxa and plant communities. Also, some information regarding plant use is simply unavailable from the ancient plant record (e.g., season when available, dependability, specific qualities that might appeal to humans). Therefore, we have instituted a number of modern environmental studies to provide a broader information base from which to understand and interpret the prehistoric record. Four projects currently in progress are discussed below; two additional projects scheduled for implementation are also outlined.

Modern Experimental Gardens

Van West (1990; Van West and Lipe, this volume) has utilized modern ethnographic information and historic dryland crop data from the area to model yields of corn (*Zea*) and beans (*Phaseolus*) under a dry-land farming regime. Experimental gardens are now underway to assess these yield figures, using Native American varieties and simulating Native American farming practices. These data, tied to modern weather records, will also provide perspectives on how morphological characters of crops might be affected by different growing conditions; currently, morphological data are heavily relied upon in characterizing specific prehistoric crop types, though the effects of temperature and precipitation on morphology remain poorly understood.

Fuelwood Availability and Qualities

Some Sand Canyon locality records of fuel use reveal over a dozen types of trees and shrubs burned in some individual hearths; others reveal only a single type. Pine (*Pinus*) and juniper (*Juniperus*) charcoal and corn (*Zea*) cobs are nearly ubiquitous in the Pueblo III sites. Patterns of occurrence undoubtedly reflect a number of situations. Humans can be quite selective with regard to fuelwood needs for tasks where specific qualities of wood are required. They are also pragmatic when it comes to needs that can be met by whatever fuelwood is most easily obtainable. If the pool of available fuelwood changed over time, because of heavy collecting or land clearance for agriculture, we might

expect a changing record of wood types to document such environmental perturbations. A series of interrelated projects has been initiated to evaluate independently some of the above concerns, including: average rate of deadwood production/tree and shrub species in the locality; qualities of each species, such as amount of heat produced, length of time heat is given off, characteristics of the smoke, etc; and relative production of identifiable charcoal specimens among the different species. With insights from these studies, interpretations of fuelwood patterns in prehistoric Sand Canyon locality sites can be enhanced.

Supply and Distribution of Construction Elements

A project to evaluate the availability of construction elements (e.g., roofing beams, lintel supports, ramada posts and roofing) in pinyon-juniper communities is currently underway (Hovezak 1990). Characteristics (length, width, etc.) of Anasazi primary, secondary, and tertiary beams, as well as lintels, have been acquired from available archaeological literature and from modern measurements of remaining elements preserved in Pueblo III cliff dwellings in the Mesa Verde area. Estimates of construction element needs will be made for Sand Canyon Pueblo. The estimated modern forest supply of construction elements can then be compared to the inferred Sand Canyon demand, taking into consideration rates of regeneration of construction elements in "pristine" forests and in forests impacted by fire, agricultural clearance, heavy fuelwood depletion, etc. The size of the catchment necessary to provide adequate elements will be modeled under various assumed forest conditions in the period of Sand Canyon construction, considering also the building timber needs of immediately prior occupants of the area, as well as the needs of the residents of nearby contemporaneous settlements.

Recovery of Plant Communities after a Fire

It seems likely that at times the Anasazi purposefully or inadvertently burned their vegetation communities. Clearance of an area for an agricultural field, burning to attract animals to recovering vegetation, and fostering a diversity of native plants in a single community type are three reasons for intentional burning. The sequence and rate of vegetation recovery, along with the qualities and relative availability of specific plants, would undoubtedly have been of interest to the Anasazi. The first year of a projected five-year study of vegetation recovery after a natural fire on the Mesa Verde (K. Adams 1991b) has focused in part on the ethnobotanical significance of the recovering vegetation. A number of taxa (*Chenopodium*, *Nicotiana* [native tobacco], members of the mustard family, plus others) displayed increased availability, along with an abundance of fuelwood and possibly some usable construction elements.

Seasonality and Productivity Observations

Timing of availability, predictability, and knowledge of average harvestable amounts of particular plants could have easily influenced the use of and reliance on a specific resource by the Anasazi of the Sand Canyon locality. These data are being gathered for key native plant resources commonly recovered from the archaeological record. The modern data will be tied to modern climatic observations to help us understand any relative effects of different precipitation and temperature regimes on specific resources. Relative drought and cooler temperatures may not affect all plant resources in the same way; some may be enhanced while others are reduced. It is hoped that these studies, in conjunction with modern gardening experiments, will enable us to better assess the ability of key native plants to buffer a season of poor agricultural return.

Resource Distribution Studies (Planned)

The information collected above will be more meaningful when a detailed understanding of the distribution of resources within the Sand Canyon locality can be acquired. Animal populations have the advantage of mobility and can move if plant community composition is altered; animal species also have habitat preferences that are generally known. Although the Soil Conservation Service has some information on the associations of plant taxa and soils, this information is incomplete for our purposes. A study to perceive the associations of key native plant resources (as defined by the archaeobotanical record) with landforms (defined by substrate, slope, aspect, and elevation) in the region is needed to understand the selectivity or ubiquity of plants in terms of where they grow. Relative density will

be evaluated for different landforms. It is proposed that this study of plant distribution be accompanied by a search of historical documents and oral interviews to assess the potential impacts of historic forces on these modern distributions. Together, these approaches will place us in a much better position to model distribution and yield of key elements of the plant environment under differing conditions of climate and human exploitation.

Site-Formation Studies

Archaeologists often lack information on the links between human behavior and formation of a particular archaeological record, as well as insight into all the forces that can act on and alter that record from the time of original deposition. Environmental archaeologists are in a good position to plan studies that assess some of these factors. For example, we plan to learn something about the relative preservation potential of the different wood types available in the Sand Canyon locality by a series of controlled burning and burial experiments. We have already begun this work by collaborating on a project in which pottery was fired in pit kilns constructed on the Crow Canyon campus. Any role that highly alkaline environments (such as those produced by burning corn cobs) play in wood preservation will also be examined. Experiments that provide information about pollen transport on harvested plant parts will help us interpret the pollen record. Repeated food processing in the pit structure that has been constructed by Crow Canyon archaeologists and educators can be monitored for any pollen records these activities produce. Results of these studies will have value for other archaeologists beyond the Sand Canyon locality.

9

Modeling Prehistoric Climate and Agriculture in Southwestern Colorado

Carla R. Van West and William D. Lipe

Introduction

The Anasazi abandonment of the northern San Juan area at the end of the Pueblo III period poses one of the classic problems in Southwestern archaeology. That these people left the area in the late thirteenth century A.D. is well known; what is not known with certainty, however, is why they left. It has long been suspected that such a widespread and seemingly sudden depopulation of this large area must have had its roots in an environmental crisis caused by natural climatic fluctuations, such as the "Great Drought" of A.D. 1276–1299 (Douglass 1929).

This chapter partially summarizes a larger work (Van West 1990) in which an attempt was made to reconstruct the agricultural environment available to Anasazi farmers in the heartland of the northern San Juan area before and during the period of abandonment. To approach this problem, Van West (1990) created a quantitative, high-resolution model of potential prehistoric agricultural productivity and sustainable population for an 1816-km^2 (701-mi^2) area in the dry-farming region of southwestern Colorado (Figure 9.1). Although the results are applicable to the entire study area, they are actually based on the portion of it for which good soils data were available—approximately 1470 km^2.

While efforts to reconstruct climatic variation and its influence on agricultural productivity and population or settlement in the Mesa Verde area have been made before (e.g., Herold 1961; Cordell 1975; Burns 1983; Schlanger 1985; Petersen 1988), none to date has had the opportunity to use both the high-quality environmental data and the spatial data-management systems now available. Without these recently derived environmental data and state-of-the-art computing technology, this research could not have been done. The data are too many, the calculations too complex, and the accurate evaluations of the options too numerous to be processed or displayed in a single lifetime. Thus, computer technology, especially Geographic Information Systems (GIS) hardware and software, plays an important role in this research. This chapter briefly summarizes the methods used to build the model that integrates climatic and soils data to produce estimates of agricultural productivity and population, then focuses on the results of the modeling effort and on their implications for understanding the Anasazi abandonment of southwestern Colorado. In the longer presentation of the model (Van West 1990), three scales of analysis are used. These are (1) the entire study area; (2) two small areas (18 km^2 and 26 km^2) where complete archaeological surveys have been done, so that estimates of actual prehistoric population can be compared with estimates of carrying capacity generated by the model; and (3) eight individual site catchments, where patterns of tree-ring-dated occupation and abandonment can be compared with modeled variation in agricultural productivity for those catchments. In this chapter, the results of only the first two approaches are summarized.

The methods employed to build the model are fully described elsewhere (Van West 1990). Below, the principal elements of the model are summarized.

Modeling Climate, Agriculture and Population

The model (Figure 9.2) integrates climatic data derived from tree-ring series with data on the water-holding capacity of soil classes to calculate Palmer Drought Severity Indices (PDSI). These indices are calculated for June of each year from A.D. 901 to 1300 for each of 36,759 4-ha cells that make up the actual spatial database for the model.

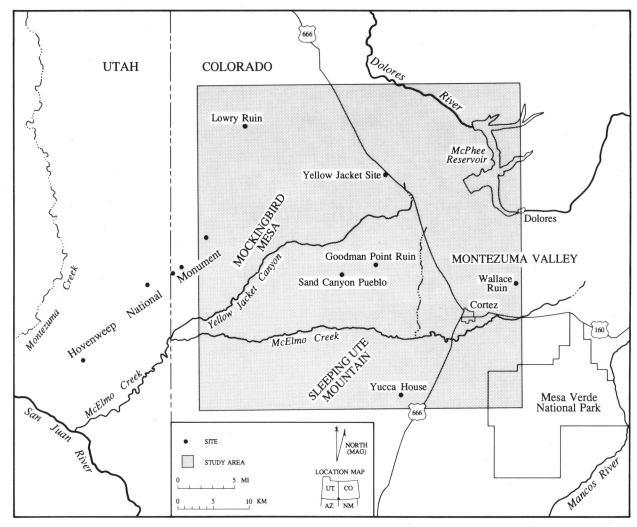

Figure 9.1. Prehistoric climate and agriculture study area.

Calibrations of natural plant productivity estimates and historic agricultural yield values for specific soil types under varying soil moisture conditions are used to retrodict potential prehistoric agricultural yields under reconstructed moisture conditions for all 4-ha cells in the database. From the cumulated prehistoric agricultural production estimates, potential population sizes and densities are calculated, using a variety of assumptions about levels of maize cultivation, consumption, and storage.

Soil Data

The study area (Figure 9.1) includes 45,400 4-ha cells, but as noted above, adequate soils data were not available for some of them. The USDA Soil Conservation Service (SCS) had mapped 98 soil types in the study area as of 1988. Each 4-ha cell was considered to have a single soil type, based on the dominant soil type by area in the unit. The 98 soil types were grouped into 11 soil classes based on available water-holding capacity (AWC), for the purpose of calculat-

ing PDSI values. Later, estimated agricultural yields for each of the original 98 soil types under five different growing-season conditions were used to "translate" spatially and temporally sensitive PDSI values into quantitative estimates of bean and maize production for each of the 4-ha cells. The sum of the individual values for all cells in the study area provided estimates of yields for the total study area.

The Palmer Drought Severity Index

The Palmer Drought Severity Index (Palmer 1965) was used as a way of quantifying variation in effective soil moisture. The PDSI has been shown to have a higher correlation with variation in tree-ring series than do annual and seasonal precipitation or temperature per se (Rose et al. 1982). This is undoubtedly because the PDSI integrates both moisture and temperature conditions, as in effect do trees when they add growth rings. The PDSI was designed to be an index of meteorological drought, defined

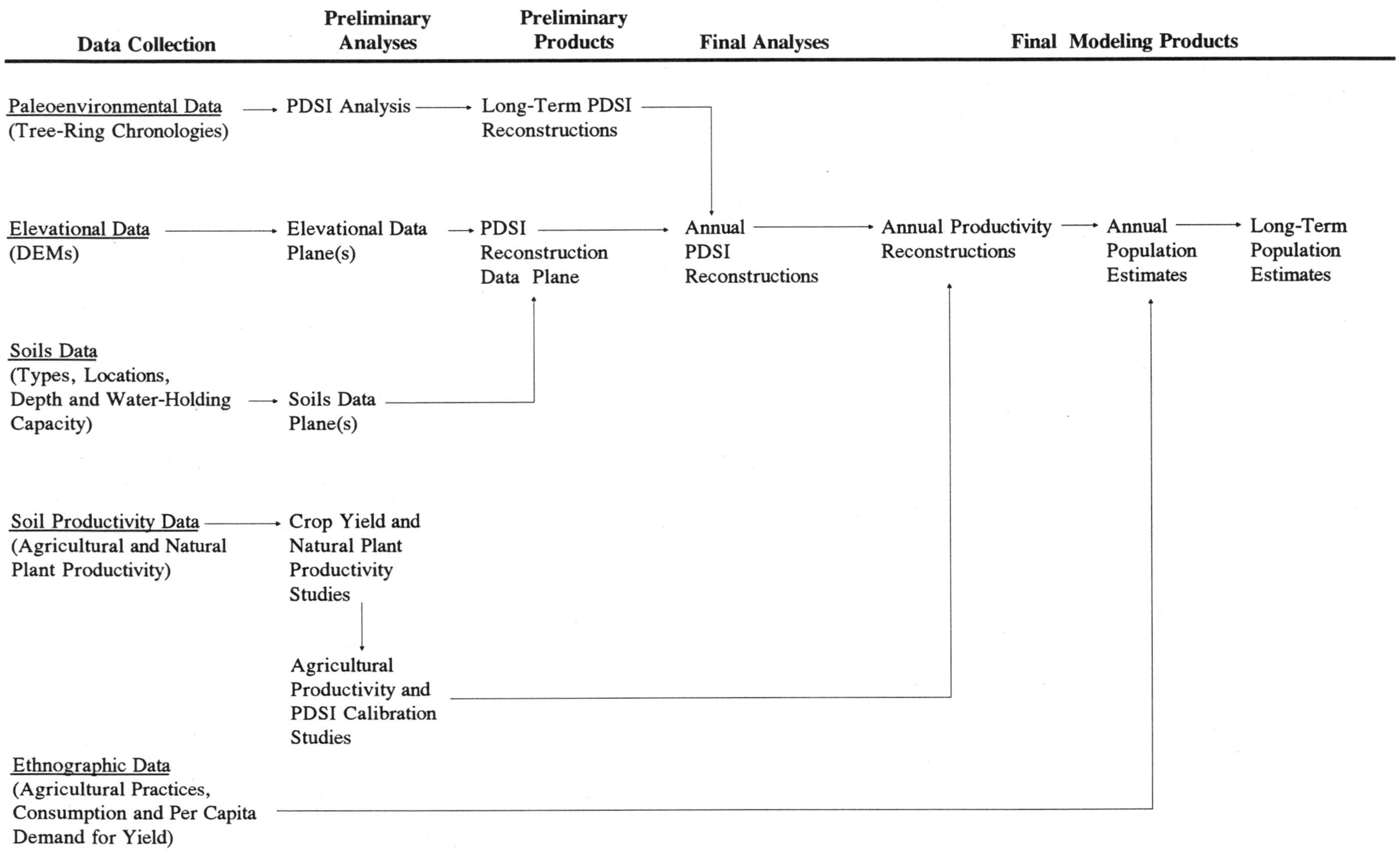

Figure 9.2. The conceptual model for reconstructing prehistoric agricultural productivity.

as "a period of prolonged and abnormal moisture deficiency" (Palmer 1965:1). The index is based on a water-balance, or hydrological accounting, approach to modeling soil moisture conditions (Palmer 1965:6) that takes the water holding capacities of particular soils into consideration. The PDSI value for a particular soil will vary depending on the cumulated balance of water added monthly by precipitation and subtracted monthly by evapotranspiration, which varies with temperature.

Because the PDSI values represent departures from the long-term mean condition of a given place, they do not provide a basis for comparing the absolute amounts of water in soils at different places having differing climatic regimes. Thus, a PDSI indicating moderate drought for a soil in Iowa may be based on more actual soil moisture than a PDSI indicating a wet period for a soil in southwestern Colorado.

The 1470-km^2 portion of the study area for which good soils data are available ranges in elevation from approximately 1500 m at the lowest to 2365 m at the highest. This results in a substantial range of elevation-related differences in annual precipitation and temperature. Consequently, PDSI values for the 11 AWC soil classes were calculated separately for five elevation zones, each of which could be characterized by historic climatic data from a weather station located in or near the study area. The weather stations are Bluff, Utah; and Cortez, Ignacio, Mesa Verde, and Ft. Lewis, in Colorado. These calculations resulted in the production of 55 long-term reconstructions of PDSI representing the full length of the tree-ring record (A.D. 901 to 1970), including the 400-year period of interest. The 55 reconstructions insured that the climatic variation characteristic of different elevation zones would be taken into account, and that PDSI values for particular soils would be expressed in relation to the long-term mean soil moisture condition for that soil in that elevation zone. Thus, soils with different water-holding capacities from different elevation zones could be characterized on a scale ranging from extreme drought to extreme wetness, relative to the long-term norms for each soil in its elevation zone.

Tree-Ring Data and Calibration of PDSI Values

The tree-ring data used to model past climate were eigenvector amplitudes (i.e., factor scores) that resulted from a principal components analysis of seven tree-ring chronologies from the southern Colorado Plateau. The data set was created by Martin Rose in conjunction with research undertaken by the Laboratory of Tree-Ring Research (Rose et al. 1982).

The reconstruction of PDSI values for representative soils in the study area by using modern precipitation and temperature data and tree-ring chronologies was a multistep process (Fritts 1976; Meko et al. 1980; Hughes et al. 1982;

Rose et al. 1982; Graybill 1989). The process began with calculation of PDSI values for specific soils using historic climatic data from a specific weather station. In this step, actual PDSI values were determined for every month and every year in the instrumented series.

Second, PDSI values from a selected month were correlated with tree-ring values for a common period of time in order to generate an initial multiple regression equation that could be used as a transfer function to predict (or in this case, to retrodict) PDSI values in the prehistoric and preinstrumented time period. Here the tree-ring data were treated as independent variables and the PDSI values as the dependent variable. In this "initial calibration," a portion of the historic record was used to build the initial regression equation, and another portion was used to test it.

Third, "verification" of the initial calibration equation took place. Correlation coefficients and probability tests were used to assess the strength of the initial equations to faithfully predict the actual values generated by the original instrumented PDSI data for years not used in the creation of the original calibration equations.

Fourth, a "full calibration" period regression equation was created for the entire period of instrumented record that overlaps with the modern end of the tree-ring data. The product of this step was the final transfer function to be used to retrodict the preinstrumented PDSI values.

Last, the retrodiction of the entire PDSI series was accomplished by applying the transfer function to the full set of tree-ring values. In this step, the tree-ring data were used as the predictor, or independent, variables and the PDSI was the predicted, or dependent, variable.

In modeling PDSI values for southwestern Colorado, the above process was repeated 55 times, once for each of the data sets (the 11 AWC types occurring in each of the five elevation zones). The conservative estimate of the explained variance (the adjusted r^2) for the 55 regression equations ranged from 32 to 62 percent, with an overall mean of 50 percent. This indicates that about 50 percent of the variation in a PDSI value can be explained by the tree-ring data, used here as a proxy for stochastic variation in climate. The adjusted r^2 values for the project compared favorably with those obtained by Rose in a reconstruction of PDSI values for the Zuni area (Martin Rose, personal communication 1989) and for southwestern Colorado (Rose et al. 1982). The program that reconstructed the entire time series for PDSI values in the study area was written by Robert Lofgren of the Laboratory of Tree-Ring Research at the University of Arizona.

Use of Geographic Information System Technology

GIS hardware and software were used to manage and analyze these large data sets and to display results. This technology has the ability to interrelate multiple spatial and nonspatial data sets concurrently, to create new information through combinations or transformations of original data, and to produce analytic products (e.g., tables, charts, graphs) in addition to map-like images.

Without GIS it would have been impossible to integrate the reconstructed drought indices and estimated agricultural yields from the actual soil classes with the locations of these soils, as mapped by the 4-ha cells used to partition the study area. By capturing, coregistering, and evaluating all data layers, as well as by creating new data layers from reclassifications and transformations of the original data, GIS technology made the fast, accurate, and consistent assignments necessary to create the model, display the results, and assess patterning across space and through time. Figure 9.3 provides an example of a GIS-generated map of potential agricultural productivity for one year—A.D. 902. To produce this map, equations were required that related agricultural productivity to soil class characteristics at differing PDSI states (see discussion below of how agricultural productivity was estimated). With GIS technology, such maps can be generated year by year for PDSI values, potential agricultural production, or potential population density.

In the GIS applications for this project, two raster (grid cell–based) programs were used to capture, store, manipulate, and display the spatially distributed data of the model. The programs—mainframe software called VICAR/IBIS and microcomputer software called EPPL7—made possible the investigation of the study area at a relatively high level of spatial resolution (4-ha cellular units). Input to the GIS was in the form of previously generated computer values entered through floppy disks, digital elevation data (DEMs) purchased from the U.S. Geological Survey on magnetic tape, and newly digitized spatial data and keyboard-entered tabular data entered directly into GIS programs. Output from the GIS consisted of color graphic displays on video monitors, black-and-white image output on dot matrix printers (e.g., Figure 9.3), and tabular data that were transferred to mainframe programs for further analysis.

Estimation of Potential Agricultural Productivity

Information on historic yields of nonirrigated bean and maize cultivation in southwestern Colorado was gathered in order to address two methodological problems that had to be solved before data on soil quality and PDSI values could be used to generate estimates of both relative agricultural productivity and actual agricultural yields. The first problem was to establish the nature and strength of the relationship between modern crop yield and modern soil moisture conditions as modeled by the Palmer Drought Severity Index—that is, the extent to which crop yields in the historic period have varied with PDSI. This would provide a basis for calibrating moisture-related variation in prehistoric crop yields. The second problem was to develop a method whereby specific yield values could be estimated for soil types and AWC classes in the study area.

For the first problem—calibrating historic crop-yield response with PDSI variation—data gathered by Burns (1983) were consulted. Burns compiled historic yield values for pinto beans and maize grown by dry-farming techniques for five counties in southwestern Colorado. Only the records for Montezuma County for the period A.D. 1931–1960 were considered in our study. This 30-year period was selected because monthly precipitation and temperature data (necessary for calculating PDSI values) were available for the Cortez, Colorado, weather station starting in 1931, and because too few maize yield data were available after A.D. 1960.

Regression analysis was used to determine the relationship between crop yields and PDSI values. The best results were obtained with partial linear regression, with time also considered as an independent variable. With partial regression techniques, the contribution to crop production of the first independent variable—time—could be controlled for and the unique contribution made by the second independent variable—soil moisture—could be assessed. This approach was taken because it was thought that time might be a proxy for the cumulative influence of modern technological changes on crop yields, or what Burns (1983) referred to as the "technology trend." Although crop production in Montezuma County prior to 1960 did not involve much use of chemical fertilizers, herbicides, or pesticides, these inputs were more likely to be used later rather than earlier. In addition, tractors and other mechanized farm equipment were increasingly employed during the 30-year period of interest.

The use of partial regression was successful in increasing the correlation coefficient (r) and index of determination (r^2) for PDSI values and crop yields. The partial regression demonstrated a significant relationship between soil moisture and maize yield (r = .70; r^2 = .49; significant at .001), but it also provided the shape of the function that needed to be fitted to the model—linear and positive.

With regard to the second problem—establishing approximate yields of nonirrigated beans and maize for the numerous soil types—several approaches were used. Estimates of average bean yield for 44 of the 98 soil types in the study area were available from the Soil Conservation Service. Using linear regression, these data were related to estimates of natural plant productivity under "average" growing-season conditions for the same soil types, also available from the SCS. The regression equation then permitted extrapolation of bean yields to the remaining 54 soil types for which only the natural productivity estimates were available. Furthermore, estimates of bean yield under notably "favorable" and "unfavorable" growing-season conditions were calculated from SCS values of natural plant

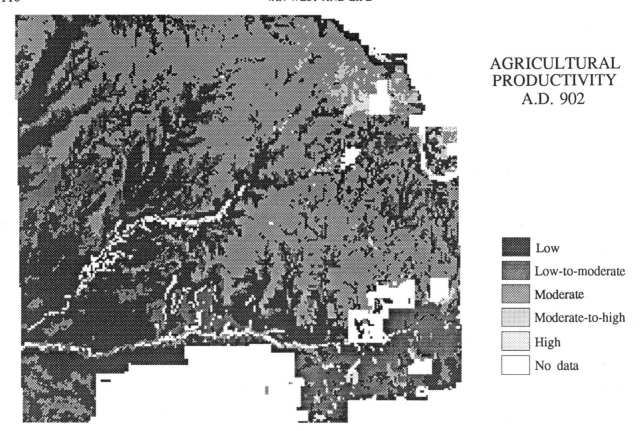

AGRICULTURAL
PRODUCTIVITY
A.D. 902

■ Low

■ Low-to-moderate

■ Moderate

▦ Moderate-to-high

□ High

□ No data

Figure 9.3. Potential agricultural productivity in the study area as reconstructed for July 1, A.D. 902.

productivity also recorded for the 98 soils in the study area. The historic data on bean and maize yield were then used to obtain a relationship between historic bean and maize yields, so that the bean yield data for various soils and moisture conditions could be used to estimate maize yields for the same soils and conditions. As a result, both soil quality and amount of stored soil moisture were taken into account when potential production of beans or maize was calculated for a given soil class in a given year.

For example, under these calibrations, a good mesa-top agricultural soil (ROB, Witt loam, 1–3 percent slopes) was estimated to produce 514 lbs/ac of beans and 1087 lbs/ac of maize, or roughly 19.4 bu/ac of maize in a favorable year, where a bushel equals 56 lbs. In metric figures, this is 576 kg/ha of beans and 1217 kg/ha of maize. In an unfavorable year, the same soil was estimated to produce 307 kg/ha of beans and 649 kg/ha of maize. This particular soil type is one of the most commonly used in dry farming today, and very likely was an important soil in prehistoric times as well.

For a poor soil, the estimated yields would be much lower. Soil type M2C (Romberg-Cragola complex) is stony, with 6 to 25 percent slopes. This soil is common in and near canyons in the study area. In a favorable year, bean production was estimated at 228 kg/ha, and maize at 483

kg/ha. In an unfavorable year, this soil was estimated to produce 72 kg/ha of beans and 152 kg/ha of maize.

Although these estimates were calibrated on the basis of historic-period crop production in southwestern Colorado, they appear to be reasonable as proxies for subsistence production by Anasazi farmers using dry-farming techniques. For example, Bradfield (1971) estimated that Hopi maize production averaged approximately 12 bu/ac (753 kg/ha) in normal years, on commonly used arable soils, in an area where both rainfall and soil quality appear consistently lower than in our southwestern Colorado study area. Bradfield (1971) also notes earlier reports that Hopi maize production averaged 10 to 12 bu/ac but reached approximately 15 bu/ac (941 kg/ha) on the best lands in the best years.

Relative agricultural productivity (e.g., low to high) for each cell was aggregated by GIS means and displayed as a map-like image (Figure 9.3) providing a visual assessment of which parts of the study area, of a locality, or of a site catchment were most and least productive in a given year. These images also permitted visual comparison of the location of productive and unproductive areas from year to year. The actual estimated yields of beans or maize were also summed by the GIS at scales ranging from a few 4-ha cells to the entire study area. Figure 9.4, for example, graphs the estimated potential annual maize production for

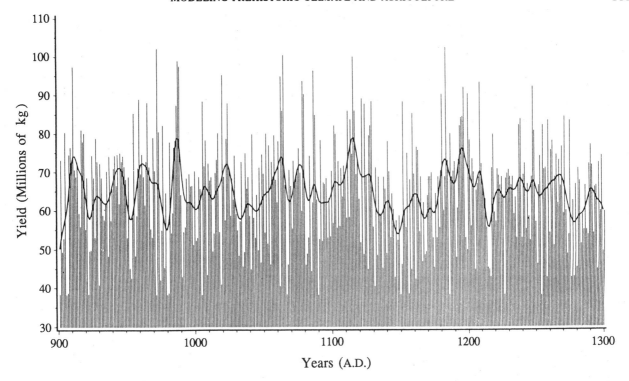

Figure 9.4. Potential maize production in the study area, A.D. 901-1300. The vertical needles represent annual maize yield. The undulating line represents a smoothed trend line (spline method) of yield values.

the study area for the period A.D. 901-1300. When these aggregated estimates were compiled, all yields that fell below a certain threshold of productivity—212 kg/ha for beans and 448 kg/ha for maize—were excluded. This is not to say that Anasazi farmers never used areas with low-yielding soils. It was felt that these areas were much less likely to be used, however, and that it was desirable to err on the side of conservatism in estimating the potential agricultural yields of the study area.

Estimation of Potential Human Population

Once an estimate of the potential annual supply of maize was obtained (excluding the contribution of the lowest-yielding cells, as noted above), a method for determining the maximum annual demand for that potential yield had to be devised. Human demand for the supply necessarily includes consideration of land use and cultivation practices, predictable postharvest crop losses, seed-retention rates, storage levels, and human consumption rates. Consequently, a number of assumptions were made so that these parameters could be modeled. These six assumptions are outlined below.

First, it was assumed that only 50 percent of the lands potentially usable for raising crops were ever cultivated in any year. This estimate was also used by Kohler et al. (1986:528) in a recent attempt to model agricultural productivity in the vicinity of the Dolores Archaeological Project, and it reflects ethnographic observations of land use by the Hopi (Forde 1931:370), San Juan Pueblo (Ford 1968:157), and maize-growing Mexican peasants (Sanders 1976:141-143).

Second, although it is not known precisely in what proportions the major prehistoric cultigens of maize, beans, and squash were grown, it seems clear from a variety of archaeological evidence that maize was the major food crop grown by Pueblo III Anasazi in the Mesa Verde region. In this study, it is assumed that 80 percent of the lands that were cultivated were devoted to maize. This value is supported ethnographically by Hack (1942), who reports that Hopi farmers of the early twentieth century devoted 72 percent of their farmland to growing maize. Williams (1989) uses an estimate of 80 percent for a sixteenth-century Aztec community, and Sanders (1976) uses the same figure in the prehistoric Basin of Mexico.

Third, not all maize harvested was available for consumption. Some would have been lost in transport, or to pests and spoilage. In this study, we followed Williams (1989) and Hassan (1981) in reducing the annual estimated gross maize yield by 10 percent to account for losses.

Fourth, of what is harvested, stored, and potentially available for consumption, a percentage must have been reserved for seed for the following year, and perhaps also for replanting in the same season or subsequent seasons if there is a crop failure. It is assumed here that 10 percent of the potential net yield was reserved for planting subsequent crops.

Fifth, although minimum daily caloric requirements vary from person to person and depend on factors such as age, gender, metabolism, and level of activity, it is assumed here that an average of 160 kg of maize was used to sustain the average person in the prehistoric populations of the study area. This value is equal to .4384 kg per day, or 1534 calories per day, where 1 kg of maize yields 3500 calories (Cook and Borah 1979:164). The estimate of 160 kg per person per year was used by Sanders (1976:145) as an aggregate statistic based on a range of ethnographic data on preindustrial maize farmers. Assumptions about average calorie needs per person per day vary but generally fall in the range of 2000 to 2500 (e.g., Schlanger 1985; Kohler et al. 1986; Hassan 1981). The estimate of 1534 calories per day from maize that is used here implies a diet based from 61 to 77 percent on maize, similar to recent estimates for Pueblo-period Anasazi (e.g., Kohler et al. 1986; Decker and Tieszen 1989).

Sixth, this study considers the possibility of storing a portion of edible harvest for one or even two years beyond the needs of the current year (cf. Burns 1983). The goal of attempting annually to grow enough maize to last two years is often cited by ethnographers as the Pueblo ideal (e.g., Hough 1915; Forde 1931; Parsons 1936; Whiting 1939; Titiev 1944; Ford 1968; Bradfield 1971). Incorporating these goals in the model results in substantially reduced estimates of potential population size and density, as compared with modeling population on the assumption that people only wished to grow enough to have one year's supply of maize on hand at the end of harvest. One way to visualize the implications of increased storage goals is to relate production goals to amount of land cultivated. If it was necessary from time to time to harvest greater amounts of maize in order to have a two- or three-year supply of maize at the end of harvest, the household would have had to control a greater amount of arable land than if planting was always designed to yield just one year's supply at harvest. Hence, maximum population density decreases as storage goals increase.

In this study, three estimates of population size were made, based on differing assumptions about storage goals and, hence, about amount of agricultural production desired. The first estimate (POP1YR) assumed that the adjusted net yield was fully consumed by the next harvest, and that long-term storage was not a goal. The second estimate (POP2YR) assumed that planting was sufficient ordinarily to produce enough maize for consumption both in the current harvest year and for one additional year. The third estimate (POP3YR) assumed a goal of obtaining enough maize for the current harvest year and for two additional years.

Even if the amount of production was not governed by explicit storage goals, it seems likely that more maize was typically grown than would have been needed to support the producers just for the current harvest year. Maize was grown not only for household consumption but to fulfill kin reciprocity and ceremonial obligations within the community, as well as for trade and exchange transactions (Kavena 1980; Bradfield 1971). In addition, the hazards faced by farmers in a semiarid environment (e.g., drought, pests, storms) may have promoted planting enough maize to provide adequate food in a bad, rather than normal, year. This strategy would ordinarily result in production beyond the needs for the year succeeding the harvest. Consequently, it seems likely that the POP2YR estimates, or even the POP3YR estimates, are likely to be more realistic than the POP1YR.

Results

The Study Area

Annual values for total maize yield for the study area were estimated (Figure 9.4). From these figures, estimates can be made of the maximum number and maximum density of people who could be supported by that yield for a population requiring one year, two years, or three years of maize in storage at the end of harvest (Figure 9.5). By definition, population size varies directly with maize production in these estimates. In some years, maximum potential yield and maximum potential population are quite high, and in some years they are much lower; this shift often happens quickly. It is clear, however, that the size of a real population could not vary from year to year in this manner. Rather, longer-term trends in productivity control the real size of a population that can be sustained in a given place. Consequently, long-term trends were derived from the 400-year series of values.

The 400-year mean value, the 400-year minimum value, and a range of values equivalent to 20 percent through 60 percent of the 400-year mean value were taken for POP1YR, POP2YR, and POP3YR to represent the maximum carrying capacity, the critical carrying capacity, and the optimal carrying capacity, respectively (Table 9.1). These data better approximate a sustainable population size than do productivity estimates from any individual year.

In this study, the concepts of maximum, critical, and optimal carrying capacity have been adapted from Hassan (1981: 166–168) to estimate sustainable population levels over extended periods of time. *Maximum carrying capacity* is a population size estimate that is equivalent to the long-term mean value of the estimated yearly maximum population for the total period of 400 years. For a POP2YR agricultural strategy, the maximum carrying capacity for the study area as a whole is 35 ± 7 persons per km^2 (Table 9.1). This value is the upper limit on population size and represents a regional population that would frequently experience yield shortfalls when annual production fell noticeably below the mean.

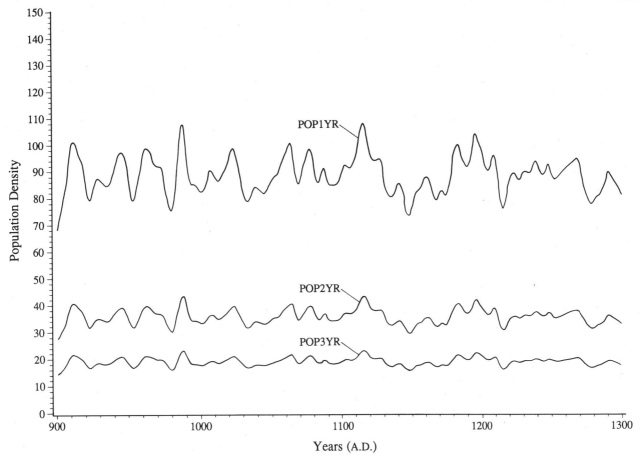

Figure 9.5. Potential population density in the study area in persons/km², A.D. 901–1300. The effects of three different levels of storage are depicted.

Critical carrying capacity is a population size estimate that is equivalent to the minimum annual population value in the 400-year period. It is a value below the maximum carrying capacity (the long-term mean) and represents the largest population that would exist throughout the entire period without experiencing significant crop shortages.

Hassan (1981) has suggested, on the basis of cross-cultural data, that groups that are able to maintain their numbers over an extended period of time usually have population sizes well below the limit of fluctuating productivity. The range of values within which such populations fall can be referred to as the *optimal carrying capacity*. Its upper limit is roughly equivalent to the critical carrying capacity. Its lower limit is not specified, but the populations studied by Hassan (1981) fell between 20 percent and 60 percent (and most commonly, between 40 and 60 percent) of the long-term mean population level that can be calculated for their sustaining area (Hassan 1981:175).

In Table 9.1, critical carrying capacity is set at the minimum population value modeled during the 400-year period from A.D. 901 to 1300. Using the POP2YR set of values, the low of 21 persons/km² occurs 15 times during this period. Values nearly as low—22 and 23 persons per km²—occur an additional 12 times. Occasionally two (but never three) of these population lows occur two years in a row (A.D. 906–907; 980–981). Other lows occur at close intervals (e.g., A.D. 901 and 906–907; A.D. 972 and 980–981; A.D. 1062 and 1067; A.D. 1146, 1150, 1156, and 1161; and A.D. 1254 and 1258). By contrast, there are a few fairly long intervals when the three lowest population values do not occur (A.D. 1020–1061; A.D. 1091–1130; A.D. 1187–1216; A.D. 1228–1253) and a number of periods of 15 or more years when the minimum population supportable was, in fact, reasonably high (Figure 9.5). Generally, however, the very low values occur once every 10 to 25 years, a time likely to be recalled by adults in the population.

The long-term minimum value, or critical carrying capacity, thus represents the long-term maximum number of people whose demands for maize could always have been met from the resources of the study area, under the assumptions about land use, consumption rate, etc., described previously. The maximum carrying capacity—the long-term mean—is theoretically the highest long-term population size that could have been sustained most, but

Table 9.1. Comparison of Population and Carrying Capacity Values for the Study Area, Sand Canyon Upland Survey Area, and Mockingbird Mesa Survey Area, A.D. 901–1300

	Study Area		Sand Canyon Upland Survey Area		Mockingbird Mesa Survey Area	
Area (km^2)	1470.36		26.08		17.96	
TOTPROD (kg)	64,925,217 $\pm$ 13,936,845		1,779,087 $\pm$ 337,524		801,336 $\pm$ 204,994	
C.V.	21.5		19.0		25.6	
	POPKM	POPNUM	POPKM	POPNUM	POPKM	POPNUM
POP1YR[a]						
Mean and S.D.	88 $\pm$ 19	131,473 $\pm$ 28,222	137 $\pm$ 26	3,602 $\pm$ 683	89 $\pm$ 23	1,622 $\pm$ 415
Range	52–141	77,439–207,382	93–198	2,437–5,174	46–142	834–2,553
POP2YR[b]						
Mean and S.D.	35 $\pm$ 7	53,246 $\pm$ 11,429	55 $\pm$ 10	1,458 $\pm$ 276	36 $\pm$ 9	656 $\pm$ 168
Range	21–57	31,363–83,989	37–80	987–2,095	18–57	337–1,034
POP3YR[c]						
Mean and S.D.	19 $\pm$ 4	28,752 $\pm$ 6,172	29 $\pm$ 5	787 $\pm$ 149	19 $\pm$ 5	354 $\pm$ 90
Range	11–30	16,936–45,354	20–43	532–1,131	10–31	182–558
Maximum value	57		80		57	
Maximum CC						
(Mean value)	35		55		36	
Critical CC						
(Minimum value)	21 (60%[d])		37 (67%[d])		18 (50%[d])	
Optimal CC						
60% of mean	21		33		22	
40% of mean	14		22		14	
20% of mean	7		11		7	

NOTE: All population values (POP1YR, POP2YR, POP3YR) and carrying capacity estimates are truncated integers.

Carrying capacity values in the lower part of the table are persons/km^2 and assume POP2YR levels of production.

CC = Carrying capacity.

C.V. = Coefficient of variation (the ratio of the standard deviation to the mean multiplied by 100 and rounded to the nearest tenth).

S.D. = Standard deviation.

TOTPROD = Total mean productivity of maize rounded to the nearest whole number.

POPKM = Number of persons per km^2.

POPNUM = Number of persons per study area or locality.

[a] ((TOTPROD $\times$ .324)/160)/area.

[b] (((TOTPROD $\times$ .324) $\times$ .81)/320)/area.

[c] (((TOTPROD $\times$ .324) $\times$ .6561)/480)/area.

[d] Percent of mean value rounded to the nearest whole number.

not all, of the time without change in the parameters of maize production and consumption. It is the least realistic of the three levels of carrying capacity, but it does provide an upper threshold for estimating aggregate population for the study area as a whole.

The population density and size values provided in Table 9.1 are high—higher than some researchers might think possible, particularly toward the end of the thirteenth century, when the Mesa Verde area was permanently abandoned by Anasazi populations. The estimates for POP1YR are probably the least realistic because we suspect that prehistoric Puebloans did attempt to store at least two years of maize at the end of harvest, in case production was low or failed the following season. Consequently, POP2YR is likely to be a better estimator of sustainable population. We suggest that the POP2YR values also represent a more likely estimate than POP3YR, since they seem to reflect the ethnographically reported attempts by historic Puebloan

farmers to buffer risk, while acknowledging that most people do what is minimally required to protect themselves against disaster.

Thus, some 21,300 to 31,360 persons, representing an optimal density of some 14 to 21 persons per km^2 for the 1470-km^2 study area, could have been supported in any given year within the A.D. 901–1300 time period. For both number and density, the lower value represents 40 percent of the long-term mean, or maximum carrying capacity, and hence falls within the optimal carrying capacity range (20 to 60 percent of the mean). The upper value also represents critical carrying capacity. The upper value for the study area is similar to the value recently suggested by Rohn (1989) for the population of the Montezuma Valley in the Pueblo III period. As he defines it, however, the Montezuma Valley is more extensive than the study area; it extends from the east slopes of the Abajo Mountains in southeastern Utah to the valley bottom drained by upper

McElmo Creek, below the northern escarpment of the Mesa Verde in southwestern Colorado. Rohn asserts that 30,000 people is a conservative estimate of the number of people who lived in the Montezuma Valley in the thirteenth century (Rohn 1989:166), an estimate derived from his knowledge of archaeological survey data in the Montezuma and Dolores county areas. Further, this estimate of 30,000 does not include the numbers of people he estimates for nearby Mesa Verde and the Mancos valley. Therefore, it would seem that the POP2YR estimates are generally in line with the only recent general estimates of Pueblo III period population for the heartland of the Mesa Verde Anasazi.

Several tentative conclusions can be drawn from this preliminary analysis of the data for the study area as a whole. First, climatically induced variation in soil moisture and its effects on agricultural production do not present a sufficient cause for the depopulation of the Mesa Verde Anasazi region in the late thirteenth century A.D. Within the parameters of the model, there was always enough productive land to support thousands of people in the study area, even during the difficult times of the middle A.D. 1100s, which coincide with the collapse of the Chacoan system, and during the so-called Great Drought of the late 1200s, which coincides with the major and final depopulation of the area. It is possible, of course, that other climatic or environmental variables, such as cooling temperatures related to the onset of the Little Ice Age (Petersen 1988; Damon 1990) or arroyo cutting in alluvial valleys (Hack 1942; Karlstrom 1988), might have operated independently or in concert with reduced soil moisture to cause or contribute to depopulation. Furthermore, crop failures due to plant disease or pests are not addressed by the model, nor is the possibility of human-induced decline in agricultural productivity due to depletion of soil fertility or erosion of cropland (e.g., Stiger 1979).

Second, the modeling effort demonstrates that the distribution of the most productive land changed somewhat from year to year, but that there were locations in the study area that were consistently productive and others that were consistently unproductive. Therefore, it may be concluded that guaranteed access to consistently productive land, or at least to the crops grown on such land, was essential as the landscape "filled up" with people (cf. Kohler 1989; Adler 1990). If mobility and access to consistently productive lands were restricted, or if redistribution systems were not in place to support populations living in less productive and reliable areas, then the potential aggregate population figures would overestimate the actual regional population that could have been supported. These issues fall as much in the sociopolitical realm of human cultural systems as in the environmental realm and force us to consider seriously the complex interactions of climatic variation, environment, and human behavioral systems (Dean 1988; Gumerman 1988).

Locality Block-Survey Areas

The agricultural productivity model was also applied to recently surveyed portions of two localities within the study area—the Sand Canyon and Mockingbird Mesa localities. Demographic reconstructions have been made for both block-survey areas; these provide a basis for comparing modeled carrying capacity with actual (or at least estimated actual) population sizes.

The upland block survey in the Sand Canyon locality, as digitized in this study, covers a 26-km^2 area surrounding two large Pueblo III sites: Sand Canyon Pueblo and Goodman Point Ruin (Figure 1.3). The survey was carried out by the Crow Canyon Archaeological Center in 1986 and 1987 (Adler, this volume; Van West et al. 1987; Adler 1988, 1990). The Mockingbird Mesa block survey, as digitized for this study, covers an area of approximately 18 km^2, coterminous with the mesa-top surface of Mockingbird Mesa (Figure 9.1). The Bureau of Land Management conducted a block survey of this area between 1981 and 1984; the work was reported by Fetterman and Honeycutt (1987).

Adler developed average momentary population estimates for several time periods in the Sand Canyon upland survey (Adler, this volume; Adler 1988, 1990). He proposed two series of estimates—one based on an assumption of a 20-year habitation-site use life and one based on an assumed 50-year use life. Using the Mockingbird Mesa survey data, Fetterman and Honeycutt (1987) estimated population on the basis of 12-year and 100-year use-life estimates for all Anasazi habitations. Schlanger (1985, 1988) also used a sample of the Mockingbird Mesa site data to make estimates of average momentary population for a number of time periods, on the assumption that habitation sites were occupied for 20 years. Although Schlanger's assumptions and methods of estimating population were not identical to those used by Adler, they were closer than those used by Fetterman and Honeycutt (1987). Consequently, Schlanger's population estimates for Mockingbird Mesa were used here, as were Adler's for the Sand Canyon upland survey area.

Table 9.1 summarizes and compares the 400-year mean maize yield and estimated potential population values for the two block survey areas with those of the study area as a whole. The POP2YR density values predicted by the productivity model for the Mockingbird Mesa survey area are nearly identical with those for the study area as a whole, but the POP2YR density values predicted for the Sand Canyon upland survey area are markedly higher. This suggests that Mockingbird Mesa is generally representative of average conditions in the study area as a whole, although it does not include the extremes of elevation and soil productivity that are found in the larger area.

It also demonstrates that there are places within the study area that are better than others insofar as productive land is concerned. The Sand Canyon upland survey area is a more productive and more predictable location in which to farm than is the area that was surveyed on Mockingbird Mesa. The higher coefficient of variation for maize yields on Mockingbird Mesa indicates there is more overall variation associated with this area than with the Sand Canyon uplands.

Table 9.1 provides the maximum, critical, and optimal carrying capacity values for the three areas expressed as persons/km^2 for a population requiring two years' maize at the end of harvest (POP2YR). At any time within the A.D. 901–1300 period, Mockingbird Mesa could have supported a population density of at least 18 persons/km^2. This minimum value, or critical carrying capacity, is equal to 50 percent of the long-term mean value of 36 persons/km^2. The critical carrying capacity value occurs 16 times over the 400-year time span, in a pattern similar to that of the study area as a whole.

By contrast, the data indicate that the Sand Canyon upland survey area could have always supported at least 37 persons/km^2 at any time during the 400-year period, a value equal to 67 percent of the long-term mean of 55 persons/km^2. This minimum, or critical carrying capacity, value occurs 29 times in the period A.D. 901–1300, nearly twice as often as the minimum value occurred in the modeled Mockingbird Mesa population. In absolute terms, the long-term critical carrying capacity of the Sand Canyon upland area is twice as high as the comparable figure for Mockingbird Mesa. This is a good indicator of the higher long-term agricultural productivity of the Sand Canyon area.

Figure 9.6 plots estimated actual momentary population densities for the Sand Canyon upland survey area for each of the archaeological time periods established by Adler (this volume; Adler 1990). Two series of estimates are given, based on assumptions of 20- and 50-year use lives for habitation sites. Varien's data (Varien et al., this volume) suggest that the shorter use life is probably the more realistic.

In Figure 9.6, the population estimates for the Sand Canyon area are overlaid on a plot of the maximum value, the long-term mean value (maximum carrying capacity), and the minimum value (critical carrying capacity) calculated for the 400-year period from the annual population density values associated with the POP2YR assumptions. Also depicted are those intervals when the minimum value (critical carrying capacity) "lifts" for a period of time from its low of 37 persons/km^2 to some greater value.

These episodes of higher minimum values were identified and plotted as follows. Using population density data for POP2YR, the minimum potential population value for a consecutive series of 10 years was recorded for each 10-year period beginning in A.D. 901. For example, the minimum potential population value for A.D. 901–910 is 37 persons/km^2. Similarly, the minimum value for each run-

ning set of 10-year periods (A.D. 902–911; 903–912; 904–913; etc.) was recorded. When the minimum level changed (e.g., from A.D. 908 to 917 the minimum value is 46 rather than 37), that new minimum value was plotted at the final year of the 10-year period (e.g., 46 was plotted at A.D. 917) and was allowed to stay at that level until a new 10-year minimum value was recorded. We chose to plot the minimum value at the end of the 10-year period, rather than at the beginning or middle, to simulate an effective 10-year memory that might have been drawn on to make decisions about current or future agricultural behavior. In this short-term view of time—a frame of reference more appropriate to a human lifetime and human recollection—this "temporary" lifting of the long-term minimum value may be perceived as normal or stable, depending on the length of time that the condition persists. If the archaeological chronology were detailed enough, it would be interesting to see if evidence of population increase, settlement of new areas, or episodes of construction were associated with periods of heightened critical carrying capacity.

An examination of Adler's average momentary population estimates based on 20-year habitation site lifespans indicates that at no time did the population of the Sand Canyon upland survey area approach the critical carrying capacity of 37 persons/km^2, despite steady population growth during the 400 years. However, the estimates based on 50-year site use lives reveal a different situation. Local population requirements for maize at the POP2YR level would have been met adequately during the earlier part of the sequence, but the minimum value of 37 persons/km^2 was exceeded at times within the final A.D. 1150–1300 period, when these estimates indicate a population density of 40 persons/km^2. This indicates that there would have been years of some shortage in meeting the demands of a population requiring two years of maize at the end of harvest if the population was as large as the 50-year use life assumption indicates. The years of shortage (i.e., years with a POP2YR potential population of less than 40 persons/km^2) in the final period are: A.D. 1150, 1156, 1176, 1185, 1191, 1215, 1227, 1254, and 1295.

It must be kept in mind that Adler's population estimates give the average number of people present in the survey area at any one time during a period. Although the pottery chronology used on survey did not allow precise placement within this period for sites with relatively small surface-sherd assemblages, it seems likely that population was lower in the late 1150s than in the 1200s. Hence, the average for the whole period may understate the actual momentary population density for the 1200s. On the other hand, as remarked above, the 50-year site use life assumption probably overstates the actual case and results in too high an estimate of population in general. Overall, however, it would appear that the Sand Canyon upland survey area was a highly productive and predictable farming location and that potentially quite large local populations could have lived well below the limits imposed by the productive environment.

Figure 9.6 also plots Schlanger's (1985) estimates of average momentary population density estimates for Mockingbird Mesa, using the assumption of a 20-year habitation-site use life. Estimates based on a 50-year span were not made. As with the Sand Canyon locality, the estimates of actual population are overlaid on a plot of the long-term mean value of potential population (the maximum carrying capacity), the maximum value, and the minimum value (critical carrying capacity), calculated for the 400-year period using POP2YR assumptions. Again, periods of elevated critical carrying capacity are depicted.

A comparison of Schlanger's population estimates for Mockingbird Mesa with the long-term estimates generated by the model reveals a different scenario than that recon-

structed for the Sand Canyon uplands. Schlanger's estimates indicate that two periods of major population growth were followed by two periods of major population decline. In both cases, in the periods of major growth—A.D. 980–1025 and A.D. 1175–1250—the population (estimated from the archaeological data to average 28.5 and 53 persons/km² for the periods, respectively) exceeded the POP2YR productive capabilities of the Mockingbird Mesa survey area. This area has a 400-year critical carrying capacity of only 18 persons/km² and a variable 10-year critical carrying capacity that was always less than 35 persons/km². The earlier period of high population density was followed by a period (A.D. 1025–1100) of very low density, whereas the later high population period (A.D. 1175–1250) was followed by a time of unknown population density (A.D. 1250–1300), during which the Mesa Verde and Four Corners regions are known to have been abandoned. These data suggest a

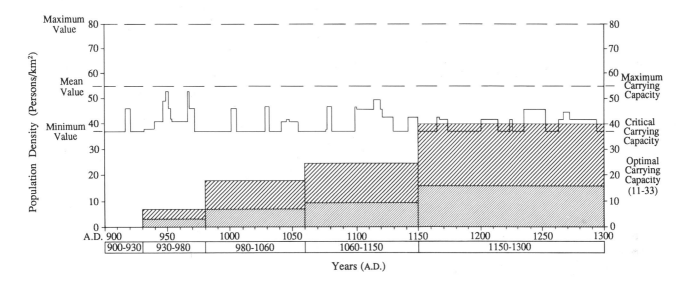

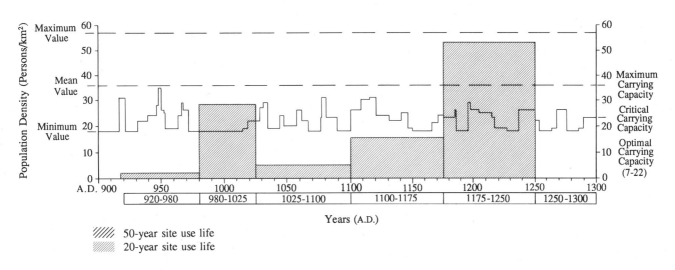

Figure 9.6. Estimates of carrying capacity for Sand Canyon upland survey area (*above*) and Mockingbird Mesa survey area (*below*).

repeated history of population overshoot and collapse when human demand exceeded agricultural supply.

In summary, comparison of modeled with estimated actual population in these two survey areas suggests two quite different histories of population in the 400 years examined. This is particularly interesting, since the areas are relatively close to each other (about 15 km apart from center to center) and both possess excellent soils with relatively high available water capacities. However, the Sand Canyon upland survey area is 124 to 385 m higher in elevation than the Mockingbird Mesa area and is not as circumscribed by canyon topography. This preliminary comparative study at the scale of small localities indicates that there are places within the study area that are more productive and predictable than others, and that even among the better locations there are some that are consistently superior.

A number of issues remain to be researched if this type of study is to be pursued further. First, pottery chronologies need to be improved, so that the survey data can be better compared with the more finely controlled environmental chronology. Second, we need sounder estimates of habitation-site use life. We hope that Varien's work with the Site Testing Program (Varien et al., this volume) will put this aspect of demographic estimation on a sounder footing. Third, survey coverage needs to be expanded around both the existing Sand Canyon upland and Mockingbird Mesa block survey areas. Both have heavy Pueblo III occupation that extends essentially to the edge of the survey block. If Pueblo III (or any other period) population density falls off rapidly outside the present survey area, the populations we have been discussing may have had a larger agricultural sustaining area available to them, and hence have had lower population density relative to this sustaining area. If, on the other hand, high density population continues outside the existing survey areas, the estimates discussed above will be supported.

Conclusions

The modeling effort described above indicates that within the study area agricultural productivity varied considerably from place to place and from year to year. It also is clear that there was always enough productive land to produce sufficient maize to support a very large population (for example, an estimated 31,360 persons at a density of 21 persons/km^2 over the 400-year period), even in the relatively dry times of the middle twelfth and late thirteenth centuries. If mobility and access to productive land were not restricted, or if redistribution systems were in place to support dispersed populations or uneven production, then the prehistoric productive environment could have always sustained many people, even during the so-called Great Drought of A.D. 1276–1299. If, however, mobility and

access to productive resources were severely restricted and extensive intercommunity food sharing was not regularly practiced, then there would have been times when the demand for maize by some populations that were confined to living in certain places might not have been met by their agricultural production. Nevertheless, it is important to emphasize that there were always locations somewhere within the study area that could produce adequate maize crops, and at no time was the "potential dry-farming belt" (Petersen 1988) completely pinched out due to fluctuations in moisture supply. In other words, rainfall and soil moisture fluctuations as they affected crop production in and of themselves cannot be used as a sole and sufficient cause for the total abandonment of the northern San Juan region at the end of the thirteenth century.

Studies at the level of individual site catchments (reported in Van West 1990, but not reviewed in this chapter) suggest that Anasazi populations were aware of the differential productivity of places on the landscape and tended to select those locations that would consistently produce good yields of maize. This may indicate that populations considered only the most arable soils as worth farming. Perhaps as their populations increased in a given area, the prehistoric Puebloan farmers of the study area were unwilling to meet their annual maize requirements by working more land of lower productive potential—that is, by lowering their cost-benefit ratio. Instead of turning to less productive soils or intensifying production on the better soils (e.g., by decreasing fallow, increasing cultivation effort, or building water and soil control features), they may have moved to places where high productivity was more predictable. This would have occasioned both local abandonments and relocations within the region and ultimately, perhaps, the abandonment of the northern San Juan region itself. The model described above can generate precise characterizations of the most productive soils for given periods. Focused survey could then determine whether prehistoric land use patterns indicate that Anasazi farmers were concentrating just on these soils or were less selective in their land use.

An alternative to the scenarios sketched above is that environmental factors other than soil quality and soil moisture were the limiting factors in sustaining a large population in the study area. Environmental resources suggested elsewhere as potentially limiting include scarcity of potable water relative to population size (Herold 1961), wood resource depletion (Kohler and Matthews 1988), soil nutrient depletion in pinyon-juniper woodland zones (Matson et al. 1988), animal protein deficiency (Speth and Scott 1985, 1989), and cooling temperatures, resulting in growing seasons that were too short for agriculture in upland locations (Petersen 1988). While possible shortages of drinking water and reduced growing seasons are linked to meteorological conditions, the other factors—shortages of wood for construction and fuel, shortages of animal protein, and depletion of soil nutrients—appear more closely linked to human overuse of the environment and poor resource management practices than to limits imposed by the natural environment as such. It is possible, of course, that several of these factors, including meteorological drought, acted together in the late thirteenth century. If so, the estimates of potential population currently generated by the model would be too high. Survey data suggest that in at least two relatively favorable localities, thirteenth-century populations were well into the zone of optimal carrying capacity. Hence lesser carrying capacities than those modeled may well have put a number of populations at risk.

Unless there was a truly large drop in temperature in the late 1200s, it would appear that environmental factors were incapable of causing a complete and rapid depopulation of the entire region, as evidently happened. That is, if populations were having problems because their numbers exceeded optimal or critical carrying capacity, then death or emigration of some portion of those populations should have enabled those remaining to adapt. There is no evidence that the high populations of the Pueblo III period resulted in irreversible soil erosion or depletion. There is abundant, uneroded soil in the area today, and it supports commercial dry-farm agriculture over large areas in the northern San Juan drainage.

Another possibility is that social or cultural factors were responsible for the ultimate abandonment of the region—either alone or in combination with environmental factors.

Comparison of the Mockingbird Mesa and upper Sand Canyon areas suggests that, in some locations, the growing populations of the thirteenth century may have "overshot" the productive capacity of their local environment. If the best alternative locations were already occupied because of regional population growth, the populations that were having difficulty would have had to join existing groups—with the possibility of conflict or difficulties of integration—or move out of the area. There is evidence that large Pueblo settlements were forming in the Rio Grande and in the Western Pueblo area during the late 1200s and early 1300s (Dickson 1979; Crown and Kohler 1990; E. C. Adams 1989; Lipe and Lekson 1990). Some of these settlements appear to be on "new lands" having little previous occupation, suggesting that land was available. In other cases, existing settlements appear to have increased substantially at this time, perhaps in part by absorbing immigrants. There are hints in architectural and community pattern changes (e.g., the increasing prominence of the central plaza and the decreasing ratio of kivas to rooms [Lipe 1989; E. C. Adams 1989]) that new forms of community integration, probably employing new or elaborated forms of religious ritual, may have characterized these growing Puebloan communities to the south. Perhaps new lands and dynamic new communities to the south provided a "pull" on northern San Juan populations that reinforced whatever "push" was being exerted by environmental or other problems in their homeland.

10

Summary and Concluding Comments

William D. Lipe

As described in Chapter 1, the long-term research goals of the Sand Canyon Project are (1) to define the community or communities that occupied the Sand Canyon locality during the period A.D. 1150-1300 and to characterize their sociocultural organization and sustaining environments; (2) to identify social, cultural, and environmental changes that took place in the Sand Canyon locality during the period A.D. 1150–1300, with a special focus on the abandonment of the locality in the late 1200s; and (3) to relate the locality's patterns of organization and change to larger patterns in the Pueblo Southwest, as well as to theoretical frameworks that promote understanding and interpretation of both locality and area-wide configurations. Some of the research (e.g., Adler, this volume; Gleichman and Gleichman, this volume) also provides data on community organization and change prior to A.D. 1150. In addition, the project includes (4) a number of instrumental studies, such as chronology building and analysis of assemblage-formation processes, that provide necessary foundations for the inferences required to address the three primary problem domains.

Chapters 2 through 9 of this monograph present brief summaries of the fieldwork and environmental modeling conducted through 1990. The tentative interpretations presented in these chapters are largely at the subproject level—e.g., results of survey and results of site testing. As noted in Chapter 1, a number of studies that utilize data from multiple subprojects and from the literature are in process or planned, and a synthesis of Sand Canyon Project results will be written in 1995. An attempt here to write a preliminary synthesis, in the sense of a systematic treatment of each research domain, is premature; the goal of this volume is to describe the research goals and structure of the Sand Canyon Project and to document progress on the basic data-gathering and environmental modeling op-

erations. Nevertheless, some brief comments on where we stand in the broader problem domains are appropriate and will serve to summarize and integrate some of the research results presented in the preceding chapters. Such comments are offered below on the primary problem domains—community organization and change in the Sand Canyon locality, as well as broader theoretical and regional perspectives on these phenomena.

Community Organization and Change in the Sand Canyon Locality A.D. 1150–1300

Research domains 1 and 2—Pueblo III community organization and organizational change—will be considered together. Because systematic survey coverage has been confined to the central part of the locality, our knowledge of community structure during the Pueblo III and preceding periods is largely confined to this surveyed area.

Adler (this volume; Adler 1990; Adler and Varien 1991) has suggested that communities can be identified by the spatial clustering of habitations in the vicinity of good springs and farmlands and by the presence of public architecture centrally located in the settlement clusters (see also Rohn 1965, 1977; Lipe 1970; Eddy 1977; and Neily 1983 for related approaches to defining communities). Communities defined in this way can be considered "first-order" or "face-to-face" communities, following Murdock (1949; Murdock and Wilson 1972). They are by definition relatively small scale, both in population size and in geographic extent. Such communities represent the maximal number of people who reside together in the sense of regular face-to-face interaction and who derive social identity from shared membership in the community.

On the basis of a cross-cultural study, Adler (1990, 1992) argues that such communities have a decision-making capability above the level of their primary economic units. Functionally, this decision-making capacity gives the community a primary role in "the definition of resource access rights for its members, and the defense of the rights or mediation of conflicts over necessary natural resources in the area within and around the community" (Adler 1992). Therefore, the community is "not just a territorial entity, but an active social theater in which claims of resource access rights are mediated above the level of the primary residential or kin groups" (Adler 1992). Cross-culturally, public architecture is often involved both in symbolically defining the social identity of the community and in providing sanctified space in or around which important integrative messages can be conveyed and disputes mediated (Adler 1989, 1990; Adler and Wilshusen 1990; Hegmon 1989a).

Three such "first-order" communities can be identified in the central portion of the Sand Canyon locality: Upper Sand Canyon, Goodman Point, and Lower Sand Canyon. Each of these communities probably included between 150 and 1000 inhabitants and underwent a certain amount of settlement pattern change through time.

Upper Sand Canyon Community

Survey data (Adler, this volume; Adler and Varien 1991) indicate that a distinct site cluster was present in the upper Sand Canyon area as early as the Pueblo II period. The testing (Varien et al., this volume) and intensive excavation programs (Huber and Lipe, this volume; Bradley, this volume) of the Sand Canyon Project have been focused in this area, so this community cluster is better known than the other two. A great kiva occurs in this settlement cluster, and surface pottery indicate it may have been built in the A.D. 1000s.

In the late Pueblo II period (late A.D. 1000s and early 1100s), the Casa Negra site—a probable Chacoan-style architectural complex with a small great house—probably served as the center of the Upper Sand Canyon community. Casa Negra is not large enough to have been a major habitation itself. The bulk of the community's members appear to have continued to live in small hamlets dispersed in the uplands around the head of Sand Canyon. The unexcavated great kiva referred to above is located several hundred meters from the Casa Negra great house. Although it may have been constructed before the great house itself, it may have continued in use after the great house was built.

The character of community organization between approximately A.D. 1150 and 1200 is problematical; few sites that clearly date to this period have been encountered in survey or testing. This may be the result of problems in recognition of ceramic styles characteristic of this interval or, possibly, of frequent later reoccupation of these sites,

so that they are difficult to recognize from surface evidence. It is also possible, however, that the Upper Sand Canyon area saw a decrease in population at this time.

Although it is clear that a number of small hamlets were occupied in the uplands surrounding the head of Sand Canyon in the early A.D. 1200s (Varien et al., this volume), it is not clear that a community center (defined by the presence of public architecture) was present in this area at that time. It is possible that a distinct first-order community existed here but had no archaeologically visible integrative center; or that the Casa Negra complex continued to be used during this period; or that the Upper Sand Canyon settlement cluster was part of a larger community cluster that was centered elsewhere—perhaps at Goodman Point Pueblo. It does appear that in the early A.D. 1200s, the average number of rooms in habitation sites in the upper Sand Canyon area increased.

Sand Canyon Pueblo was built about A.D. 1250 and served as a residential and integrative center for the Upper Sand Canyon community until the abandonment of the site, community cluster, and locality, probably in the A.D. 1280s. At its peak, Sand Canyon Pueblo appears to have had a residential population numbering in the several hundreds. It also had a variety of examples of public architecture (Bradley, this volume). A number of small habitations that are located within the Upper Sand Canyon site cluster appear to be at least in part contemporaneous with Sand Canyon Pueblo (Varien et al., this volume; Huber and Lipe, this volume; Hegmon 1991). The majority of the Upper Sand Canyon community's population probably lived at Sand Canyon Pueblo, however, and the proportion of the community population that lived there probably increased during this site's occupation.

The middle and late A.D. 1200s also witnessed the shift of most Upper Sand Canyon habitations from the uplands near the canyon to the canyon itself. Sand Canyon Pueblo is built on and just under the canyon rim at the head of a small side canyon of upper Sand Canyon. The site also encloses a spring. The smaller sites occupied in the mid- and late 1200s are located on benches or talus tops within the main canyon further downstream. Testing at several of these sites has provided evidence of light use during the Pueblo II and/or early Pueblo III periods, but they probably were not habitations at that time (Varien et al., this volume; Huber and Lipe, this volume).

Reconnaissance in areas west of Sand Canyon Pueblo indicates that scattered small cliff dwellings and open sites that date to the Pueblo III period also occur in canyon settings. It is not clear whether these should be considered part of the Upper Sand Canyon community cluster or part of a separate cluster. The former alternative implies a larger community, in spatial extent and population size, than we have inferred to date. To the extent that these western sites postdate A.D. 1250 (and some appear to), it would also change the ratio of population residing in Sand Canyon

Pueblo relative to that in the dispersed small sites. Additional systematic survey, with attention to precise site dating, is needed in the area west of Sand Canyon Pueblo.

Goodman Point Community

The Goodman Point community cluster appears to be well established by about A.D. 1000 and to undergo gradual growth in population and size of individual habitations during the Pueblo II and III periods. The degree of spatial clustering of habitation sites also increases (Adler, this volume; Adler 1990). The Goodman Point Ruin proper appears to have been built primarily in the 1200s, though it is not well dated. The styles present in surface pottery indicate that a number of the habitation sites outside the main Goodman Point Ruin were occupied in the 1200s. The present evidence does not permit a firm judgment as to whether occupation at these sites ended in the early, middle, or late 1200s.

Earlier excavations at several small habitations in the Goodman Point cluster have yielded tree-ring dates. Work by Colorado Mountain College at 5MT3807, located just north of the Goodman Point Unit of the National Park Service, yielded two cutting dates in the early 1100s and one in the early 1200s (Adler 1990:261). The context of these samples is poorly known, however. A burned kiva at the Mustoe Site, a unit-type pueblo located just southwest of the Goodman Point Unit boundary, yielded two clusters of tree-ring dates, one at A.D. 1173–1175 and the other at A.D. 1229–1231 (Gould 1982:373–374). Gould (1982:345–348) interpreted this evidence as indicating construction in the late A.D. 1100s, with remodeling in the early 1230s. The site appears to have been abandoned soon after burning of the kiva (Gould 1982:350–351). These findings indicate that occupation continued in the Goodman Point community cluster until at least the A.D. 1230s. Later occupation at some of the other sites in the cluster cannot be ruled out on the basis of present evidence, and it seems likely that at least some continued into the middle or late 1200s. Both the upper Sand Canyon and Goodman Point site clusters undergo similar settlement shifts from dispersed mesa-top sites to a large site built around a spring near the head of a canyon. This suggests that the occupation chronologies of the two areas are likely to be similar.

Integrative architecture is concentrated in and around the current Goodman Point Unit of the National Park Service (Figure 1.3). Site 5MT3807, which is located on private land just north of the Park Service unit boundary, appears to have been a large site-complex that may have included a possible great house structure and a great kiva (Adler 1990). A road segment that extends from near the Casa Negra site above the head of Sand Canyon appears to have terminated at 5MT3807. Unfortunately, this large site-complex has been largely destroyed by agricultural activities and by excavation for artifacts.

The area within the National Park Service unit includes a possible Pueblo II or early Pueblo III great kiva, as well as the Pueblo III features associated with Goodman Point Ruin. Public architecture here consists of a great kiva, an enigmatic above-ground circular structure associated with it, a site-enclosing wall, and several possible informal plazas. The precise date at which this large (80–90 kivas, 300+ rooms) site formed is not clear, but the bulk of evidence suggests occupation in the A.D. 1200s; contemporaneity with Sand Canyon Pueblo cannot be ruled out. Surface pottery, though sparse, indicate that there might also have been occupation at this location in the late 1100s. It is certainly possible that the predominantly thirteenth-century architecture at the site incorporates or has covered up a smaller number of structures that date to the twelfth or even the late eleventh centuries. More precise dating of Goodman Point Ruin and of the small sites in its community cluster would add greatly to our understanding of organization and change in this community and of its relationships to the Upper Sand Canyon community.

Lower Sand Canyon Community

The Lower Sand Canyon settlement cluster consists of a number of small Pueblo III sites in lower Sand and East Rock canyons and adjacent portions of McElmo Canyon (Gleichman and Gleichman, this volume; Adler and Metcalf 1991). These include cliff dwellings as well as open sites. Because only a small amount of systematic survey has been done in McElmo Canyon proper, it is not clear how far the Lower Sand Canyon cluster extends east and west along McElmo Creek and whether it has well-defined boundaries in that area. Pueblo II sites occur in the McElmo valley within 2 km upstream from the mouth of Sand Canyon (Wayne Howell, personal communication), outside the area surveyed by the Gleichmans (this volume) and Adler and Metcalf (1991). At this time, the earliest definite community cluster of habitation sites that we can recognize in the lower Sand Canyon area dates to the Pueblo III period.

In addition to the small Pueblo III sites that have been noted, there is a medium-size central site—Castle Rock Pueblo (Kuckelman et al. 1991). Located in McElmo Canyon at the mouth of Sand Canyon, Castle Rock Pueblo is by far the largest site in this cluster, with 10 to 15 kivas and 50 to 75 surface rooms (Kuckelman et al. 1991). Castle Rock Pueblo has several elements of public architecture and qualifies as a community integrative center under Adler's definition (Adler, this volume; Adler 1990). Tree-ring dates and architectural styles indicate an occupation in the late A.D. 1200s and show that it was contemporaneous with Sand Canyon Pueblo's occupation. The possibility that the occupation of Castle Rock Pueblo began before A.D. 1250 cannot be ruled out on the basis of present evidence. Tree-ring and ceramic-style evidence (Varien et al., this volume; Hegmon 1991) suggest that several of the small sites in this cluster may also have had occupations postdating A.D. 1250.

Dimensions of Organizational Variation

Scale

The three tentatively defined first-order communities described above appear to have had populations in the order of a few hundred people and a geographic extent in the order of 10–15 km². In the late 1200s, when Sand Canyon Pueblo and several outlying small settlements were occupied contemporaneously, the population of the Upper Sand Canyon community may well have exceeded 500 people. The Lower Sand Canyon community appears to have been smaller at that time in both population and area, although its full geographic extent has probably not been included in surveys to date. The issue of boundary definition, of course, has a large bearing on estimates of both population size and geographic extent. All of the three community clusters proposed for the central Sand Canyon locality may in fact extend outside the boundaries of the area surveyed.

If we take large sites with public architecture (see Varien et al. 1990, 1991) as marking the centers of first-order Pueblo III communities in southwestern Colorado and assume that community boundaries conform roughly to the Thiessen polygons drawn between adjacent centers, then we must conclude that the geographic extent, and almost certainly the populations, of such communities were larger than indicated above. Adler (1992), working with data on large sites and public architecture assembled by Varien et al. (1990, 1991) for the central portion of the northern San Juan region, used this type of approach to defining community scale. From his research, he inferred that in the late Pueblo II period (A.D. 1000–1125), most community territories in the core area ranged from 40 km² to somewhat over 150 km² (Adler 1992). He also estimated that by late in this period, the demographic scale of these communities ranged between 150 and 300 people (Adler 1992). During the Pueblo III period (A.D. 1125–1300), the geographic scale of communities probably stayed approximately the same, but population increased somewhat, with the size of most communities probably falling between 200 and 600 people (Adler 1992). Adler's population estimates are based on partial survey data. It may well be that full survey of the areas around and between community centers would increase these population estimates.

Additional research on the issue of community size in the Sand Canyon Project should include expansion of the intensive survey, application of Hegmon's newly refined ceramic chronology (Hegmon 1991) to surface collections from surveyed sites, and refinements in our estimates of momentary population sizes for habitation sites. Recent work by Lightfoot (1992), for example, suggests that population estimates based on room count may often be too high and that estimates based on floor area may be more accurate for Pueblo habitation sites in the Mesa Verde area.

As noted in Chapter 1, there is another aspect of scale—the size of the catchment, or the area from which material items were imported. From our excavations in Pueblo III sites so far, very few items can be identified as having come from outside the northern San Juan region—or from outside the Sand Canyon locality, for that matter. The relative similarity of ceramic technology throughout the northern San Juan region in the Pueblo III period could mask imports from other localities within this region. Nonlocal lithic materials are present in the collections, but most are not of types known to occur at substantial distances from the locality. Obsidian, which must come from outside the northern San Juan area, is extremely rare. Likewise, other exotic items such as shell or turquoise very seldom occur and appear to be even less common in Pueblo III contexts than in sites dating to earlier periods in this general area. For example, the 1991 excavations at two sites that appear to have substantial occupations in the A.D. 1100s— the G and G and Kenzie Dawn sites—indicate that ornaments and items of imported materials are relatively more common there than at sites dating to the A.D. 1200s (Mark Varien, personal communication).

Differentiation

Differentiation as part of the definition of social complexity needs to be distinguished from other kinds of complicatedness. A hunter-gatherer band may have a very complicated subsistence economy, settlement pattern, and archaeological expression. But it is not a socially complex entity. In reference to social systems, *horizontal* differentiation is the "functional specialization among parts of equal rank," while *vertical* differentiation refers to "rank differences among functionally diverse parts" (Blanton et al. 1981:21; see also Plog 1974 and Blau 1975). Vertical differentiation implies inequality of access to economic, ideological, or military sources of power (Mann 1986).

By partitioning social space, architecture provides some reflection of the nature of the social order (Hegmon 1989a; Rapoport 1982). Because buildings embody varying investments of time and energy and are long lasting and visible, they may also be used to communicate messages about differential power, wealth, or sanctity (Wilson 1988). As with other symbolic media, they may of course also be used to hide or obscure social differences. Nevertheless, the analysis of architectural forms and their arrangement in settlements is a useful starting point in the study of social differentiation. Evidence and inferences from architecture can then be compared with evidence and inferences from other sources of data, such as artifacts, food remains, and regional level locational analysis.

As Prudden recognized long ago (Prudden 1903), the basic Anasazi residential facility in the San Juan drainage is the *unit-type pueblo,* consisting of a kiva and a few (generally fewer than 12) associated surface rooms. This pattern forms in the Pueblo I period and lasts through Pueblo III, but does not transfer to the large settlements that occur in the Rio Grande and Western Pueblo areas after the abandonment of the San Juan (Lipe 1989; E. C. Adams 1989). Most if not all of these Pueblo I–III unit-type pueblos, or "kiva units," probably represent the facilities used by a household or set of closely allied households, organized around an extended family (Lipe 1989; Lightfoot 1992). As Prudden (1903, 1914, 1918) noted, these kiva units often occur singly and thus constitute a settlement, or they may be joined in roomblocks of varying size. In turn, the individual kiva units and blocks of such units may occur in clusters of varying tightness, ranging from "site clusters" to a maximally aggregated state, as large pueblos.

Formation of large aggregates of kiva units is especially pronounced in the late Pueblo I and mid- to late Pueblo III periods. Adler (1990) argues that in large Pueblo III sites such as Goodman Point Ruin and Sand Canyon Pueblo, the roomblocks are clusters of domestic kiva units that are probably equivalent to the site clusters of the earlier, more dispersed community pattern.

The question arises as to whether all kiva units are functionally and socially equivalent. On the functional side, Wilshusen (1989) has argued that not all Pueblo I–III kivas were domestic structures, but that some were more specialized for ritual and were probably used by larger groups. He calls these "community kivas" (not to be confused with great kivas). It is only these more specialized kivas that are functionally comparable to Pueblo IV and historic Western Pueblo kivas. Consequently, we might expect that in the large Pueblo III sites, the majority of kiva units would be domestic, but that some kivas might have a more specialized function and be used by groups such as medicine or dance societies that drew membership from a number of localized kin groups (Ferguson 1989).

For Sand Canyon Pueblo, Bradley (this volume; Bradley 1991b) has used a preliminary analysis of room-to-kiva ratios, amounts of construction labor, and degree of spatial integration of the structures within excavated kiva units to argue that several of the units excavated so far (those in the 100 and 200 blocks) are likely to have had specialized nondomestic functions. Excavated kiva units in the 500, 1000, and 1200 blocks appear to be domestic, whereas the rooms and kiva excavated in the 300 block may have been domestic or part of a suprahousehold storage area. Bradley thus provides evidence for architectural differentiation at the level of the kiva unit. If his interpretation is correct, the "specialized" kiva units may document the presence of sodalities such as dance or medicine societies that may have promoted integration among kin and residence groups. However, they would not necessarily document the presence of functional differentiation among basic social segments.

Preliminary analysis of pollen and botanical remains from the excavated units provides only partial support for these architecturally based distinctions (K. Adams, personal communication 1991). Analysis of faunal remains (Walker 1990a; Brand 1991) reveals variation among the kiva units tested so far at Sand Canyon Pueblo, but interpretation of these data awaits the results of ongoing studies of faunal assemblage-formation processes at this site. The architectural model of kiva-unit function at Sand Canyon Pueblo is also being tested by comparing stone and bone tool assemblages from both midden and floor contexts of several kiva units (Turner 1991). Another ongoing study (Chao 1991) is comparing ceramic vessel sizes and styles at several kiva-unit middens to determine if there is more evidence of feasts or other socially diverse gatherings (cf. Blinman 1989; Hegmon 1989b; Plog 1989) at the architecturally "nondomestic" units.

The possibility of vertical social differentiation at Sand Canyon Pueblo has received less attention. In general, the occupants of this site appear to have been rather relentlessly egalitarian, at least in terms of foregoing the wearing of durable ornaments and the possession of exotic artifacts of either local or nonlocal manufacture. The previously discussed variation in kiva-unit architecture analyzed by Bradley (this volume; Bradley 1991b) could mark status differences, but the more architecturally specialized complexes are smaller than the domestic ones, which does not seem to be consistent with the tendency for high-status leaders to have larger households (Lightfoot 1984). It is possible that the smaller, more specialized kiva units in fact represent small households or ones in an early stage of the domestic cycle. In any case, the overall similarity in the size and architectural characteristics of the kiva units that have been excavated so far does not appear to indicate vertical social differentiation among these basic "building blocks" of the settlement. There are what appear to be several very large kivas downslope from the D-shaped structure in the western portion of the site. It is possible that these represent larger and more elaborate households, or that they are examples of the nondomestic "community kivas" postulated by Wilshusen (1989) and implied by Bradley's analysis of the variation among the excavated kiva units. The possibility that the D-shaped structure itself was a residence is also briefly discussed below.

At Sand Canyon Pueblo, there is clear architectural differentiation between the kiva units discussed above and the elements of *public architecture* found at the site. This term refers to nonresidential structures thought to have played a role in the social and ceremonial integration of the community (Flannery and Marcus 1976; Bradley and Lipe 1990). At Sand Canyon Pueblo, these structures include a great kiva, an informally bounded plaza, a D-shaped biwalled structure, and a masonry wall that encloses the site. In addition, the 300 block may at least initially have been a suprahousehold storage facility, perhaps one that served the entire community. The interpretation of this complex remains somewhat unclear. Architectural evidence (Bradley, this volume; Bradley 1986) suggests it may have grown by accretion, a pattern perhaps not entirely expectable if it was built as a centrally controlled storage facility.

The plaza, great kiva, D-shaped structure, and possible storage complex all cluster in the western portion of the site, perhaps defining a "civic" or "ceremonial" area differentiated from the residential portions of the site. Bradley (this volume) also suggests that the possibly "specialized" kiva complexes also occur primarily in the western portion of the site.

In the summer of 1991, test excavations were carried out in and around the great kiva that is located in the western part of the site. The kiva was found to be partially surrounded by rooms (Bradley, this volume; Bradley 1991a). Excavations to date suggest that these rooms are more likely to have been used for storage rather than habitation. If so, this would be an example of a substantial storage complex not clearly associated with a household-level residential complex.

Construction and control of these "public" facilities implies some degree of community-level decision making and authority, but probably not beyond the kind found in many egalitarian, nonranked, "tribal" societies (Adler 1989, 1992; Kosse 1992). Conceivably, this interpretation could be challenged by the results of future excavations in the D-shaped structure. Test excavations in 1991 (Bradley 1991a) revealed that the outer portion of the D probably stood considerably higher than the ordinary surface structures at the site and consisted of probable storerooms. A wall divides the interior of the D into two courtyard areas, each of which contains a burned kiva. If these kivas show evidence of domestic use, and if domestic midden deposits are found with this structure, this complex could be interpreted as an unusual form of dwelling, clearly differentiated in size and form from the ordinary kiva units at the site. By implication, this architecture would mark the residents of the complex as different from the ordinary residents of the site as well. Additional sample excavations in and around the D-shaped structure are planned for the summer of 1992 and may clarify its function and use history.

The presence of a possible centralized storage complex (the 300 block) and the possible storage rooms associated with the great kiva may also indicate a level of centralized economic control beyond that found in many egalitarian societies. Although the kivas excavated in the 100 and 200 blocks had fewer than the usual number of surface rooms, the units studied in the 500, 1000, and 1200 blocks

appeared to have as many surface storage rooms as most Pueblo II and III kiva units. This implies that even if there was some type of centralized storage facility at the site, the extended family-based residence units had their own storage facilities as well. Further analysis of the materials from the 300 block and the great kiva, and perhaps further excavations in these areas, will be needed to better examine the possibility that suprahousehold centralized storage facilities existed at the site.

Castle Rock Pueblo, which was tested in 1990 and 1991 (Kuckelman et al. 1991) has 12–15 kivas and perhaps 75 surface rooms and appears to be contemporaneous, at least in part, with Sand Canyon Pueblo. Like the latter site, it has elements of public architecture that may define a "civic" space differentiated from the primarily residential areas. These include an informal plaza, a large D-shaped enclosure that was walled with rough stones but probably never roofed, and several low walls and boulder alignments that connect structures or partially enclose spaces. Most of these elements are clustered on the north side of the rock outcrop around which the site is built.

Another potential dimension of differentiation is between the large aggregated pueblos, such as Sand Canyon and Castle Rock, and the small sites that have been tested or partially excavated, such as Lillian's, Shorlene's, and Green Lizard. A number of these are slightly earlier than Sand Canyon and Castle Rock pueblos, but several—Green Lizard, Lester's, Lookout House, Troy's Tower, Saddlehorn, and Mad Dog Tower—appear to be at least partially contemporary with the late aggregated pueblos (Hegmon 1991; Varien et al., this volume). All the small tested sites show good evidence of having been year-round habitations in the Pueblo III period, except for the two tower-kiva complexes—Troy's Tower and Mad Dog Tower (Varien et al., this volume). These may have had only seasonal occupation or another function that is as yet not understood.

The smaller habitation sites differ from the large aggregates in size, of course, but also in their lack of recognizable public architecture. They consist of one or a few kiva units, which resemble the kiva units found at the larger sites. Architecturally, there may be a tendency for structures at the smaller sites to have a lower level of labor investment and architectural formality (Huber 1991; Varien et al., this volume), and the small, late talus-top sites have a lower ratio of rooms to kivas (Varien et al., this volume) than is found at many of the large aggregates.

Studies of artifact and ecofact assemblages have concentrated on basic identifications and site-by-site data compilations. The studies are standardized, however, to facilitate intersite comparisons. Preliminary comparisons of artifacts and ecofacts from the large and small sites show that the assemblages are broadly similar. Sand Canyon Pueblo has a somewhat higher frequency of artiodactyl remains than do the set of small sites that were involved in a comparison made by Brand (1991). Since the small sites compared were somewhat earlier, this may be a case of the shift toward dependence on larger animals contingent on settlement aggregation noted by Speth and Scott (1989, cited in Brand 1991). Fuller and more intensive comparative studies of architecture, artifacts, and ecofacts may reveal aspects of functional or even vertical differentiation that are not yet apparent.

Integration

Integration refers to the degree of interdependence of structural units in a society and to the manner in which the interdependence is accomplished. As noted in Chapter 1, integration can be accomplished through common ideology and cultural norms, reinforced by ritual; through regular flows of information, material, energy, or people among units, making them interdependent; through organizations such as sodalities that crosscut local social segments; through organizational devices that extend consensual decision making beyond the small-group level; or through formal, centralized, managerial control. Below, we briefly consider the evidence for integration at the intracommunity and intercommunity levels in the Sand Canyon locality in the context of the central Mesa Verde area.

At the intracommunity level, we have argued (Lipe 1989; Lipe and Hegmon 1989) that ordinary small Pueblo III Mesa Verde kivas probably functioned in rituals and other activities that helped integrate very small groups, such as extended family households. These structures probably were also used in domestic activities, in addition to possessing features of religious symbolism and being the locus of household-level rituals. By providing such small social segments with control of powerful religious symbols, this pattern may have actually worked against strong community-level integration (Lipe 1989). The arguments for and against the presence of some nonresidential kivas at Sand Canyon Pueblo have been reviewed above (see also Bradley, this volume, and Bradley 1991b).

Researchers on the Dolores Project (Kane 1988, 1989; Kane and Robinson 1988; Wilshusen 1989) found Pueblo I period "oversized" protokivas that may have been used in rituals or other activities that helped integrate groups above the household level. Following Western Pueblo ethnographic analogy (Ferguson 1989), such structures may have been used by religious sodalities that drew membership from across the community. An alternative interpretation is that these large structures were part of the household architecture of powerful, high-status localized kin groups that had both political and religious power or influence in the community. Artifactual and other architectural data provided little support, however, for the presence of vertical differentiation at the Dolores communities where these structures occurred (Orcutt et al. 1990). Patterns of ceramic discard associated with these structures suggested to Blinman (1989) that they had been involved

in suprahousehold level feasting, perhaps of a "potluck" sort associated with gatherings for ceremonies. This interpretation is not inconsistent with control of the oversized protokivas by either large localized kin groups or sodalities.

The research on Pueblo I period integrative structures from the Dolores Project leads us to expect that similar structures involved in suprahousehold integration might be found in later Mesa Verde Anasazi settlements. This may be an error; patterns of integration, or at least their architectural expressions, may have been somewhat different in the communities of the two periods. To date, no "oversized" Pueblo III kivas have been excavated as part of the Sand Canyon Archaeological Project, and they appear to be rare, if present at all, in sites of this period elsewhere in the Mesa Verde region. As noted above, however, there is surface evidence of several large kivas in the central western portion of Sand Canyon Pueblo, but their size has not been confirmed by testing.

At the community level, Adler (this volume; Adler 1990, 1992; Adler and Varien 1991) uses settlement clustering and the presence of centralized public architecture as indicators of first-order, or face-to-face, communities (Murdock 1949). The public architecture seems likely to have been involved in some way with religious rituals that contributed to community integration. Certainly, individuals or groups must have organized and controlled these rituals, and political decisions that affected whole communities must have been made. This does not mean, however, that ritual and political power was necessarily centralized or that a permanent political hierarchy was in place. Small-scale, nonranked societies can organize and carry out fairly complex collective activities on the basis of consensual decision making through a process Johnson (1982) has called "sequential hierarchy," whereby representatives of lower-order social segments can form a higher-order consensual decision-making body. Religious rituals can support and promote this process by reinforcing community identity and values and by providing a sanctified context for group decision making and dispute resolution.

On the basis of a cross-cultural survey, Kosse (1992) argues that some type of centralized and institutionalized political control is almost always present in polities of 3000 or more members, but that it is increasingly less likely to occur with decreasing group size. The community sizes inferred by Adler (1992) indicate a low probability for centralized political institutions in the Pueblo III communities of the Sand Canyon locality and the core Mesa Verde area.

This argument for lack of large-scale sociopolitical integration would be weakened, however, if it could be shown that several first-order communities (e.g., Goodman Point, Upper Sand Canyon, and Lower Sand Canyon) were linked to form a higher-order social unit. The existence of a road extending from the area of Casa Negra, in the Upper Sand Canyon cluster, to the area of site 5MT3807, in the

Goodman Point cluster, suggests that at some point in the late Pueblo II or Pueblo III periods there was some type of integration of these two first-order communities. At present, the chronology of construction and use of this road segment is not understood, nor is its function.

For the late Pueblo III period, we have little or no evidence for or against the idea of intercommunity integration in the central Sand Canyon locality. If warfare was endemic, it should have promoted the formation of alliances or mergers among communities and have made it more difficult for relatively small communities such as Lower Sand Canyon to remain independent adjacent to a larger community such as Upper Sand Canyon. There is possible evidence of violence against some individuals at the end of the occupation of Sand Canyon Pueblo (Annie Katzenberg, personal communication 1991). However, we lack evidence of whether warfare was widespread in the 1200s or whether it was more common at this time than in earlier times, when settlement was largely dispersed. Haas and Creamer (1990) have proposed that there was increased Anasazi warfare in the late A.D. 1200s, based on evidence from the Kayenta area.

The aggregation that occurred in the 1200s may have been a response to warfare, but to use this as evidence of warfare would simply be circular reasoning. In the Mesa Verde area, the location of sites in defensible positions does appear to be more frequent in the Pueblo III period than in Pueblo II, but whether this can be taken as evidence of an increase in warfare is debatable.

A study of settlement patterns and site-size hierarchies on the regional level might help determine whether or not first-order communities formed the highest level of maintained sociopolitical integration. If each major site is associated with several medium-size and a number of small sites, and if these distributions do not appear merely to map differences in abundance of arable land or other resources, a case could begin to be made that some type of supracommunity organization was present. This supposition would be strengthened if certain types of public architecture were present only at the top-ranked settlements. The argument would gain strength if other lines of evidence indicated the presence of some degree of vertical differentiation, as discussed above.

Although we are unable to evaluate the possibility that supracommunity social organization existed in the Sand Canyon locality or central Mesa Verde area, it does appear that there was a high degree of cultural similarity throughout this area. Pottery and architectural styles are quite similar over the central Mesa Verde area, from Montezuma Canyon in southeastern Utah to the Mesa Verde proper. West of Montezuma Canyon, pottery styles are still clearly Mesa Verdean but differ in detail from those in the core area, whereas architectural forms appear more variable. These are subjective impressions and are not based on systematic comparative studies. The degree of similarity does suggest that material culture technology and symbolic systems expressed in material culture were shared by a large number of communities and that intercommunication was frequent enough so that changes were more or less synchronous over the area. These similarities imply that a cultural basis for interaction among individuals and communities probably existed. It does not imply, however, that a supracommunity level of social organization must have existed, or that relationships among communities in this area were always harmonious.

Intermarriage and exchange of goods among individuals and social segments from different communities may establish a number of linkages between communities, even in the absence of more formal political links. As noted above, common cultural patterns in the area may have facilitated the former type of relationships. Neily (1983) surveyed portions of the Hovenweep-Cross Canyon area on the Colorado-Utah border to investigate intercommunity exchange relationships. He found that lithic and ceramic assemblages from neighboring site clusters became somewhat more differentiated during the Pueblo III period. This suggested to him that intercommunity exchange networks were contracting in the Pueblo III period. In turn, this would imply a decrease in the level of informal, interaction-based integration among first-order communities in the central Mesa Verde area during the Pueblo III period.

Intensity

Intensity refers to the amounts of population, material, information, or energy use per unit area or per capita. The per-unit-area formulations of subsistence intensity have been employed in numerous theories of sociocultural evolution (e.g., Earle 1980; Johnson and Earle 1987). The per capita approach can be used to characterize "standard of living." It has been used extensively to document the unequal access to resources characteristic of vertical differentiation (e.g., Johnson 1989) but has had less use in the comparisons of whole communities or societies. Economists, of course, often compare money-based economies in terms of per capita income, consumption, savings rates, etc.

Many studies would be relevant to this topic, but only two have been done to date: Adler's (this volume; Adler 1990) reconstruction of population size and density for the central Sand Canyon locality and Van West's study of potential agricultural productivity in the central Mesa Verde region (Van West and Lipe, this volume; Van West 1990, 1992).

Adler's population reconstruction indicates substantial and apparently fairly steady population growth in the central Sand Canyon locality from the early 1000s through the 1200s. Therefore, by definition, humans were extracting more resources from a given unit of area in the Pueblo III period than in early Pueblo II. If the supply of arable land and of wild plant and animal resources remained more or less constant, the supply and demand relationships must have changed.

Van West's study (Van West and Lipe, this volume; Van West 1990) indicates that climatic fluctuations affected the amounts of arable land in the area, but that overall there was sufficient productive land to accommodate the growing population documented by Adler and others. Use of the overall study area figure as an estimate for the area's carrying capacity of course assumes that the population had unlimited residential mobility or distribution systems that could be used to even out spatial and temporal fluctuations in production within the area. A comparison of archaeologically estimated population in the Sand Canyon and Mockingbird Mesa localities indicated that there were times in which the occupants of the latter area might have suffered production shortfalls if they did not have access to additional lands or to distribution systems (Van West and Lipe, this volume; Van West 1992). Under these circumstances, we might expect some changes in resource use or in economic organization as populations adapted to changes in resource supply and demand that were driven both by population growth and by climatic fluctuations. As resource use per unit area increased, anthropogenic changes in vegetation, game populations, and soil quality may also have occurred.

Agricultural terraces, checkdams, and other indicators of intensified land use are not common in the survey portion of the Sand Canyon locality, but such examples as occur appear to date from the late Pueblo II and Pueblo III periods (see Rohn 1963 for evidence of intensified soil and water control at this time on Chapin Mesa). Haase (1985) notes the relatively frequent occurrence of reservoirs in association with large Pueblo III settlement clusters; these may be evidence of intensified management of domestic water as populations increased.

The studies of floral and faunal remains currently being undertaken by Karen Adams and associates (see Chapter 8) are designed to detect changes in biological resource use that may be a response to increased demand attendant on population growth—e.g., shifts to less desirable but more abundant plant or animal species (cf. Kohler and Matthews 1988) or increases in long-distance resource procurement. Comparison of the incidence of turkey bones in Pueblo I period contexts in the nearby Dolores valley (Neusius 1986) with occurrences in late Pueblo III contexts in the Sand Canyon locality (Walker 1990a; Brand 1991) indicates a substantial increase through time that may reflect substitution of domesticated turkey for local wild game. This may have been a strategy for extracting more animal protein from a given size area than would be possible if only wild game were relied upon; it could also have helped maintain per capita consumption of animal protein as population grew. The tentative evidence for increased artiodactyl procurement at Sand Canyon Pueblo (Brand 1991) may

reflect the organization of long-distance hunting parties as the area surrounding the aggregated settlement became depleted of larger game (cf. Speth and Scott 1989).

Current and projected "rate-of-accumulation" studies by Varien show considerable promise in the area of calibrating per capita intensities. If certain per capita or per household constants can be established-e.g., discard of cooking pot sherds per household per year—then discard rates for other resource residues and for various types of material culture can be compared in relation to this constant. This approach showed some promise in research on the Pueblo I period occupation of the Dolores valley. For example, Blinman (1988) showed that if the per-household discard rate of gray ware sherds was assumed to be constant, the amount of animal bone discarded per household per year decreased as population density increased. On the other hand, he found that fragmentation of the bone—presumably an indicator of intensity of processing—increased as population grew (Blinman 1988).

The Abandonment Question

In the thirteenth century A.D., the Four Corners area of the American Southwest (Figure 1.1) was abandoned by the Anasazi. The abandonment of an area of over 60,000 km^2, centered on the drainage basin of the San Juan River, has stimulated archaeological interest for over a century. Not only the geographic and demographic scale of the abandonment, but its rapidity remain to be satisfactorily explained. Anasazi populations numbering minimally in the several tens of thousands occupied the Four Corners area as late as the middle A.D. 1200s. Yet, by A.D. 1290 or 1300, these populations had disappeared, by in situ decline, by migration to the Rio Grande and Little Colorado drainages farther south, or through some combination of both processes.

Research on the Sand Canyon Project provides a detailed case study of several communities that participated in the regional abandonment of the late 1200s and that must have been affected by whatever processes caused this abandonment. By undertaking a detailed study of the organization and abandonment of thirteenth-century communities in the Sand Canyon locality, researchers from the Crow Canyon Center hope to gain information that will contribute to understanding of the regional abandonment. Likewise, insights gained by archaeologists working elsewhere in the region may help us understand events in the Sand Canyon locality. The paragraphs that follow characterize the abandonment of the Upper Sand Canyon community, provide a minimal regional context for abandonment of the Sand Canyon locality, and survey some processes that might have contributed to the abandonment of both the locality and the larger northern San Juan (Mesa Verde) region.

Our best evidence on abandonment in the Sand Canyon locality is from the Upper Sand Canyon community. Here, most of the smaller Pueblo III settlements appear to have been abandoned before the end of occupation at Sand Canyon Pueblo. These smaller sites (Varien et al., this volume; Kuckelman et al. 1991) typically show a pattern of abandonment in which few usable artifacts were left on occupation surfaces and the roofs of most kivas were not burned but were intentionally dismantled, with the beams probably being put into use at nearby settlements either as construction materials or as fuel.

At Sand Canyon Pueblo, building was still going on as late as the middle 1270s, on the basis of tree-ring dating evidence (Bradley, this volume; Bradley 1991b). Tree-ring dates also indicate that Lester's site, located on the talus top just outside the wall enclosing Sand Canyon Pueblo, was built or added to in the early 1270s (Varien et al., this volume). This suggests that the aggregation of population in and around Sand Canyon Pueblo was still continuing as late as the early 1270s.

Abandonment of Sand Canyon Pueblo probably took place sometime between the middle 1270s and the middle or late 1280s. Some architectural complexes appear to have been abandoned rapidly, probably at or very near the end of site abandonment. For example, the kiva unit excavated in the 500 block had numerous usable artifacts on occupation surfaces, the kiva roof was burned rather than being dismantled, and most of the structures in the complex appear to have continued in use until abandonment (Bradley, this volume). On the other hand, the complex excavated in the 1000 block provided evidence that most structures in this unit went out of use as habitation or storage areas before neighboring units were abandoned. Several of the 1000-block structures became used for refuse deposition, presumably by people living in adjacent kiva units, and several were used as "cemeteries" with formal and informal placement of the dead. Relatively few complete or usable artifacts were found on occupation surfaces in the 1000 block, suggesting that residents moved to nearby locations, or that abandonment assemblages were scavenged by people living at the site or in the vicinity of the site (Bradley, this volume).

Of the 22 skeletons recovered from the site, some appear not to have been given a formal burial. Most skeletons do not show evidence of trauma, but several do show perimortem injuries to the skull that cannot be accounted for by wall or roof collapse over the body (Anne Katzenberg, personal communication). Studies of the human remains and of the manner in which they entered the archaeological record are continuing.

The roofs of the majority of the kivas that have been excavated at Sand Canyon Pueblo had been burned (Bradley, this volume). A good case can be made that most or all of these burnings were the result of a "closing-down" ritual rather than being an act of violence. It seems very unlikely that they represent accidental conflagrations.

Overall, the evidence so far indicates that Sand Canyon Pueblo was probably abandoned relatively rapidly, but not all at once. The abandonment may have extended over several years, and the sections of the site that have been excavated so far show a variety of abandonment patterns. In several of the units that have been excavated, there is tentative evidence that trauma affected individuals at or near the end of occupation.

A survey of existing data on settlement and demography in the Mesa Verde region (Varien et al. 1990, 1991) provides qualitative support for Rohn's (1983, 1989) interpretations of population history—that large populations, probably in the range of several tens of thousands of people, were still living in the core part of the region in the mid–1200s A.D. The population may even have been at or near its peak at that time. Alternative interpretations (e.g., Lipe 1978, 1983) that saw Mesa Verde region population peaking in the early 1100s and then steadily declining through the late 1100s and 1200s do not seem to be supportable. There may have been some decline in population in the middle or late 1100s—the evidence is not good one way or the other—but, clearly, there were large populations in the area in the 1200s. The implication is that the depopulation of the region in the late 1200s must have been very rapid. A recent compilation of tree-ring dates from the Southwest as a whole (Robinson and Cameron 1991) shows that in the Four Corners area there are many dates from the early 1270s but only a few in the late 1270s and early 1280s, and none after the mid-1280s. This indicates that building came to a halt rather rapidly. The Mesa Verde area was probably largely or entirely abandoned by the late 1280s or 1290.

My impression is that, like Sand Canyon Pueblo, other late thirteenth-century sites lack clear evidence of a catastrophic end. But I am not sure we know how the effects of an adaptive catastrophe—say, three successive years of near-complete crop failure—would look archaeologically. Nor do we know how an in-place dwindling of population due to excess of mortality over births would look in the archaeological record. I am not suggesting that these events happened, just that I am not sure we could distinguish the archaeological record left by these processes from that left by the orderly emigration of intact families and communities. We need a better cross-cultural understanding of what happens in communities and households when these things happen, and we need to model their archaeological expression.

What caused the dramatic depopulation of the Four Corners area—an event, or a roughly synchronous series of events, that has generated hundreds if not thousands of undergraduate term papers and countless media evocations of a sublime and impenetrable mystery? It seems to me that there are two main kinds of possible causes: (1) those related to environmental problems and adaptive stress in the Four Corners area itself, and (2) those related to the attractiveness of new Puebloan social, religious, or economic systems forming farther to the south in the late thirteenth century. Each of these kinds of explanations are briefly reviewed below.

Adaptive Problems Related to Environmental Change

The long-recognized Great Drought (Douglass 1929) of the late 1200s (A.D. 1276–1299) coincides remarkably well with the abandonment of the Mesa Verde area and the whole Four Corners region. There also is evidence that a cycle of arroyo cutting was under way at this time (Euler et al. 1979; Dean et al. 1985). Finally, Petersen (1987, 1988, 1989) has made a case for significant cooling in the 1200s. These three factors could have significantly reduced the abundant agricultural resources of the Mesa Verde region. Cooling would have shortened growing seasons, affecting dry farming at high elevations and increasing the effects of cold-air drainage in the valleys. Drought would have affected dry farming at the middle elevations, while arroyo cutting would have reduced or eliminated farming based on floodwater or groundwater in the alluvial valleys. Drought would probably also have reduced the flow of springs, which were the primary source of domestic water over most of the area. With the large population sizes that have been projected for this period, domestic water supplies may have been a critical resource (K. Adams 1991b).

It is hard to believe, however, that some farming areas would not have remained viable even under this worst-case scenario. In southwestern Colorado, the summer of 1989 was the driest on modern record, yet the majority of dry farmers at the higher elevations (for example, in the central part of the Sand Canyon locality) obtained at least partial crops of pinto beans or wheat. Even in an extremely dry year, most of the Mesa Verde region has more rainfall than does the area that has been farmed by the Hopi since prehistoric times. Van West's studies (Van West and Lipe, this volume; Van West 1990) of past soil moisture conditions indicate that the drought of the middle 1100s was worse than the Great Drought of the late 1200s. Her simulation also indicates that, in any case, enough arable land was available to support thousands of people even in both of these dry periods.

Recent evidence from temperature-sensitive tree-ring series in northern New Mexico (Grisson-Mayer, personal communication; K. Adams 1991b) indicates that there was a substantial decline in temperatures in the late A.D. 1200s, but that its magnitude was similar to that of other cool periods that occurred during the Pueblo I–III periods. Settlement pattern evidence indicates that the majority of Mesa Verde area communities appear to have been dependent on dry farming or small-watershed, upland-runoff farming rather than on the alluvial valley soils that were susceptible to arroyo cutting.

Although the environmental conditions of the late A.D. 1200s may not have been worse than those during other difficult periods in Anasazi prehistory, it does seem quite likely that this was a time of adaptive stress for some or perhaps most communities. Furthermore, there may have been some significant differences in the ability of the Mesa Verde Anasazi to respond to this stress, as compared to earlier periods.

The region probably had higher population density and, possibly, stronger intracommunity integration and more intercommunity conflict than in previous periods of environmental difficulty. Higher population density would have reduced the fall-back options available in case of crop failure. Surely, only a tiny fraction of the thirteenth-century population in the Mesa Verde region could have survived entirely on the basis of hunting and gathering. Furthermore, it appears that during the A.D. 1200s, the region had larger first-order communities with stronger patterns of intracommunity integration than in earlier times (Adler 1992) and that patterns of intercommunity exchange were weaker (Neily 1983). If intercommunity warfare also increased during this time (Haas and Creamer 1990), then it would have been more difficult for the basic social units of production and consumption (probably extended-family households) to disperse, join other communities, or recombine into new communities in order to make best use of existing patches of arable land. Yet, such patterns may have been adaptive at times when the overall supply of arable land was reduced, its distribution was patchier, and there was less year-to-year congruence in the location of productive lands (Van West and Lipe, this volume; Van West 1990, 1992). Consequently, the demographic and community structure of the period may have inhibited optimal responses to the environmental problems presented by drought, cooler temperatures, and arroyo cutting.

Even though we can make a case for environmental problems and, possibly, for some limitations on adaptive response, this still does not add up to a satisfactory scenario for a complete depopulation of the region, due to in-place starvation, or to failure to reproduce, or to forced emigration. A decrease in population by any of these means should have reduced the extent and severity of the problems, enabling the remaining population to readapt.

Perhaps, however, the population and social organization of the Four Corners region had become a "large interactive system" that had reached a state of "self-organized criticality" (Bak and Chen 1991). This type of explanation has been used to understand the dynamics of systems as disparate as the earth's crust, the stock market, and ecosystems. Many kinds of large composite systems evolve to a state of criticality, in which a minor event may start a chain reaction that can have effects ranging from small to very large (Bak and Chen 1991). In other words, as elements are added to the system and interconnections increase, so does the probability that a small perturbation will have dramatic effects. Bak and Chen (1991) use the graphic example of placing dominos at random on a field of finite size. When the density of dominos is low and one is toppled, there is a very low probability that the "domino effect," or chain reaction, will spread to more than a few other pieces. As more dominos are added, however, the probability increases that the chain reaction will spread through the field and affect many or all of the dominos. The important point is that in all cases, the "kicker" is the same—the toppling of a single domino—but the effects vary widely, depending on the state of the system. Also, repeated trials, even in a single system state, will result in a range of effects, from small to large.

Perhaps something analogous happened in the Four Corners area in the thirteenth century (see Davis [1965] for a related idea). Increases through time in the density of elements (people, households, or communities) can be demonstrated, but what is the nature of the interconnections? The work done on the Sand Canyon Project so far indicates that the basic unit of consumption and production probably stayed small—one or a few cooperating households—and that either economic or political relationships among neighboring communities were weakly developed or such relationships are difficult to measure archaeologically. On the other hand, Adler (1990) does make a case that the basic unit of production and consumption may have increased in the A.D. 1100s and 1200s, as indicated by the increase in size of residential roomblocks, and that the community of several hundred people became both better integrated and more important as a social survival vehicle.

In conclusion, it is tempting to see the Four Corners abandonment as merely at the large end of a range of lesser abandonments that can be documented in Anasazi prehistory (e.g., Matson et al. 1988; Schlanger 1990). Perhaps we err in seeking causes proportionate to the scale of the effects and need to pay greater attention to regional system characteristics. Changes in these characteristics may have produced widely differing responses to similar environmental and demographic "kickers."

Attraction of New Sociocultural Systems Farther South

We who work in the northern San Juan (Mesa Verde) region tend to think of it as the center of the Anasazi world, when in fact it is on the periphery. By the late A.D. 1200s, large Pueblo communities were beginning to form in the Rio Grande, Mogollon Rim, Western Pueblo, and Salado areas. These communities display evidence of new forms of community social and religious organization (E. C. Adams 1989, 1991; Crown 1992) and much stronger systems of interlocality and interregional exchange. For the first time, the Mesa Verde people had cultural (and perhaps actual) kinsmen living in Puebloan settlements that matched their own in size and may have been more attractive in other

respects. If these new communities farther south were actively recruiting immigrants in order to build their political or religious power, a drought-harassed Mesa Verde population may have been fair game. Mass acceptance of a new religious ideology (an early version of the Kachina cult?) might account for the speed and completeness of the late 1200s abandonment.

It seems clear that the Anasazi of the Four Corners region are linked culturally, and probably biologically, to the Pueblo peoples occupying the Rio Grande and Western Pueblo areas today. In this sense, the problem is not explaining the disappearance of the Anasazi—they didn't disappear, they just became Pueblo Indians (Ladd 1991; Judge 1991). Yet much needs to be learned about the direction, kind, and degree of these linkages (Ford et al. 1972; Ellis 1967), as well as the relative magnitude of population movement out of the Four Corners area. The similarities between Mesa Verde Black-on-white and Galisteo Black-on-white and the rapid rise in population in the Rio Grande area in the late thirteenth and fourteenth centuries have been used as evidence that large numbers of people moved from the Mesa Verde area to the Rio Grande (Mera 1935 and Smiley et al. 1953, cited in Dutton 1964). But the stylistic similarities between these two pottery types appear to be no greater than the similarity between earlier types—e.g., Mancos Black-on-white and Kwahe'e Black-on-white (Dutton 1964; Dean Wilson, personal communication). Large-scale population movement probably does not explain the stylistic similarity in pottery designs present during the Pueblo II period, and it is therefore less than conclusive for tracing population movements in the late thirteenth century.

To better understand the abandonment of the Mesa Verde region, we need to continue to improve our understanding of its late thirteenth-century depopulation. In the Sand Canyon Project, we need to continue research on the locality and central Mesa Verde area environments, and especially on the temporal and spatial distribution of possible critical variables such as arable land, domestic water supplies, and wild food resources (Adams, this volume; K. Adams 1991b).

We also need to continue to study abandonment at specific sites and localities and to attempt to understand what type of depopulation the archaeological record is documenting—emigration of small groups such as households; emigration of larger groups or communities; dwindling of population in place; or catastrophic events such as famine, widespread disease, and loss of life in warfare.

Furthermore, understanding the abandonment of the Mesa Verde area and the Four Corners region as a whole will probably require a better understanding of environments, demography, and social interaction in the greater Southwest. Populations respond to opportunities and attractions, as well as to pressures and stresses. If the former are primarily to be found in other areas, population movements may result. A recent conference at the Crow Canyon Center, sponsored by the Wenner-Gren Foundation (Lipe and Lekson 1990), brought together a number of Southwestern archaeologists to discuss the entire area where Puebloan sites are found in the period A.D. 1150 to 1350. The papers from this meeting are currently being edited for publication. This meeting began to lay the foundations for a larger-scale, more integrated view of Puebloan prehistory, one that needs to be much more fully developed in the future (Lekson 1992) as a strategy for understanding the major events in Southwestern prehistory, such as the Four Corners abandonment.

References

Adams, E. C.

1983 Archeological Research Design. Ms. on file, Crow Canyon Archaeological Center, Cortez, Colorado.

1984 *Plan of Operations for Work to be Conducted on Bureau of Land Management Administered Land.* Crow Canyon Campus, Center for American Archaeology, Cortez, Colorado. Report submitted to the Bureau of Land Management, San Juan Resource Area Office, Durango, Colorado.

1985a *Annual Report of Test Excavations at 5MT765, Sand Canyon Pueblo, and Archaeological Survey in T36N, R18W, Sections 12 & 24, and T36N, R16W, Sections 29 & 30.* Crow Canyon Archaeological Center, Cortez, Colorado. Report submitted to the Bureau of Land Management, San Juan Resource Area Office, Durango, Colorado.

1985b Sand Canyon Pueblo: A Thirteenth Century Anasazi Ceremonial Center in Southwestern Colorado. Paper presented at the 50th Annual Meeting of the Society for American Archaeology, Denver.

1986 Report to the National Geographic Society on Excavations at Sand Canyon Pueblo, an Anasazi Ceremonial Center in Southwestern Colorado. Ms. on file, Crow Canyon Archaeological Center, Cortez, Colorado.

1989 Changing Form and Function in Western Pueblo Ceremonial Architecture from A.D. 1000 to A.D. 1500. In *The Architecture of Social Integration in Prehistoric Pueblos*, edited by W. D. Lipe and M. Hegmon, pp. 155–160. Occasional Papers of the Crow Canyon Archaeological Center, no. 1. Cortez, Colorado.

1991 *The Origin and Development of the Pueblo Katsina Cult.* University of Arizona Press, Tucson.

Adams, K. R.

1989a Plant Remains from Four Small Pueblo III Sites (5MT3918, 5MT3930, 5MT3936, 5MT3951) in Southwestern Colorado. Ms. on file, Crow Canyon Archaeological Center, Cortez, Colorado.

1989b Plant Remains from the Green Lizard Site (5MT3901), a Pueblo III Anasazi Habitation Site in Southwestern Colorado. Ms. on file, Crow Canyon Archaeological Center, Cortez, Colorado.

1989c Plant Remains from Sand Canyon Pueblo (5MT765), a Mesa Verde Phase Pueblo III Site in Southwestern Colorado. Ms. on file, Crow Canyon Archaeological Center, Cortez, Colorado.

1989d Report on Sand Canyon Flotation Samples Analyzed Fall 1989. Ms. on file, Crow Canyon Archaeological Center, Cortez, Colorado.

1991a Environment and Anasazi Abandonment of Southwest Colorado in the 13th Century A.D. Research proposal submitted to the National Science Foundation. Ms. on file, Crow Canyon Archaeological Center, Cortez, Colorado.

1991b Mesa Verde Fire Effects: An Ecological and Ethnobotanical Study of Vegetation Recovery After the Long Mesa Fire of July 1989. Crow Canyon Archaeological Center, Cortez, Colorado. Report submitted to Mesa Verde National Park, Mesa Verde, Colorado.

Adler, M. A.

1988 *Archaeological Survey and Testing in the Sand Canyon Pueblo/Goodman Point Ruin Locality, Montezuma County, Colorado, 1987 Field Season.* Crow Canyon Archaeological Center, Cortez, Colorado. Report submitted to the Bureau of Land Management, San Juan Resource Area Office, Durango, Colorado.

1989 Ritual Facilities and Social Integration in Nonranked Societies. In *The Architecture of Social Integration in Prehistoric Pueblos*, edited by W. D. Lipe and M. Hegmon, pp. 35–52. Occasional Papers of the Crow Canyon Archaeological Center, no. 1. Cortez, Colorado.

1990 *Communities of Soil and Stone: An Archaeological Investigation of Population Aggregation Among the Mesa Verde Region Anasazi, A.D. 900–1300.* Unpublished Ph.D. dissertation, Department of Anthropology, University of Michigan, Ann Arbor.

1992 Fathoming the Spatial and Demographic Scale of the Northern Anasazi Community. Paper presented at the Third Southwest Symposium, Tucson.

Adler, M. A., and M. Metcalf

1990 *Archaeological Survey in the Lower Sand Canyon Area, Southwestern Colorado.* Crow Canyon Archaeological Center, Cortez, Colorado. Letter report submitted to the Bureau of Land Management, San Juan Resource Area Office, Durango, Colorado.

1991 *Draft Report on Archaeological Survey of Lower East Rock and Sand Canyons, Montezuma County, Colorado.* Crow Canyon Archaeological Center, Cortez, Colorado. Report submitted to the Bureau of Land Management, San Juan Resource Area Office, Durango, Colorado.

Adler, M. A., and M. D. Varien

1991 The Changing Face of the Community in the Mesa Verde Region, A.D. 1000–1300. Paper presented at the Anasazi Symposium, Mesa Verde National Park, Colorado.

Adler, M. A., and R. H. Wilshusen

1990 Large-Scale Integrative Facilities in Tribal Societies: Cross-cultural and Southwestern US Examples. *World Archaeology* 22(2):133–145.

Ahlstrom, R. V. N.

1985 *The Interpretation of Archaeological Tree-Ring Dates.* Unpublished Ph.D. dissertation, Department of Anthropology, University of Arizona, Tucson.

Bak, P., and K. Chen

1991 Self-Organized Criticality. *Scientific American* 264(1):46–53.

Barth, F.

1978 Conclusions. In *Scale and Social Organization*, edited by F. Barth, pp. 253–283. Universitetsforlaget, Oslo.

Betancourt, J. L., T. R. Van Devender, and P. S. Martin (editors)
1990 *Packrat Middens, the Last 40,000 Years of Biotic Change*. The University of Arizona Press, Tucson.

Blalock, H. M.
1979 *Social Statistics*. 2d rev. ed. McGraw-Hill, New York.

Blanton, R. E., S. A. Kowalewski, G. Feinman, and J. Appel
1981 *Ancient Mesoamerica: A Comparison of Change in Three Regions*. Cambridge University Press, Cambridge.

Blau, P. M.
1975 Parameters of Social Structure. In *Approaches to the Study of Social Structure*, edited by P. M. Blau, pp. 220–253. Free Press, New York.

Blinman, E.
1986 Additive Technologies Group Final Report. In *Dolores Archaeological Program: Final Synthetic Report*, compiled by D. A. Breternitz, C. K. Robinson, and G. T. Gross, pp. 53–101. Bureau of Reclamation, Engineering and Research Center, Denver.
1988 *The Interpretation of Ceramic Variability: A Case Study from the Dolores Anasazi*. Unpublished Ph.D. dissertation, Department of Anthropology, Washington State University, Pullman.
1989 Potluck in the Protokiva: Ceramics and Ceremonialism in Pueblo I Villages. In *The Architecture of Social Integration in Prehistoric Pueblos*, edited by W. D. Lipe and M. Hegmon, pp. 113–124. Occasional Papers of the Crow Canyon Archaeological Center, no. 1. Cortez, Colorado.

Bloomer, W. B.
1988 Green Lizard (5MT3901) Granulometric Analysis. Ms. in author's possession.

Boserup, E.
1965 *The Conditions of Agricultural Growth*. Aldine, Chicago.

Bradfield, M.
1971 *Changing Patterns of Hopi Agriculture*. Royal Anthropological Institute Occasional Paper, no. 30. Royal Anthropological Institute of Great Britain and Ireland. London.

Bradley, B. A.
1986 *Annual Report of Test Excavations at Sand Canyon Pueblo (5MT765)*. Crow Canyon Archaeological Center, Cortez, Colorado. Report submitted to the Bureau of Land Management, San Juan Resource Area Office, Durango, Colorado.
1987 *Annual Report of Excavations at Sand Canyon Pueblo (5MT765)*. Crow Canyon Archaeological Center, Cortez, Colorado. Report submitted to the Bureau of Land Management, San Juan Resource Area Office, Durango, Colorado.
1988a *Annual Report on the Excavations at Sand Canyon Pueblo, 1987 Field Season*. Crow Canyon Archaeological Center, Cortez, Colorado. Report submitted to the Bureau of Land Management, San Juan Resource Area Office, Durango, Colorado.
1988b Wallace Ruin Interim Report. *Southwestern Lore* 54(2):8–33.
1989 Architectural Petroglyphs at Sand Canyon Pueblo (5MT765), Southwestern Colorado. *Kiva* 54:153–161.
1990 *Annual Report of the 1989 Excavations at Sand Canyon Pueblo (5MT765)*. Crow Canyon Archaeological Center, Cortez, Colorado. Report submitted to the Bureau of Land Management, San Juan Resource Area Office, Durango, Colorado.

1991a Excavations in Public Architecture at Sand Canyon Pueblo: The 1991 Field Season. Ms. on file, Crow Canyon Archaeological Center, Cortez, Colorado.
1991b Planning, Growth, and Functional Differentiation at a Prehistoric Pueblo: A Case Study from SW Colorado. *Journal of Field Archaeology*, in press.

Bradley, B. A., and W. D. Lipe
1990 Investigating 13th Century Anasazi Public Architecture at Sand Canyon Pueblo. Proposal submitted to the National Geographic Society. Ms. on file, Crow Canyon Archaeological Center, Cortez, Colorado.

Brand, M. J.
1991 Zooarchaeology of Sand Canyon Pueblo (5MT765), Shorlene's Site (5MT3918), Roy's Ruin (5MT3930), Lillian's Site (5MT3936) and Troy's Tower (5MT3951), Colorado. Honor's Essay, Archaeology 499, Department of Archaeology, Simon Fraser University, Burnaby, British Columbia.

Breternitz, D. A., C. K. Robinson, and G. T. Gross (compilers)
1986 *Dolores Archaeological Program: Final Synthetic Report*. Bureau of Reclamation, Engineering and Research Center, Denver.

Breternitz, D. A., A. H. Rohn, Jr., and E. A. Morris (compilers)
1974 *Prehistoric Ceramics of the Mesa Verde Region*. Museum of Northern Arizona, Ceramic Series, no. 5. Flagstaff, Arizona.

Brew, J. O.
1946 *Archaeology of Alkali Ridge, Southeastern Utah*. Papers of the Peabody Museum of American Archaeology and Ethnology, Harvard University, vol. 21. Cambridge.

Brown, B. M.
1987 Population Estimation from Floor Area: A Restudy of "Naroll's Constant." *Behavior Science Research* 22(1–4):1–49.

Burns, B. T.
1983 *Simulated Anasazi Storage Behavior Using Crop Yields Reconstructed from Tree-Rings: A.D. 652–1968*. Ph.D. dissertation, University of Arizona. University Microfilms, Ann Arbor.

Cameron, C. M.
1990 The Effect of Varying Estimates of Pit Structure Use-Life on Prehistoric Population Estimates in the American Southwest. *Kiva* 55:155–166.

Carlson, R. L.
1963 *Basket Maker III Sites Near Durango, Colorado*. University of Colorado Studies, Series in Anthropology, no. 8. Boulder.

Casselberry, S. E.
1974 Further Refinement of Formulae for Determining Population from Floor Area. *World Archaeology* 6:118–122.

Cattanach, G. S., Jr.
1980 *Long House, Mesa Verde National Park, Colorado*. Publications in Archeology, no. 7H. National Park Service, Washington, D.C.

Chao, V. S.
1991 Stylistic and Functional Variability Within Sand Canyon Pueblo. Ms. on file, Crow Canyon Archaeological Center, Cortez, Colorado.

Connolly, M.
1990 A Historic Land Use Study of Goodman Point. Ms. on file, Crow Canyon Archaeological Center, Cortez, Colorado.

Cook, S. F.
1972 *Prehistoric Demography*. McCaleb Modules in Anthropology, no. 16. Addison-Wesley, Reading, Mass.

Cook, S. F., and W. Borah
1979 *Essays in Population History: Mexico and California*. University of California Press, Berkeley.

Cordell, L. S.
1975 Predicting Site Abandonment at Wetherill Mesa. *The Kiva* 40:189–202.

Cordell, L. S., and F. Plog
1979 Escaping the Confines of Normative Thought: A Reevaluation of Puebloan Prehistory. *American Antiquity* 44:405–429.

Crown, P. L.
1992 Change in Ceramic Technology in the 13th to 14th Century Southwest. Paper presented at the Third Southwest Symposium, Tucson.

Crown, P. L., and T. A. Kohler
1990 Community Dynamics, Site Structure and Aggregation in the Northern Rio Grande. Paper presented at the Second Southwest Symposium, Albuquerque.

Damon, P. E.
1990 The New Warm Epoch: Solar Activity Versus the Greenhouse Effect. In *Earth Observations and Global Change Decision Making, 1989: A National Partnership*, edited by I. W. Ginsberg and J. A. Angelo, pp. 269–274. Krieger, Malabar, Florida.

Davis, E. L.
1965 Small Pressures and Cultural Drift as Explanations for Abandonment of the San Juan Area, New Mexico and Arizona. *American Antiquity* 30:353–355.

Dean, J. S.
1988 A Model of Anasazi Behavioral Adaptation. In *The Anasazi in a Changing Environment*, edited by G. J. Gumerman, pp. 25–44. School of American Research Advanced Seminar Series. Cambridge University Press, Cambridge.

Dean, J. S., R. C. Euler, G. J. Gumerman, F. Plog, R. H. Hevly, and T. N. V. Karlstrom
1985 Human Behavior, Demography, and Paleoenvironment on the Colorado Plateaus. *American Antiquity* 50:537–554.

Decker, K. W., and L. L. Tieszen
1989 Isotopic Reconstruction of Mesa Verde Diet from Basketmaker III to Pueblo III. *Kiva* 55:33–47.

DeNiro, M. J.
1987 Stable Isotopy and Archaeology. *American Scientist* 75:182–191.

Dickson, D. B., Jr.
1979 *Prehistoric Pueblo Settlement Patterns: The Arroyo Hondo, New Mexico, Site Survey*. Arroyo Hondo Archaeological Series, vol. 2. School of American Research Press, Santa Fe.

Dittert, A. E., Jr., J. J. Hester, and F. W. Eddy
1961 *An Archaeological Survey of the Navajo Reservoir District, Northwestern New Mexico*. Monographs of the School of American Research and the Museum of New Mexico, no. 23. Santa Fe.

Douglass, A. E.
1929 The Secret of the Southwest Solved by Talkative Tree-Rings. *National Geographic* 54:737–770.

Dutton, B.
1964 Las Madres in the Light of Anasazi Migrations. *American Antiquity* 29:449–454.

Dykeman, D. D.
1986 *Excavations at 5MT8371, an Isolated Pueblo II Pit Structure in Montezuma County, Colorado*. Studies in Archaeology, no. 2. San Juan County Archaeological Center and Library, Bloomfield, New Mexico.

Earle, T. K.
1980 A Model of Subsistence Change. In *Modeling Change in Prehistoric Subsistence Economies*, edited by T. K. Earle and A. L. Christenson, pp. 1–29. Studies in Archaeology. Academic Press, New York.

Eddy, F. W.
1966 *Prehistory in the Navajo Reservoir District, Northwestern New Mexico*. Museum of New Mexico Papers in Anthropology, no. 15, parts 1 and 2. Santa Fe.

1977 *Archaeological Investigations at Chimney Rock Mesa: 1970–1972*. Memoirs of the Colorado Archaeological Society, no. 1. Boulder.

Eddy, F. W., A. E. Kane, and P. R. Nickens
1984 *Southwest Colorado Prehistoric Context: Archaeological Background and Research Directions*. Office of Archaeology and Historic Preservation, Colorado Historical Society, Denver.

Ellis, F. H.
1967 Where Did the Pueblo People Come From? *El Palacio* 74(3):35–43.

1981 Discussion. In *The Protohistoric Period in the North American Southwest, A.D. 1450–1700*, edited by D. R. Wilcox and B. Masse, pp. 410–433. Anthropological Research Papers, no. 24. Arizona State University, Tempe.

Euler, R. C., G. Gumerman, T. N. V. Karlstrom, J. Dean, and R. Hevly
1979 The Colorado Plateaus: Cultural Dynamics and Paleoenvironment. *Science* 205:1089–1101.

Feinman, G., and J. Neitzel
1984 Too Many Types: An Overview of Prestate Societies in the Americas. In *Advances in Archaeological Method and Theory*, vol. 7, edited by M. B. Schiffer, pp. 39–102. Academic Press, Orlando.

Ferguson, T. J.
1989 Comment on Social Integration and Anasazi Architecture. In *The Architecture of Social Integration in Prehistoric Pueblos*, edited by W. D. Lipe and M. Hegmon, pp. 169–173. Occasional Papers of the Crow Canyon Archaeological Center, no. 1. Cortez, Colorado.

Ferguson, W. M., and A. H. Rohn
1986 *Anasazi Ruins of the Southwest in Color*. University of New Mexico Press, Albuquerque.

Fetterman, J., and L. Honeycutt
1987 *The Mockingbird Mesa Survey, Southwestern Colorado*. Cultural Resource Series, no. 22. Bureau of Land Management, Denver.

Flannery, K. V.
1972 The Cultural Evolution of Civilizations. *Annual Review of Evolution and Systematics* 3:399–426.

Flannery, K. V., and J. Marcus

1976   Evolution of the Public Building in Formative Oaxaca. In *Cultural Change and Continuity: Essays in Honor of James Bennett Griffin*, edited by C. E. Cleland, pp. 205–221. Studies in Archeology. Academic Press, New York.

Force, E. R.

1990   Holocene Fluvial Stratigraphy Using Anasazi "Guide Fossils", McElmo Canyon, Southwestern Colorado—A Progress Report. Ms. on file, Crow Canyon Archaeological Center, Cortez, Colorado.

Ford, R. I.

1968   *An Ecological Analysis Involving the Population of San Juan Pueblo, New Mexico.* Ph.D. dissertation, University of Michigan. University Microfilms, Ann Arbor.

Ford, R. I., A. H. Schroeder, and S. L. Peckham

1972   Three Perspectives on Puebloan Prehistory. In *New Perspectives on the Pueblos*, edited by A. Ortiz, pp. 19–39. School of American Research Advanced Seminar Series. University of New Mexico Press, Albuquerque.

Forde, C. D.

1931   Hopi Agriculture and Land Ownership. *Journal of the Royal Anthropological Institute* 61:357–406.

Fowler, A. P., and J. R. Stein

1990   The Anasazi Great House in Time and Space. Paper presented at the 55th Annual Meeting of the Society for American Archaeology, Las Vegas.

Fowler, A. P., J. R. Stein, and R. Anyon

1987   *An Archaeological Reconnaissance of West-Central New Mexico: The Anasazi Monuments Project.* Report submitted to State of New Mexico Office of Cultural Affairs, Historic Preservation Division, Santa Fe.

Fritts, H. C.

1976   *Tree Rings and Climate.* Academic Press, London.

Fuller, S. L.

1984   *Late Anasazi Pottery Kilns in the Yellowjacket District, Southwestern Colorado.* CASA Papers, no. 4. Complete Archaeological Service Associates, Cortez, Colorado.

1988   *Archaeological Investigations in the Bodo Canyon Area, La Plata County, Colorado.* UMTRA Archaeological Report, no. 25. U.S. Department of Energy, Washington, D.C.

1989   *Research Design and Data Recovery Plan for the Animas-La Plata Project* (with contributions by T. G. Baugh and D. V. Hill). Four Corners Archaeological Project Report, no. 15. Complete Archaeological Service Associates, Cortez, Colorado.

Gillespie, W. B.

1976   *Culture Change at the Ute Canyon Site: A Study of the Pithouse-Kiva Transition in the Mesa Verde Region.* Unpublished Master's thesis, Department of Anthropology, University of Colorado, Boulder.

Gilman, P. A.

1983   Changing Architectural Forms in the Prehistoric Southwest. Unpublished Ph.D. dissertation, Department of Anthropology, University of New Mexico, Albuquerque.

Gish, J. W.

1988   Pollen Analysis of Structure 208 at Sand Canyon Pueblo, Colorado. Ms. on file, Crow Canyon Archaeological Center, Cortez, Colorado.

1991   Pollen Results from Five Pueblo III Sites, Upper Sand Canyon, Southwestern Colorado. Ms. on file, Crow Canyon Archaeological Center, Cortez, Colorado.

Gleichman, C. L., and P. J. Gleichman

1989   *An Archaeological Inventory of Lower Sand Canyon, Montezuma County, Colorado.* Native Cultural Services, Boulder, Colorado. Report submitted to the Bureau of Land Management, San Juan Area Resource Office, Durango, Colorado.

Gooding, J. D. (editor)

1980   *The Durango South Project: Archaeological Salvage of Two Late Basketmaker III Sites in the Durango District.* Anthropological Papers of the University of Arizona, no. 34. Tucson.

Gorman, F. J. E., and S. T. Childs

1981   Is Prudden's Unit Type of Anasazi Settlement Valid and Reliable? *North American Archaeologist* 2(3):153–192.

Gould, R. R.

1982   *The Mustoe Site: The Application of Neutron Activation Analysis in the Interpretation of a Multi-Component Archaeological Site.* Unpublished Ph.D. dissertation, Department of Anthropology, University of Texas, Austin.

Grady, J.

1986   Photogrammetric Mapping of Sand Canyon Pueblo, 5MT765. Ms. on file, Crow Canyon Archaeological Center, Cortez, Colorado.

Graybill, D. A.

1989   The Reconstruction of Prehistoric Stream Flow. In *The 1982–1984 Excavations at Las Colinas, Environment and Subsistence*, edited by D. A. Graybill, D. A. Gregory, F. L. Nials, S. K. Fish, C. H. Miksicek, R. E. Gasser, and C. R. Szuter, pp. 25–38. Archaeological Series 162, vol. 5, part 1. Cultural Resource Management Division, Arizona State Museum, University of Arizona, Tucson.

Gumerman, G. J. (editor)

1988   *The Anasazi in a Changing Environment.* School of American Research Advanced Seminar Series. Cambridge University Press, Cambridge.

Haas, J., and W. Creamer

1990   The Irritating Role of Warfare in the Pueblo III Period. Paper presented at the Conference on Pueblo Cultures in Transition: A.D. 1150–1350 in the American Southwest, Crow Canyon Archaeological Center, Cortez, Colorado.

Haase, W. R.

1985   Domestic Water Conservation Among the Northern San Juan Anasazi. *Southwestern Lore* 51(2):15–27.

Hack, J. T.

1942   *The Changing Physical Environment of the Hopi Indians of Arizona.* Papers of the Peabody Museum of American Archaeology and Ethnology, vol. 35, no. 1. Harvard University, Cambridge.

Hassan, F. A.

1981   *Demographic Archaeology.* Studies in Archaeology. Academic Press, New York.

Hayes, A. C.

1964   *The Archeological Survey of Wetherill Mesa, Mesa Verde National Park, Colorado.* Archeological Research Series, no. 7-A. National Park Service, Washington, D.C.

1981   A Survey of Chaco Canyon Archeology. In *Archeological Surveys of Chaco Canyon, New Mexico*, edited by A. C. Hayes, D. M. Brugge, and W. J. Judge, pp. 1–68.

Publications in Archeology no. 18A, Chaco Canyon Studies. National Park Service, Washington, D.C.

Hayes, A. C., and J. A. Lancaster

1975   *Badger House Community, Mesa Verde National Park.* Publications in Archeology, no. 7E. National Park Service, Washington, D.C.

Hegmon, M.

1989a   Social Integration and Architecture. In *The Architecture of Social Integration in Prehistoric Pueblos*, edited by W. D. Lipe and M. Hegmon, pp. 5–14. Occasional Papers of the Crow Canyon Archaeological Center, no. 1. Cortez, Colorado.

1989b   The Styles of Integration: Ceramic Style and Pueblo I Integrative Architecture in Southwestern Colorado. In *The Architecture of Social Integration in Prehistoric Pueblos*, edited by W. D. Lipe and M. Hegmon, pp. 125–141. Occasional Papers of the Crow Canyon Archaeological Center, no. 1. Cortez, Colorado.

1991   Six Easy Steps to Dating Pueblo III Ceramic Assemblages: Working Draft. Ms. on file, Crow Canyon Archaeological Center, Cortez, Colorado.

Herold, J.

1961   *Prehistoric Settlement and Physical Environment in the Mesa Verde Area.* Anthropological Papers, no. 53. University of Utah, Salt Lake City.

Hill, J. N.

1970   *Broken K Pueblo: Prehistoric Social Organization in the American Southwest.* Anthropological Papers of the University of Arizona, no. 18. Tucson.

Hillier, B., and J. Hanson

1984   *The Social Logic of Space.* Cambridge University Press, Cambridge.

Hoffman, J. M.

1985   Preliminary Report on Human Skeletal Remains from Sand Canyon Pueblo (5MT765) and the Duckfoot Site (5MT3868): 1984 Excavations of the Crow Canyon Center for Southwestern Archeology. Ms. on file, Crow Canyon Archaeological Center, Cortez, Colorado.

1987   Preliminary Report on Human Skeletal Remains from Sand Canyon Pueblo (5MT765): 1985 Excavations of the Crow Canyon Archaeological Center. Ms. on file, Crow Canyon Archaeological Center, Cortez, Colorado.

1990a   Final Report: The Human Skeletal Remains from the Duckfoot Site (5MT3868). Ms. on file, Crow Canyon Archaeological Center, Cortez, Colorado.

1990b   Report on Human Skeletal Remains from Sand Canyon Pueblo (5MT765): 1987 Excavations of the Crow Canyon Archaeological Center. Ms. on file, Crow Canyon Archaeological Center, Cortez, Colorado.

Hough, W.

1915   *The Hopi Indians.* Little Histories of North American Indians, no. 4. The Torch Press, Cedar Rapids, Iowa.

Hovezak, M. H.

1990   Thesis Prospectus for Master of Arts in Anthropology. Ms. on file at the Department of Anthropology, Northern Arizona University, Flagstaff.

Huber, E. K.

1989   *Preliminary Report of Excavations: 1987 and 1988 Seasons at Green Lizard (5MT3901), Montezuma County, Colorado.* Crow Canyon Archaeological Center, Cortez, Colorado. Report submitted to the Bureau of Land Management, San Juan Resource Area Office, Durango, Colorado.

1990   Green Lizard (5MT3901) Pollen Analysis Data Sheets. Ms. on file, Crow Canyon Archaeological Center, Cortez, Colorado.

1991   Site Size Differences and Community Organization in 13th Century Pueblo Sites of the Northern Southwest. Paper presented at the 56th Annual Meeting of the Society for American Archaeology, New Orleans.

Huber, E. K., and W. W. Bloomer

1988   *Annual Report of Investigations at Green Lizard (5MT3901), Montezuma County, Colorado.* Crow Canyon Archaeological Center, Cortez, Colorado. Report submitted to the Bureau of Land Management, San Juan Resource Area Office, Durango, Colorado.

Hughes, M. K., P. M. Kelly, J. R. Pilcher, and V. C. LaMarche, Jr. (editors)

1982   *Climate from Tree Rings.* Cambridge University Press, Cambridge.

Iorns, W. V., C. H. Hembree, D. A. Phoenix, and G. L. Oakland

1964   *Water Resources of the Upper Colorado River Basin: Basic Data.* U.S. Geological Survey Professional Paper, no. 442. Washington, D.C.

Irwin-Williams, C.

1973   *The Oshara Tradition: Origins of Anasazi Culture.* Eastern New Mexico University Contributions in Anthropology, vol. 5, no. 1. Portales.

Irwin-Williams, C. (editor)

1972   *The Structure of Chacoan Society in the Northern Southwest: Investigations at the Salmon Site—1972.* Eastern New Mexico University Contributions in Anthropology, vol. 4, no. 3. Portales.

Johnson, A. W., and T. Earle

1987   *The Evolution of Human Societies: From Foraging Group to Agrarian State.* Stanford University Press, Stanford.

Johnson, G. A.

1982   Organizational Structure and Scalar Stress. In *Theory and Explanation in Archaeology*, edited by C. Renfrew, M. J. Rowlands, and B. A. Segraves, pp. 389–421. Academic Press, New York.

1989   Dynamics of Southwestern Prehistory: Far Outside—Looking In. In *Dynamics of Southwest Prehistory*, edited by L. S. Cordell and G. J. Gumerman, pp. 371–389. School of American Research Advanced Seminar Series. Smithsonian Institution Press, Washington, D.C.

Jope, E. M.

1986   Sample Credentials Necessary for Meaningful High-Precision ^{14}C Dating. *Radiocarbon* 28:1060–1064.

Judge, W. J.

1989   Chaco Canyon-San Juan Basin. In *Dynamics of Southwest Prehistory*, edited by L. S. Cordell and G. J. Gumerman, pp. 209–261. School of American Research Advanced Seminar Series. Smithsonian Institution Press, Washington, D.C.

Judge, W. J. (moderator)

1991   *The Anasazi—Why Did They Leave, Where Did They Go? A Panel Discussion at the Anasazi Heritage Center, Dolores, Colorado.* Southwest Natural and Cultural Heritage Association, Albuquerque.

Judge, W. J., W. B. Gillespie, S. H. Lekson, and H. W. Toll
    1981   Tenth Century Developments in Chaco Canyon. In
           Collected Papers in Honor of Erik Kellerman Reed, edited
           by A. H. Schroeder, pp. 65–98. Papers of the Archaeological
           Society of New Mexico, vol. 6. Albuquerque.

Kane, A. E.
    1983   Introduction to Field Investigations and Analysis. In
           *Dolores Archaeological Program: Field Investigations and
           Analysis—1978*, prepared under the supervision of D. A.
           Breternitz, pp. 1–37. Bureau of Reclamation, Engineering
           and Research Center, Denver.
    1986   Prehistory of the Dolores River Valley. In *Dolores
           Archaeological Program: Final Synthetic Report*, compiled
           by D. A. Breternitz, C. K. Robinson, and G. T. Gross, pp.
           353–435. Bureau of Reclamation, Engineering and Re-
           search Center, Denver.
    1988   McPhee Community Cluster Introduction. In *Dolores
           Archaeological Program: Anasazi Communities at Dolores:
           McPhee Village*, compiled by A. E. Kane and C. K.
           Robinson, pp. 1–59. Bureau of Reclamation, Engineering
           and Research Center, Denver.
    1989   Did the Sheep Look Up? Sociopolitical Complexity in
           Ninth Century Dolores Society. In *The Sociopolitical Struc-
           ture of Prehistoric Southwestern Societies*, edited by S.
           Upham, K. G. Lightfoot, and R. A. Jewett, pp. 307–361.
           Investigations in American Archaeology. Westview Press,
           Boulder.

Kane, A. E., and C. K. Robinson (compilers)
    1988   *Dolores Archaeological Program: Anasazi Communi-
           ties at Dolores: McPhee Village*. Bureau of Reclamation,
           Engineering and Research Center, Denver.

Karlstrom, T. N. V.
    1988   Alluvial Chronology and Hydrologic Change of Black
           Mesa and Nearby Regions. In *The Anasazi in a Changing
           Environment*, edited by G. J. Gumerman, pp. 45–91. School
           of American Research Advanced Seminar Series. Cam-
           bridge University Press, Cambridge.

Kavena, J. T.
    1980   *Hopi Cookery*. University of Arizona Press, Tucson.

Kent, S.
    1986   New Dates for Old Pots: A Comment on Cortez Black-
           on-White. *The Kiva* 51:255–262.

Kice, D. A.
    1990   Preliminary Report on Human Skeletal Remains from
           Sand Canyon, Colorado: 1988 Excavations of the Crow
           Canyon Archaeological Center. Ms. on file, Crow Canyon
           Archaeological Center, Cortez, Colorado.
    1991   Preliminary Report on Human Skeletal Remains from
           Sites 5MT765, 5MT3901, 5MT3930 and 5MT3936: 1988
           Excavations of the Crow Canyon Archaeological Center.
           Ms. on file, Crow Canyon Archaeological Center, Cortez,
           Colorado.

Kidder, A. V.
    1927   Southwestern Archaeological Conference. *Science*
           68:489–491.

Kleidon, J., and B. A. Bradley
    1989   *Annual Report of the 1988 Excavations at Sand Canyon
           Pueblo (5MT765)*. Crow Canyon Archaeological Center,
           Cortez, Colorado. Report submitted to the Bureau of Land
           Management, San Juan Resource Area Office, Durango,
           Colorado.

Kohler, T. A. (editor)
    1989   *Bandelier Archaeological Excavation Project: Re-
           search Design and Summer 1988 Sampling*. Reports of
           Investigations, no. 61. Department of Anthropology, Wash-
           ington State University, Pullman.

Kohler, T. A., and E. Blinman
    1987   Solving Mixture Problems in Archaeology: Analysis of
           Ceramic Materials for Dating and Demographic Recon-
           struction. *Journal of Anthropological Archaeology* 6:1–28.

Kohler, T. A., and M. H. Matthews
    1988   Long-Term Anasazi Land Use and Forest Reduction: A
           Case Study from Southwest Colorado. *American Antiquity*
           53:537–564.

Kohler, T. A., J. D. Orcutt, E. Blinman, and K. L. Petersen
    1986   Anasazi Spreadsheets: The Cost of Doing Business in
           Prehistoric Dolores. In *Dolores Archaeological Program:
           Final Synthetic Report*, compiled by D. A. Breternitz, C. K.
           Robinson, and G. T. Gross, pp. 525–538. Bureau of Recla-
           mation, Engineering and Research Center, Denver.

Kosse, K.
    1992   Middle Range Societies from a Scalar Perspective.
           Paper presented at the Third Southwest Symposium, Tuc-
           son.

Kuckelman, K. A., and J. N. Morris (compilers)
    1988   *Archaeological Investigations on South Canal*. 2 vols.
           Four Corners Archaeological Project Report, no. 11. Com-
           plete Archaeological Service Associates, Cortez, Colorado.

Kuckelman, K. A., J. Kleidon, M. D. Varien, and R. R. Lightfoot
    1991   *1990 Sand Canyon Project Site Testing Program: Pre-
           liminary Report on the Excavations at Saddlehorn
           (5MT262), Mad Dog Tower (5MT181), Castle Rock Pueblo
           (5MT1825), Lester's Site (5MT10246), Lookout House
           (5MT10459), and Cougar Cub Alcove (5MT1690)*. Crow
           Canyon Archaeological Center, Cortez, Colorado. Report
           submitted to the Bureau of Land Management, San Juan
           Resource Area Office, Durango, Colorado.

Ladd, E.
    1991   On the Zuni View. In *The Anasazi—Why Did They
           Leave, Where Did They Go? A Panel Discussion at the
           Anasazi Heritage Center, Dolores, Colorado*, moderated by
           W. J. Judge, pp. 34–36. Southwest Natural and Cultural
           Heritage Association, Albuquerque.

Lancaster, J. A., and Philip F. Van Cleave
    1954   Excavation of Sun Point Pueblo. In *Archeological Ex-
           cavations in Mesa Verde National Park, Colorado, 1950*,
           edited by J. A. Lancaster, J. M. Pinkley, P. F. Van Cleave,
           and D. Watson, pp. 87–111. Archeological Research Series,
           no. 2. National Park Service, Washington, D.C.

Lange, F., N. Mahaney, J. B. Wheat, and M. L. Chenault
    1986   *Yellow Jacket: A Four Corners Anasazi Ceremonial
           Center*. Johnson Books, Boulder.

Lekson, S. H.
    1984   *Great Pueblo Architecture of Chaco Canyon*. Publica-
           tions in Archeology, no. 18B. National Park Service, Wash-
           ington, D.C.
    1988   The Idea of the Kiva in Anasazi Archaeology. *The Kiva*
           53:213–234.
    1992   Scale and Process in the Southwest. Paper presented at
           the Third Southwest Symposium, Tucson.

Leonard, R. D., and G. T. Jones
1987   Elements of an Inclusive Evolutionary Model for Archaeology. *Journal of Anthropological Archaeology* 6:199–219.

Lightfoot, K. G.
1984   *Prehistoric Political Dynamics: A Case Study from the American Southwest*. Northern Illinois University Press, DeKalb.

Lightfoot, K. G., and S. Upham
1989a   Complex Societies in the Prehistoric American Southwest: A Consideration of the Controversy. In *The Sociopolitical Structure of Prehistoric Southwestern Societies*, edited by S. Upham, K. G. Lightfoot, and R. A. Jewett, pp. 3–30. Investigations in American Archaeology. Westview Press, Boulder.

1989b   The Sociopolitical Structure of Prehistoric Southwestern Societies: Concluding Thoughts. In *The Sociopolitical Structure of Prehistoric Southwestern Societies*, edited by S. Upham, K. G. Lightfoot, and R. A. Jewett, pp. 583–593. Investigations in American Archaeology. Westview Press, Boulder.

Lightfoot, R. R.
1989   Crow Canyon Archaeological Center Proposal for Test Excavations at Goodman Point Pueblo. Proposal submitted to the National Park Service, Rocky Mountain Region, Denver. Ms. on file, Crow Canyon Archaeological Center, Cortez, Colorado.

1990   Abandonment Processes at the Duckfoot Site. Paper presented at the 55th Annual Meeting of the Society for American Archaeology, Las Vegas.

1992   *Archaeology of the House and Household: A Case Study of Assemblage Formation and Household Organization in the American Southwest*. Unpublished Ph.D. dissertation, Department of Anthropology, Washington State University, Pullman.

Lightfoot, R. R., and M. D. Varien
1988   *Report of 1987 Archaeological Investigations at the Duckfoot Site (5MT3868), Montezuma County, Colorado*. Crow Canyon Archaeological Center, Cortez, Colorado. Report submitted to the Bureau of Land Management, San Juan Resource Area Office, Durango, Colorado.

Lindsay, A. J., Jr., and J. S. Dean
1971   Changing Patterns of Human Settlement in the Long House Valley, Northeastern Arizona. In *The Distribution of Prehistoric Population Aggregates*, edited by G. J. Gumerman, pp. 111–125. Prescott College Anthropological Reports, no. 1. Prescott, Arizona.

Lipe, W. D.
1970   Anasazi Communities in the Red Rock Plateau, Southeastern Utah. In *Reconstructing Prehistoric Pueblo Societies*, edited by W. A. Longacre, pp. 84–139. School of American Research Advanced Seminar Series. University of New Mexico Press, Albuquerque.

1978   The Southwest. In *Ancient Native Americans*, edited by J. D. Jennings, pp. 327–401. W. H. Freeman and Co., San Francisco.

1983   The Southwest. In *Ancient North Americans*, edited by J. D. Jennings, pp. 421–493. W. H. Freeman and Co., San Francisco.

1989   Social Scale of Mesa Verde Anasazi Kivas. In *The Architecture of Social Integration in Prehistoric Pueblos*, edited by W. D. Lipe and M. Hegmon, pp. 53–71. Occasional Papers of the Crow Canyon Archaeological Center, no. 1. Cortez, Colorado.

Lipe, W. D., and B. A. Bradley
1986   Prehistoric Pueblo Organization, Goodman Point Locality, Southwestern Colorado. Proposal submitted to the National Science Foundation. Ms. on file, Crow Canyon Archaeological Center, Cortez, Colorado.

1988   Prehistoric Pueblo Organization, Sand Canyon Locality, Southwestern Colorado. Proposal submitted to the National Science Foundation. Ms. on file, Crow Canyon Archaeological Center, Cortez, Colorado.

Lipe, W. D., and C. D. Breternitz
1980   Approaches to Analyzing Variability Among Dolores Area Structures, A.D. 600–950. *Contract Abstracts and CRM Archeology* 1(2):21–28.

Lipe, W. D., and M. Hegmon
1989   Historical and Analytical Perspectives on Architecture and Social Integration in the Prehistoric Pueblos. In *The Architecture of Social Integration in Prehistoric Pueblos*, edited by W. D. Lipe and M. Hegmon, pp. 15–34. Occasional Papers of the Crow Canyon Archaeological Center, no. 1. Cortez, Colorado.

Lipe, W. D., and T. A. Kohler
1984   Method and Technique: Prehistory. In *Dolores Archaeological Program: Synthetic Report 1978–1981*, prepared under the supervision of D. A. Breternitz, pp. 7–20. Bureau of Reclamation, Engineering and Research Center, Denver.

Lipe, W. D., and S. H. Lekson
1990   Southwestern Pueblo Cultures in Transition: Report of a Conference. Paper presented at the 55th Annual Meeting of the Society for American Archaeology, Las Vegas.

Lipe, W. D., T. A. Kohler, M. D. Varien, J. N. Morris, and R. R. Lightfoot
1988   Synthesis. In *Dolores Archaeological Program: Anasazi Communities at Dolores: Grass Mesa Village*, compiled by W. D. Lipe, J. N. Morris, and T. A. Kohler, pp. 1213–1276. Bureau of Reclamation, Engineering and Research Center, Denver.

Longacre, W. A. (editor)
1970   *Reconstructing Prehistoric Pueblo Societies*. School of American Research Advanced Seminar Series. University of New Mexico Press, Albuquerque.

Luebben, R. A., and P. R. Nickens
1982   A Mass Interment in an Early Pueblo III Kiva in Southwestern Colorado. *Journal of Intermountain Archeology* 1:66–79.

Mann, M.
1986   *The Sources of Social Power*. Vol. 1: *A History of Power from the Beginning to A.D. 1760*. Cambridge University Press, Cambridge.

Marshall, M. P., J. R. Stein, R. W. Loose, and J. E. Novotny
1979   *Anasazi Communities of the San Juan Basin*. Public Service Company of New Mexico and Historic Preservation Bureau, Planning Division, Department of Finance and Administration of the State of New Mexico, Santa Fe.

Martin, C. W.
1976   Archaeological Inventory of the Sand Canyon Cliff Dwelling Area, Montezuma County, Colorado. Ms. on file, Bureau of Land Management, San Juan Resource Area Office, Durango, Colorado.

Martin, P. S.
　1936　*Lowry Ruin in Southwestern Colorado* (with reports by Lawrence Roys and Gerhardt von Bonin). *Field Museum of Natural History, Anthropological Series, vol. 23, no. 1.* Chicago.
　1938　*Archaeological Work in the Ackmen-Lowry Area, Southwestern Colorado, 1937.* Field Museum of Natural History, Anthropological Series, vol. 23, no. 2. Chicago.

Matson, R. G., and W. D. Lipe
　1978　Settlement Patterns on Cedar Mesa: Boom and Bust on the Northern Periphery. In *Investigations of the Southwestern Anthropological Research Group: An Experiment in Archaeological Cooperation*, edited by G. J. Gumerman and R. C. Euler, pp. 1–12. Museum of Northern Arizona Bulletin, no. 50. Flagstaff, Arizona.

Matson, R. G., W. D. Lipe, and W. R. Haase IV
　1988　Adaptational Continuities and Occupational Discontinuities: The Cedar Mesa Anasazi. *Journal of Field Archaeology* 15:245–264.

Matthews, M. H.
　1986　The Dolores Archaeological Program Macrobotanical Data Base: Resource Availability and Mix. In *Dolores Archaeological Program: Final Synthetic Report*, compiled by D. A. Breternitz, C. K. Robinson, and G. T. Gross, pp. 151–184. Bureau of Reclamation, Engineering and Research Center, Denver.

Meko, D. M., C. W. Stockton, and W. R. Boggess
　1980　A Tree-Ring Reconstruction of Drought in Southern California. *Water Resources Bulletin* 16:594–600.

Mera, H. P.
　1935　*Ceramic Clues to the Prehistory of North Central New Mexico.* Laboratory of Anthropology Technical Series Bulletin, no. 8. Santa Fe.

Mills, P.
　1987　*Use-Wear Analysis of Stone Axes from Sand Canyon Pueblo Ruin (5MT765), Southwestern Colorado.* Unpublished Master's thesis, Department of Anthropology, Washington State University, Pullman.

Minnis, P. E.
　1989　Prehistoric Diet in the Northern Southwest: Macroplant Remains from Four Corners Feces. *American Antiquity* 54:543–563.

Morris, E. H.
　1939　*Archaeological Studies in the LaPlata District, Southwestern Colorado and Northwestern New Mexico.* Carnegie Institution of Washington Publication, no. 519. Washington, D.C.

Morris, E. H., and R. F. Burgh
　1954　*Basket Maker II Sites Near Durango, Colorado.* Carnegie Institution of Washington Publication, no. 604. Washington, D.C.

Morris, J. N.
　1991　*Archaeological Excavations on the Hovenweep Laterals.* Four Corners Archaeological Project Report, no. 16. Complete Archaeological Service Associates, Cortez, Colorado.

Murdock, G. P.
　1949　*Social Structure.* The Macmillan Company, New York.

Murdock, G. P., and S. F. Wilson
　1972　Settlement Patterns and Community Organization: Cross Cultural Codes. *Ethnology* 11:254–295.

Naroll, R.
　1962　Floor Area and Settlement Population. *American Antiquity* 27:587–589.

National Park Service
　1990　*Statement for Management, Hovenweep National Monument, Colorado-Utah.* National Park Service, Rocky Mountain Region, Denver.

Neily, R. B.
　1983　*The Prehistoric Community on the Colorado Plateau: An Approach to the Study of Change and Survival in the Northern San Juan Area of the American Southwest.* Unpublished Ph.D. dissertation, Department of Anthropology, Southern Illinois University, Carbondale.

Netting, R. M.
　1987　Population, Permanent Agriculture, and Polities: Unpacking the Evolutionary Portmanteau. Paper prepared for the Advanced Seminar, The Development of Political Systems in Prehistoric Sedentary Societies, April 20–24, 1987, School of American Research, Santa Fe.

Neusius, S. W.
　1986　The Dolores Archaeological Program Faunal Data Base: Resource Availability and Resource Mix. In *Dolores Archaeological Program: Final Synthetic Report*, compiled by D. A. Breternitz, C. K. Robinson, and G. T. Gross, pp. 199–303. Bureau of Reclamation, Engineering and Research Center, Denver.

Nickens, P.
　1981　*Pueblo III Communities in Transition: Environment and Adaptation in Johnson Canyon.* Memoirs of the Colorado Archaeological Society, no. 2. Boulder.

Northrop, S. A.
　1973　Lexicon of Stratigraphic Names of the Monument Valley-Four Corners Region. In *Guidebook of Monument Valley and Vicinity, Arizona and Utah*, edited by H. L. James, pp. 157–176. New Mexico Geological Society, Twenty-Fourth Field Conference, October 4–6, 1973. New Mexico Bureau of Mines and Resources, Socorro.

Olsen, N.
　1988　*The Chappell Collection.* Anasazi Historical Society, Cortez, Colorado.

Orcutt, J. D., E. Blinman, and T. A. Kohler
　1990　Explanations of Population Aggregation in the Mesa Verde Region Prior to A.D. 900. In *Perspectives on Southwestern Prehistory*, edited by P. E. Minnis and C. L. Redman, pp. 196–212. Investigations in American Archaeology. Westview Press, Boulder.

Palmer, W. C.
　1965　*Meteorological Drought.* Research Paper, no. 45. U.S. Department of Commerce, Office of Climatology, U.S. Weather Bureau, Washington, D.C.

Parsons, E. C.
　1936　*Hopi Journal of Alexander M. Stephen.* Columbia University Contributions to Anthropology, nos. 23 and 24. Columbia University Press, New York.

Pauketat, T. R.
　1989　Monitoring Mississippian Homestead Occupation Span and Economy Using Ceramic Refuse. *American Antiquity* 54:288–310.

Petersen, K. L.
　1986　Climatic Reconstruction for the Dolores Project. In *Dolores Archaeological Program: Final Synthetic Report,*

compiled by D. A. Breternitz, C. K. Robinson, and G. T. Gross, pp. 311–325. Bureau of Reclamation, Engineering and Research Center, Denver.

1987 Summer Warmth: A Critical Factor for the Dolores Anasazi. In *Dolores Archaeological Program: Supporting Studies: Settlement and Environment*, compiled by K. L. Petersen and J. D. Orcutt, pp. 61-71. Bureau of Reclamation, Engineering and Research Center, Denver.

1988 *Climate and the Dolores River Anasazi: A Paleoenvironmental Reconstruction from a 10,000–Year Pollen Record, La Plata Mountains, Southwestern Colorado*. Anthropological Papers, no. 113. University of Utah, Salt Lake City.

1989 AT LAST! Why the Anasazi Left the Four Corners Region. *Canyon Legacy* 1:19-24.

Plog, F.

1974 *The Study of Prehistoric Change*. Academic Press, New York.

Plog, F., G. J. Gumerman, R. C. Euler, J. S. Dean, R. H. Hevly, and T. N. V. Karlstrom

1988 Anasazi Adaptive Strategies: The Model, Predictions, and Results. In *The Anasazi in a Changing Environment*, edited by G. J. Gumerman, pp. 230–276. School of American Research Advanced Seminar Series. Cambridge University Press, Cambridge.

Plog, S.

1989 Ritual, Exchange, and the Development of Regional Systems. In *The Architecture of Social Integration in Prehistoric Pueblos*, edited by W. D. Lipe and M. Hegmon, pp. 143-154. Occasional Papers of the Crow Canyon Archaeological Center, no. 1. Cortez, Colorado.

Powers, R. P., W. B. Gillespie, and S. H. Lekson

1983 *The Outlier Survey: A Regional View of Settlement in the San Juan Basin*. Reports of the Chaco Center, no. 3. Division of Cultural Research, National Park Service, Albuquerque.

Prudden, T. M.

1903 The Prehistoric Ruins of the San Juan Watershed of Utah, Arizona, Colorado and New Mexico. *American Anthropologist* 5:224-288.

1914 The Circular Kivas of Small Ruins in the San Juan Watershed. *American Anthropologist* 16:33-58.

1918 *A Further Study of Prehistoric Small House Ruins in the San Juan Watershed*. Memoirs of the American Anthropological Association, vol. 5, no. 1.

Rapoport, A.

1982 *The Meaning of the Built Environment: A Nonverbal Communication Approach*. Sage Publications, Beverly Hills.

Reed, A. D., and R. E. Kainer

1978 The Tamarron Site, 5LP326. *Southwestern Lore* 44(1 and 2):1-47.

Reed, E. K.

1958 *Excavations in Mancos Canyon, Colorado*. Anthropological Papers, no. 35. University of Utah, Salt Lake City.

Reher, C. A. (editor)

1977 *Settlement and Subsistence Along the Lower Chaco River: The CGP Survey*. University of New Mexico Press, Albuquerque.

Reid, J. J.

1985 Measuring Social Complexity in the American Southwest. In *Status, Structure and Stratification: Current Archaeological Reconstructions*, edited by M. Thompson, M. T. Garcia, and F. J. Kense, pp. 167–173. Proceedings of the Sixteenth Annual Chacmool Conference. The Archaeological Association of the University of Calgary, Alberta.

1989 A Grasshopper Perspective on the Mogollon of the Arizona Mountains. In *Dynamics of Southwest Prehistory*, edited by L. S. Cordell and G. J. Gumerman, pp. 65–97. School of American Research Advanced Seminar Series. Smithsonian Institution Press, Washington, D.C.

Roberts, F. H. H., Jr.

1929 *Shabik'eshchee Village—a Late Basket Maker Site in the Chaco Canyon, New Mexico*. Bureau of American Ethnology Bulletin, no. 92. Washington, D.C.

Robinson, W. J., and C. M. Cameron

1991 *A Directory of Tree-Ring Dated Prehistoric Sites in the American Southwest*. Laboratory of Tree-Ring Research, University of Arizona, Tucson.

Rohn, A. H.

1963 Prehistoric Soil and Water Conservation on Chapin Mesa, Southwestern Colorado. *American Antiquity* 28:441-455.

1965 Postulation of Socio-Economic Groups from Archaeological Evidence. In *Contributions of the Wetherill Mesa Archeological Project*, assembled by D. Osborne, pp. 65-69. Society for American Archaeology Memoir, no. 19. Salt Lake City.

1971 *Mug House, Mesa Verde National Park, Colorado*. Archeological Research Series, no. 7–D. National Park Service, Washington, D.C.

1977 *Cultural Change and Continuity on Chapin Mesa*. Regents Press of Kansas, Lawrence.

1983 Budding Urban Settlements in the Northern San Juan. In *Proceedings of the Anasazi Symposium, 1981*, edited by J. E. Smith, pp. 175–180. Mesa Verde Museum Association, Mesa Verde National Park, Colorado.

1989 Northern San Juan Prehistory. In *Dynamics of Southwest Prehistory*, edited by L. S. Cordell and G. J. Gumerman, pp. 149–177. School of American Research Advanced Seminar Series. Smithsonian Institution Press, Washington, D.C.

Rose, M. R., W. J. Robinson, and J. S. Dean

1982 Dendroclimatic Reconstruction for the Southeastern Colorado Plateau. Final report to Dolores Archaeological Project and Division of Chaco Research. Ms. on file, Laboratory of Tree-Ring Research, University of Arizona, Tucson.

Sanders, W. T.

1976 The Agricultural History of the Basin of Mexico. In *The Valley of Mexico: Studies in Pre-Hispanic Ecology and Society*, edited by E. R. Wolf, pp. 101–159. University of New Mexico Press, Albuquerque.

Schlanger, S. H.

1985 *Prehistoric Population Dynamics in the Dolores Area, Southwestern Colorado*. Ph.D. dissertation, Washington State University. University Microfilms, Ann Arbor.

1986 1982 Probabilistic Sampling Survey of Windy Ruin and Yellowjacket Crest Localities. In *Dolores Archaeological Program: Research Designs and Initial Survey Results*, compiled by A. E. Kane, W. D. Lipe, T. A. Kohler, and C. K. Robinson, pp. 447–470. Bureau of Reclamation, Engineering and Research Center, Denver.

1988 Patterns of Population Movement and Long-Term Population Growth in Southwestern Colorado. *American Antiquity* 53:773–793.

1990 Artifact Assemblage Composition and Site Occupation Duration. In *Perspectives on Southwestern Prehistory*, edited by P. E. Minnis and C. L. Redman, pp. 103–121. Investigations in American Archaeology. Westview Press, Boulder.

Schlanger, S. H., and J. D. Orcutt

1986 Site Surface Characteristics and Functional Inferences. *American Antiquity* 51:296–312.

Schwartz, T.

1978 The Size and Shape of a Culture. In *Scale and Social Organization*, edited by F. Barth, pp. 215–252. Universitetsforlaget, Oslo.

Scott, L. J., and D. K. Aasen

1985 Pollen and Macrofloral Analyses of Sand Canyon Pueblo: Feasibility Study and Preliminary Interpretations. Ms. on file, Crow Canyon Archaeological Center, Cortez, Colorado.

Service, E.

1962 *Primitive Social Organization*. Random House, New York.

Simmons, A. H.

1981 The "Other" Archaeology of Northwestern New Mexico: Perspectives on Aceramic Occupation of the San Juan Basin. *Contract Abstracts and CRM Archeology* 2(2):12–19.

Smiley, T. L., S. A. Stubbs, and B. Bannister

1953 *A Foundation for the Dating of Some Late Archaeological Sites in the Rio Grande Area, New Mexico: Based on Studies in Tree-Ring Methods and Pottery Analyses*. Laboratory of Tree-Ring Research Bulletin, no. 6. University of Arizona, Tucson.

Speth, J. D., and S. L. Scott

1985 The Role of Large Mammals in Late Prehistoric Horticultural Adaptations: The View from Southeastern New Mexico. In *Contributions to Plains Prehistory: The 1984 Victoria Symposium*, edited by D. V. Burley. Archaeological Survey of Alberta Occasional Paper, no. 26. Edmonton.

1989 Horticulture and Large-Mammal Hunting: The Role of Resource Depletion and the Constraints of Time and Labor. In *Farmers as Hunters: The Implications of Sedentism*, edited by S. Kent, pp. 71–79. Cambridge University Press, Cambridge.

Stein, J. R., and P. J. McKenna

1988 *An Archeological Reconnaissance of a Late Bonito Phase Occupation Near Aztec Ruins National Monument, New Mexico*. Southwest Cultural Resources Center, National Park Service, Santa Fe.

Stevenson, M. G.

1982 Toward an Understanding of Site Abandonment Behavior: Evidence from Historic Mining Camps in the Southwest Yukon. *Journal of Anthropological Archaeology* 1:237–265.

Stiger, M. A.

1979 Mesa Verde Subsistence Patterns from Basketmaker to Pueblo III. *The Kiva* 44:133–144.

Stuiver, M., and G. W. Pearson

1986 High-precision Calibration of the Radiocarbon Time Scale, A.D. 1950–500 B.C. *Radiocarbon* 28:805–838.

Stuiver, M., and P. J. Reimer

1986 A Computer Program for Radiocarbon Age Calibrations. *Radiocarbon* 28:1022–1030.

Thompson, I., M. D. Varien, S. Kenzle, and R. Swentzell

1991 Prehistoric Architecture with Unknown Function. In *Anasazi Architecture and American Design*, edited by B. H. Morrow and V. B. Price. University of New Mexico Press, Albuquerque, in press.

Titiev, M.

1944 *Old Oraibi: A Study of the Hopi Indians of Third Mesa*. Papers of the Peabody Museum of American Archaeology and Ethnology, vol. 22, no. 1. Harvard University, Cambridge.

Turner, N. A.

1991 Anasazi Abandonment and Sand Canyon Pueblo: Artifact Assemblages from Special Use vs. Habitation Structures. Ms. on file, Crow Canyon Archaeological Center, Cortez, Colorado.

Upham, S.

1982 *Polities and Power: An Economic and Political History of the Western Pueblo*. Studies in Archaeology. Academic Press, New York.

1985 Interpretations of Prehistoric Complexity in the Central and Northern Southwest. In *Status, Structure, and Stratification: Current Archaeological Reconstructions*, edited by M. Thompson, M. T. Garcia, and F. J. Kense, pp. 175–180. Proceedings of the Sixteenth Annual Chacmool Conference. The Archaeological Association of the University of Calgary, Alberta.

1989 East Meets West: Hierarchy and Elites in Pueblo Society. In *The Sociopolitical Structure of Prehistoric Southwestern Societies*, edited by S. Upham, K. G. Lightfoot, and R. A. Jewett, pp. 77–102. Investigations in American Archaeology. Westview Press, Boulder.

Van der Merwe, N. J.

1982 Carbon Isotopes, Photosynthesis, and Archaeology. *American Scientist* 70:596–606.

Van West, C. R.

1986 *Cultural Resource Inventory for the 1985 Field Season in the Crow Canyon and Sand Canyon Areas, Montezuma County, Colorado*. Crow Canyon Archaeological Center, Cortez, Colorado. Report submitted to the Bureau of Land Management, San Juan Resource Area Office, Durango, Colorado.

1990 *Modeling Prehistoric Climatic Variability and Agricultural Production in Southwestern Colorado: A G.I.S. Approach*. Unpublished Ph.D. dissertation, Department of Anthropology, Washington State University, Pullman.

1992 The Heuristic Value of Estimates of Prehistoric Agricultural Production: A Case Study from Southwestern Colorado. Paper presented at the Third Southwest Symposium, Tucson.

Van West, C. R., M. A. Adler, and E. K. Huber

1987 *Archaeological Survey and Testing in the Vicinity of Sand Canyon Pueblo, Montezuma County, Colorado, 1986 Field Season*. Crow Canyon Archaeological Center, Cortez, Colorado. Report submitted to the Bureau of Land Management, San Juan Resource Area Office, Durango, Colorado.

Varien, M. D.

1990a Measuring Site Uselife: Accumulation Rate Studies. Poster presented at the 55th Annual Meeting of the Society for American Archaeology, Las Vegas.

1990b *1988 Small Site Testing: Preliminary Descriptive Report on the Excavations at Lillian's Site (5MT3936), Roy's Ruin (5MT3930), Shorlene's Site (5MT 3918), and Troy's Tower (5MT3951).* Crow Canyon Archaeological Center, Cortez, Colorado. Report submitted to the Bureau of Land Management, San Juan Resource Area Office, Durango, Colorado.

1991 *1989 Sand Canyon Project Testing Program: Preliminary Report on the Excavations at Troy's Tower (5MT3951), Catherine's Site (5MT3967) and Stanton's Site (5MT10508).* Crow Canyon Archaeological Center, Cortez, Colorado. Report submitted to the Bureau of Land Management, San Juan Resource Area Office, Durango, Colorado.

Varien, M. D., and R. R. Lightfoot

1989 Ritual and Nonritual Activities in Mesa Verde Region Pit Structures. In *The Architecture of Social Integration in Prehistoric Pueblos*, edited by W. D. Lipe and M. Hegmon, pp. 73–87. Occasional Papers of the Crow Canyon Archaeological Center, no. 1. Cortez, Colorado.

Varien, M. D., W. D. Lipe, B. A. Bradley, M. A. Adler, and I. Thompson

1990 Southwest Colorado and Southeast Utah Mesa Verde Region Settlement, A.D. 1100 to 1300. Paper presented at the Conference on Pueblo Cultures in Transition: A.D. 1150–1350 in the American Southwest, Crow Canyon Archaeological Center, Cortez, Colorado.

1991 Regional Context. In *Sand Canyon Locality Context: Research Design and Preliminary Results*, compiled by R. R. Lightfoot, pp. 158–177. Crow Canyon Archaeological Center, Cortez, Colorado. Report submitted to the Bureau of Land Management, San Juan Resource Area Office, Durango, Colorado.

Vivian, R. Gordon

1959 *The Hubbard Site and Other Tri-Wall Structures in New Mexico and Colorado.* Archeological Research Series, no. 5. National Park Service, Washington, D.C.

Vivian, R. Gordon, and T. W. Mathews

1965 *Kin Kletso: A Pueblo III Community in Chaco Canyon, New Mexico.* Southwestern Monuments Association, Technical Series, no. 6, part 1. Globe, Arizona.

Vivian, R. Gordon, and P. Reiter

1965 *The Great Kivas of Chaco Canyon and Their Relationships.* Monograph of the School of American Research, no. 22. University of New Mexico Press, Santa Fe.

Vivian, R. Gwinn

1970 An Inquiry Into Prehistoric Social Organization in Chaco Canyon, New Mexico. In *Reconstructing Prehistoric Pueblo Societies*, edited by W. A. Longacre, pp. 59–83. School of American Research Advanced Seminar Series. University of New Mexico Press, Albuquerque.

1990 *The Chacoan Prehistory of the San Juan Basin.* New World Archaeological Record. Academic Press, New York.

Walker, D. N.

1989 Faunal Remains from the Green Lizard Site (5MT3901), Colorado. Ms. on file, Crow Canyon Archaeological Center, Cortez, Colorado.

1990a Preliminary Report on Faunal Remains from Sand Canyon Pueblo (5MT765), Colorado. Ms. on file, Crow Canyon Archaeological Center, Cortez, Colorado.

1990b Zooarchaeology of the Green Lizard Site (5MT3901), Colorado. Ms. on file, Crow Canyon Archaeological Center, Cortez, Colorado.

White, L. A.

1949 *The Science of Culture: A Study of Man and Civilization.* Grove Press, New York.

1959 *The Evolution of Culture: The Development of Civilization to the Fall of Rome.* McGraw-Hill, New York.

Whiting, A. F.

1939 *Ethnobotany of the Hopi.* Museum of Northern Arizona Bulletin, no. 15. Flagstaff.

Wilcox, D.

1981 Changing Perspectives on the Protohistoric Pueblos, A.D. 1450–1700. In *The Protohistoric Period in the North American Southwest, A.D. 1450–1700*, edited by D. R. Wilcox and W. B. Masse, pp. 378–409. Anthropological Research Papers, no. 24. Arizona State University, Tempe.

Willey, G. R., and P. Phillips

1958 *Method and Theory in American Archaeology.* University of Chicago Press, Chicago.

Williams, B. J.

1989 Contact Period Rural Overpopulation in the Basin of Mexico: Carrying-Capacity Models Tested with Documentary Data. *American Antiquity* 54:715–732.

Wilshusen, R. H.

1989 Unstuffing the Estufa: Ritual Floor Features in Anasazi Pit Structures and Pueblo Kivas. In *The Architecture of Social Integration in Prehistoric Pueblos*, edited by W. D. Lipe and M. Hegmon, pp. 89–111. Occasional Papers of the Crow Canyon Archaeological Center, no. 1. Cortez, Colorado.

Wilson, C. D.

1991 Ceramic Analysis: Hovenweep Laterals Project. In *Archaeological Excavations on the Hovenweep Laterals*, authored by J. N. Morris, pp. 677–762. Complete Archaeological Service Associates, Cortez, Colorado.

Wilson, P. J.

1988 *The Domestication of the Human Species.* Yale University Press, New Haven.

Windes, T. C., and D. Ford

1990 The Nature of the Early Bonito Phase. Paper presented at the 55th Annual Meeting of the Society for American Archaeology, Las Vegas.

Winter, J. C.

1976 *Hovenweep 1975.* Archeological Report, no. 2. San Jose State University, San Jose, California.